"Writing with the knowledge and sensitivity of a participant-observer, Paul describes every facet of firehouse culture, from the daily firehouse routine to the emotional experiences of lives saved and lost. In the end, readers also learn the story of how a young woman found—in one of the most life-threatening occupations—her own life's purpose."—*Booklist*

"A rare, fascinating look at the inner workings of an urban fire department, with plenty of thrills, adventure, and raw emotion. Between the quality of Paul's writing and the subject matter, her book will keep readers on edge until the very last page."
—*Library Journal* (starred review)

"An outstanding account of one woman's struggle to prove her personal worth and courage and to make her place in a world previously reserved exclusively for men."—*Kirkus Reviews*

"Terrific. . . . The grip of real fire fighting tensely tactilely, bruisingly described by a woman honest in examining her own thoughts, too. She confronts and homes in on what is going on and its fracturing impact."
—Edward Hoagland, author of *Notes from the Century Before* and *The Courage of Turtles.*

# FIGHTING FIRE

# CAROLINE PAUL

## St. Martin's Paperbacks

FIGHTING FIRE

Copyright © 1998 by Caroline Paul.

Library of Congress Catalog Card Number: 98-9791

ISBN: 0-312-97000-5

Printed in the United States of America

St. Martin's Press hardcover edition / May 1998
St. Martin's Paperbacks edition / June 1999

10  9  8  7  6  5  4  3  2  1

# ACKNOWLEDGMENTS

Thanks to my agent, Charlotte Sheedy, who would have made a formidable firefighter herself. Thanks also to Elaine Pfefferblit, my original editor, who has done an extraordinary job; I can't thank her enough. And to Michael Denneny, who did the final edit.

To my readers: Keith Abell, Erik Gaull, Elizabeth Leahy, Marni Hine, Katie Hubbard, Kay K., Gina Macintosh, Eric Martin, Stephen Muller, Ken Olsen (I owe you dinner), Jim Paul, and Beth Rypins—all of whom gave incisive critiques and an occasional white lie.

To Farley's Cafe, which let me use an electrical outlet and a corner table.

To the Babar writers, especially Jim, who encouraged and advised me.

And to the Green family, who keep me asking all the wacky questions of life.

To my family: Sarah Paul, Mark Paul, Alexandra, and Jonathan, for their unflagging enthusiasm and their constant support.

To the many firefighters who shared their stories and opinions.

And finally, to Trish Lee, who put up with it all.

All firefighters and fire stations have been renamed, and some events have been compressed or chronologically rearranged. Because this book spans eight years, much of the original dialogue has been forgotten. Spoken phrases are not exact quotes, but remain as true to the original circumstances as I remember.

# CONTENTS

# PREFACE

It always begins the same way. First the fire coat, one arm at a time. It is snapped—usually only three of the snaps—and clipped. From here the fingers slide upward to the collar, feeling the rough Nomex cloth and the hard, chipped paint of the name that lines the back of it.

I flip up the collar so that it hits my chin and the soft underside of my ears. Then the belt is cinched tight, the buckle jingling almost daintily against the small crash axe, which I spin to a precise place against my right thigh where it will not tangle with the air pack. Thick leather gloves, often stiff with ash, are put on, and each hand is flexed—one, two, three times—to loosen them.

Finally, there is the fire helmet. It is picked up in one quick motion with the palm outstretched. Fingers crook around the front shield—mine says RESCUE 3—and lift it to eye level. Then the head is bent, as if in prayer, and some sweep a hand across the hair to smooth it down. I do. I push back my bangs in one quick movement. Then I lean the leather against my forehead. All our helmets are leather. This is a source of pride in an era of high-tech plastics. Finally, the head is brought up and the helmet slid back, simultaneously. Most of the men leave the chin straps to dangle, but I cinch mine up with one quick pull. The helmet has yet to fit well over my array of bobby pins and hair ties.

Today is no exception. Despite the chaos as we race to the incident—the siren is at full wail and the air horn blasts angrily at each street intersection—I have reenacted these small, precise movements. My crew has done the same. Alberto is the one exception—as the rest of us jump quickly out of the rig, which has pulled to an abrupt and bumpy stop on the sidewalk, he stops and drops his helmet on from above as if it were any other old hat, and wriggles it from side to side to snare it onto his head. Then he starts a careful, deliberate walk.

I run—an odd run, with legs barely lifting off the ground to save energy—toward a crowd that has gathered in a large, fragmented half circle. I smell the smoke before I see it; it is a sour, acrid smell that conjures up false images of fireplaces and marshmallows. Then I see it. Heavy and dark gray, it pumps in round, angry thrusts out of the two upper side windows of an old Victorian-style house. It spews toward the midday sky. Over the sound of burning wood—a belching, crackling roar—I hear the collective gasp of the crowd.

Two engines are already parked in the busy intersection ahead. Flames leap from the front second-floor windows. Even on the sidewalk, it has grown hot. Momentarily we stare, mesmerized like the onlookers. Above me, flames reach out into the day. In front of me, burning wood drops into the stairwell. For a millisecond, there is nothing but this power and beauty.

Another window blows out from the force of the heat. I feel the adrenaline start to leak behind my ears and down my throat. My heart pounds. Not from fear, but from something else. Wonder. Awe. And a little bit of disbelief. There is something about fire that touches our soul and moves us in a profound, primal way. In the face of it, we want to ask the bigger questions, the *why*'s of existence—lofty, inappropriate questions like *Why am I here on this earth?* and smaller ones like *How did I get here, to this place of being a firefighter?*

My lieutenant brushes by me. All our small rituals of certainty—coat buttoned, helmet on, air pack tight—are over. Now come the vast possibilities, the meeting of chance, fate, and luck with skill and choice. Now comes the unknown of fire. There is no time for existential philosophy; I follow him into the roaring building.

*One*

# SMOKE

# BEFORE FIRE

It is 1986. My father is happy; Ronald Reagan is halfway into his second term as President of the United States and I am about to graduate from Stanford University. All of us see, from different angles, a wide-open, bright future. For me, the sheer expanse of that future is at once mortifying and exhilarating. The brightness is sometimes blinding. The President promises that it will finally be free of "evil empires," but I am not so sure. I have an evil empire of my own to face. Also known as "the career search."

For me *fire* is purely a poetic word. The only connection to career that *fire* has by graduation day is that I must *burn with ambition*. Indeed, all of us black-robed, tassel-hatted future leaders of America are *hot with promise;* we have *fire in our eyes*.

They call Stanford University "the Farm." No one minds; there is a romanticism in the hardworking, honest, close-to-the-land ethic that the words convey, but otherwise we are not here to be farmers. Every graduation speech says so. We will rise to the top, each promises. Of course. No doubt.

I stand in my black robe, looking ridiculous. It is a scalding spring day. I glance around, wishing that I had taped a funny message to my graduation hat like the people in front of me. *In debt. Thanks, Mom. I need a job.* In the stands, programs of high-quality bond flicker across the faces of parents. For them, perhaps more than for us, the big day has finally come.

The man I am in love with stands next to me. Andy is an

engineer, part French, part Persian—"Every mother's dream," my mother calls him. He smiles at me and squeezes my fingertips lightly. The woman I am in love with is somewhere in the audience. College can be a crazy time.

My twin sister, Alexandra, and my younger brother, Jonathan, sit through the pomp and circumstance somewhere above me. I imagine them in their folding chairs, giggling perhaps, or trying to find me in the rows of black hats below them. My sister will be sitting on the edge of her seat, and her long neck will be angled forward as if listening; I know this without seeing her. I am less sure about my brother; he will drape himself over the metal frame, letting his hands dangle behind him, or he will be hunched over his knees with one finger playing with the chip on his front tooth. I made that chip myself a long time ago, during a particularly vicious Water Pik fight, back when Water Piks were in fashion and my brother and I used to fight, so I notice it often, with a soft, guilty feeling in my stomach.

My father has flown in from Massachusetts, my mother from Connecticut. Divorced for ten years, my parents speak politely to each other, but most of the time they convey messages in an orbital fashion—they do not speak toward, but around each other. "Your father is taking us out to dinner," my mother says; the inference that my father does not exist in relation to her, only in relation to us, is clear. They slide away from us alternately, like buoys offshore, first my mother and then, as she drifts back, my father, in a seeming effort to avoid each other. Sometimes we wish that our parents did not both come to these events. But neither of them would have missed this day, when finally one of their kids is matriculating from university.

It is Alexandra who is supposed to be graduating. She had been accepted into Stanford five years ago. Instead, she had chosen to act. She lives in Los Angeles. She is successful there, working frequently in movies and television shows. But she knows that she is looking, through me, at a life she might have had.

We are identical twins, but next to her it is easy to feel

ungainly. Alexandra leaves a wide swath of flat-footed admirers in her wake, and Jonathan and I are no exception. All my life, I have tried to be as distinct from her as possible. Yet here I am, graduating from the college she was supposed to attend. She walks up and hugs me. "Hey, Mugsy," she says, using a code name from a secret club we had when we were kids. "Hey, Black Jack," I say.

We were born in New York City on a muggy afternoon. My father read the business section of *The New York Times* aloud to distract my mother through her twelve-hour labor. Finally, my mother was wheeled into the delivery room. Alexandra slid out after a shot of Demerol and a whiff of oxygen. My mother recalls that one of the doctors then turned to a nurse and said, "My gosh, I think there's another one," and two minutes later I appeared. "It was the most exciting moment of my life," my mother says now. "That, and skydiving."

At less than five pounds each, we were promptly put into incubators. My mother swears that we were *the most adorable* babies, but I have since seen pictures of preemies, and I am sure that we also looked like small, hairless, ratlike creatures with a strange purplish hue. My parents had not been prepared with two names, and we were instead labeled Baby A and Baby B and sent home after two weeks.

There is a photo of my mother from those early days. She has a bottle in each hand, feeding us. She looks haggard and exhausted. Later Alexandra and I developed a secret language; in certain outfits we looked cute; we called each other Caroline because we couldn't pronounce "Alexandra." Otherwise, we were unexceptional. Two and a half years later, my brother was born, weighing almost as much as his sisters at their birth combined. We are the typical affluent American family.

Only once is there a veiled portent of my incendiary future, when my brother accidentally sets fire to a back field at our Connecticut country house. The volunteer fire-fighters come. The fire chief is actually the local elementary-school janitor; his crew consisted of the butcher, the first-grade teacher, and the fathers of kids I knew. They bustled around the field importantly, lobbing water from hoses that extended from a large red fire engine. The engine had managed to drive down a path meant for our horses. It looked silly, hunkered amidst the long golden grass of summer. It did not interest me; fire engines were for school janitors and the men from other families. Instead, I stared, fascinated, at the deep black bruise that the flames left on the field. The next year the grass grew back in a vibrant, almost neon, green—a pond of color among duller grasses.

But my life is already "different." I am a twin, and this shapes my character first and foremost. Being a twin results in both a doubling and a halving of everything about oneself. I am twice what I am, and yet there is a constant, nagging feeling that I am only half of what I should be. This duality gives rise to both self-assurance and self-doubt.

Twinship promises someone who will always be there, always approve; there is a brimming, almost arrogant, confidence that comes with that. Certain kinds of loneliness and need are not felt by twins; we are, after all, born with a partner, genetically married to the companion that most humans crave. My twin provides all the connection and comfort that we invoke from the fairy godmother, the guardian angel, the imaginary playmate, the best friend, and, finally, the soul mate. Once a boyfriend of Alexandra's said in frustration that it was clear she would never really need him the way he needed her. "You have Caroline," he said, and she did not contradict him.

The mystical side of twinship lends a sense of magic and possibility to the entire world. No wonder I eventually find myself in the unlikely world of fire fighting; it is easy to expect more, to pursue (foolishly, perhaps) seemingly impossible avenues when our lives consist daily of the fantastical: We phone each other up at the same time, we choose the same chocolate truffle among dozens of possibilities while on opposite sides of the state, we get sick simultaneously. This is not to say that I never get scared or uneasy or insecure. But these feelings become diluted when shared by Alexandra. Even though she may not actually be feeling them at the moment, there is a certainty that she nevertheless has taken them on for me, much as Christians on the street promise that Jesus takes on burdens for those who come to Him.

On the other hand, what you could be walks right next to you all the time. This results in a constant feeling that there is always something more, something better, to be done. Arriving in twos offers a constant measuring stick to others, a standard by which one and then the other twin is gauged. In many ways, twins are like nags at an auction—weighed, pinched, spun around, their mouths opened wide and their teeth inspected. We are offers to the world of variations on ourselves, and people think they can eye and choose the parts and pieces they like best in each one, as if they might build a completely new person.

This fosters competitiveness. We tried to avoid it. We had different friends, liked different things. We chose separate swimming strokes to excel at so we would never race against each other. However, we sometimes erupted into yelling matches when one of us seemed to be getting more of a workout, and so was becoming "better." This competitiveness begins, I have heard, in the womb, where twins fight for space. On ultrasounds, twins have been caught throwing punches at each other. They kiss, too. I imagine the two of us, eyeing each other in our uterine water, making sure one does not learn a single fetal stroke without the other. We fight, then we curl up like seaweed, pressed together in our warm, dark lake of a world.

Now my graduation gown entangles with Alexandra's slim arms as we hug, and I let my cap fall because I pretend that I do not care how I look, or that any of this matters so much. Journalism, which I have studied here in its various forms (newspaper writing and documentary filmmaking), suits me this way; I have the cool detachment of an observer. Partly, I think, it is in response to being compared so often to a twin. Partly, it is something buried in me that I do not dislodge, though I know that it bothers people. It is not readily discernible; I am a social, outgoing person. But there is something unreachable in me. Andy feels it. My mother feels it. My journalism professor feels it. She gives me A's on my papers.

My brother, Jonathan, lopes up behind and gives us both a big squeeze, and then pulls Andy into it, too. Jonathan has shaved his beard, but not for us, though we are glad. He can't grow a full beard, and what he can grow conspires to hide what my mother calls his "good genes." Jonathan does not attempt to soothe family dynamics, as Alexandra does. And he upsets them more by talking about his latest animal-rights efforts. It is hard to enjoy my graduation thoroughly when part of me wonders if some angry hunter is going to suddenly appear and poke a rifle into my brother's ribs.

I will miss this place. Stanford University is beautiful, with elegant Spanish-style roofs and quaint Victorian houses. There are long, pillared corridors and quadrangles with square stones that make just the right echo—that serious, concise tapping that narrows and ends in a delicate point of sound that lingers long after you have stepped there. I have made good friends, and together we have struggled through these college years with something like grace. However, the grace came easily; we struggled because we realized that college is a time of struggle, and we played it like the script that it was. There was a sense that even the angst of youth was a routine expected of us.

My father waves the video camera around and tries to catch the hug in progress, but Alexandra has broken it off to look around for my mother. The news commentator Ted Koppel is about to speak at a small ceremony for my department. My father takes this as a good sign. He wants me to be the next Jane Pauley. Around me, everyone has plans. *Doctor, lawyer, businessperson,* they say with assurance. Even Andy; he gets his master's today in electrical engineering. His certainty makes me at once admiring and uneasy. I have no plans—no real plans—just a vague sense that I am on a slow trajectory, a trajectory that must belong to someone else.

I do not tell my father this; he is someone who always had a plan. Even when he worked on the General Motors assembly line in the summer during his time at Harvard business school with eighty seconds to assemble and screw on the radio antennae, he had vision, assessing how the plant could run better, putting ideas in the suggestions box until the foreman told him to quit it, he'd get fired. Eighty seconds not only for the antennae, but to put two screws in the front door on one side and then run around the back end, lift the spare tire out, spray the upholstery with glue, reload the tire, and press the carpet down. If you fumbled, there was no time to correct your mistake. He said that workers ate lunch in the back of the cars and sometimes there were wrappers or banana peels left there, but eighty seconds was not enough time to clean them out, so the lunch remains got upholstered right into the car. My father was born in the Depression and carries with him a deep sense that honesty and efficiency are almost the same ethic, so that when he tells this story he laughs, but there is an offended edge to it.

My father applied to the international banking firm of Morgan Stanley in his last year of business school. In the interview, he explained that nightmarish summer job at General Motors. Coincidentally, Morgan Stanley was a major investor in General Motors. My father assessed the assembly plant for the interviewers. The president of GM received a three-page letter, while my father was promptly hired by Morgan Stanley at a salary of five thousand dollars a year.

For my graduation, my father has bought a cutting-edge video camera with auto focus. I am touched because I know that he does not like newfangled mechanical devices; now he fumbles with the buttons and forgets to take the lens cap off. For a moment it is hard to imagine my father outside of his awkward love for us: that he worked on forty-five cars an hour, loose screws, crooked upholstery, and all; that he retired as a partner from a major investment banking firm; that he owns a farm and puts in his own fence posts. That for all his best-laid plans, he had never expected twins. That he certainly never expected this, looking at his grown children so similar to each other in looks and bearing, wedged within the frame of his camera, but on their way to different lives. We stand absolutely still, unused to this new camera that can make any family look poised and cohesive, until my father finally says "Speech," and my brother says congratulations, congratulations to the only college graduate of this Paul generation.

# SMOLDERING

It is twenty-five degrees below zero. My breath collapses against the scarf around my mouth. Momentarily the scarf stays wet, then freezes on my chin. Two miles and the sweat clings to my eyebrows in crystals. Soon I am haloed in a delicate lace, though there is nothing delicate about this bitter-cold day. At four miles, even my nose hairs are white. Ice is forming on my back; I finish the run inelegantly, slipping on the sidewalk that leads to the Lake Placid Olympic Training Center. I have an hour to eat and then I must change into my racing suit and make my way up to the luge track. Even on a cold day like this one I like to get into my racing suit. It is shiny and skintight and it makes me feel like a daunting athlete, even if I look something like a svelte garbage bag.

Luge is an obscure sport. If I could take myself less seriously, I might enjoy the perfect metaphor it represents for the twenty-one-year-old that I am. In luge, we hurtle down a thin ice track on a sled, trying to shave milliseconds off our time with slight movements of our shoulders, our chin, our toes. The sled becomes our body, and we spend hours preparing it, cutting millimeters off the fiberglass corners, filing down the edges of bolts and screws. We are obsessed manicurists of aerodynamics. German names are peppered throughout the race lingo, and we say these tangled words loudly, with earnest German accents. We launch ourselves down a single, windy track that tosses us about but ultimately leads us to the finish. Then we glance at the watch and go up to do it again. We are obsessed with refining our narrow lives to a perfection invisible to the naked eye, admired only by ourselves and the electronic clock.

It seemed like a good idea at the time—it filled up the space between college and real life. On graduation day, when everyone asks me what I plan to do, Andy says *luging,* proudly, and people smile broadly and blankly and move away. I am glad that I have an excuse not to embark on a career right away—something I am too embarrassed to admit openly. Like most college graduates, I think that the world is simultaneously at my fingertips and at my throat.

I am a terrible luger. I crash constantly and spectacularly. Curve 14 is my downfall, a neck-straining corkscrew turn that repeatedly slams me into the ice, finally tearing cartilage in my ribs. Still, I keep at it, until people gather at the curve to see my aerobatic tragedies. I enter the U.S. Nationals with my rib cage bound tightly; I move like a drunk but corseted maiden, sucking in half breaths and stepping carefully. Curve 14 bucks me off once again, so that I cross the finish line hanging on to the back of my sled by my fingertips. This is enough to make me the eleventh-ranked women's luger in the United States this year.

It is good to be terrible at a sport that not many people participate in.

No doubt about it: Luge is a peculiar choice for a diversion. Why not go to Spain, perhaps, and study the language, waitressing at night? Or France? I could read the classics in a small sidewalk café and smoke pinkie-thin cigars. *Ç'est plus chic, ça, plus responsable.* That is what most confused college graduates do.

But I have a fascination with adventure. More specifically, I have a fascination with the space in my mind between control and complete chaos—that moment when my tenuous hold on perspective narrows and sharpens to its finest resolution, just before complete fear takes over and all understanding shatters into a wide panic. I am painfully aware of how close oncoming traffic comes to the side of my car, how just a few inches to the left complete mayhem reigns. I never have an urge to turn into the oncoming car; I simply remain fascinated by its proximity. I walk along thin cliff edges, jump into dark quarries, climb spindly radio towers, all to glimpse the brief, heightened clarity that comes just before the situation is pushed too far. It is here, in that small space, that I finally shed some of the detachment, the coldness in me. There is a soft sensuousness to the precarious moment when the body is tensed, the breath is short, and the world tightens into a thin filament that consists only of what is right before you. All that matters is the next handhold, the right positioning of the feet, the precise movement of thought. It seems to me that adventure offers a small, powerful, meditative moment, one that might take a monk years to attain. It is as if that momentary peak of adrenaline holds some deep insight into the meaning of life, and my place in it.

Like some bruised prodigal daughter I luge, then travel the world. But something is missing. Despite the peaks of adrenaline that luge offers, the feeling persists that I am not connected to whatever is important in life. Confining my experience to an ice track suddenly seems ludicrous. I abruptly leave my sled in Germany and set off for Yugoslavia, Greece, and Italy. I cross the Sinai Desert. I snorkel in the Red Sea.

Later, as a firefighter, I will see people who remind me of myself at this restless age. Unlike me, they push heroin, not adrenaline, into their veins. But they, too, look for a connection. At first the heroin works. It provides a euphoria, an ecstasy that they say is beyond words. But then the heroin takes over. It becomes the meaning, not a path to the meaning; a way to hide from answers instead of finding them. Luckily, the adventure that I find to fill the void does not kill me. Like the overdose you manage to wake from, this adventure takes me to the farther ends of the earth, and there to some answers that bring me home.

# KINDLING

The jungle shimmies with sound and life. Spiders as big as my palm nest secretly in the giant bark of wide, yawning trees. Snakes flash in the eddies and then disappear. The rain explodes at night so that our new bright-blue tents turn brown and sag helplessly under the torrent. The modern world is forgotten for a while; the pressures of decision succumb to the heaving, ululating wildness of Borneo.

I am part of a white-water expedition determined to run the mythic river Boh.

I was a white-water raft guide three summers ago, after my junior year at Stanford. I like swift rivers; they career through beautiful wilderness with little in mind but speed, power, and the path of least resistance. I was not a great river guide, but I was a popular one. Tourists loved the way I awkwardly handled the boat so that it hit rocks haphazardly or pitched them into the white water. With me they could return to their cities with the exhilarating feeling that they had almost died in the wilderness. On my first trip I wrapped my boat on a rock that was so small that it did not even have a name. (Most dangerous rocks, those that constantly threaten to spill or wrap even an accomplished rafter's boat, are given heady names like Gunsight, Can Opener, and Ricochet.) I had a boatload of women who, by the time we hit the rock, had already fashioned Amazonian headdresses out of upstream bushes and were chanting aggressive earth songs. Being forced to swim from the stuck boat was simply a higher spiritual adventure for them. I was mortified at the mishap; they could not stop talking about their exciting brush with death. Of course, they didn't really believe that they had nearly died. If they had, they might have sued me, the raft company, or the State of California. This was the nature of commercial river rafting. The illusion of death was offered, with a clause ensuring that this would never happen. Stories circulated about the notorious comments made by naive, citified customers. "Where are the tracks?" someone once asked me, peering into the white water. "Tracks?" I asked, puzzled. "Yeah, tracks," he said impatiently. "The tracks this boat is on. Like Space Mountain."

However, beyond the commercial rafting circle, there are boaters who search out and expect dangerous situations. These rafters and kayakers do first descents: They run rivers that have never been run before. I am lucky enough to be asked to participate—not because I am a good rafter but because I have just the right amount of affected cool to convince people that I know what I am doing, even if I actually do not. This is how I now find myself on the Boh River, about to meet the Dayak people who live along its banks. An ABC television crew is with us. They, too, want to know how this adventure will turn out. It is not just the danger of the river that interests them; the Dayaks are the legendary "headhunters of Borneo."

As we approach the bend before the village, we brush our hair and smooth our Gore-Tex shorts. We have boated through easy waters to get here. Now we will stay with these indigenous people and prepare for the dangerous part of the descent.

For all the research we have done, nothing prepares us for the sight of several hundred people on the banks of the river. They peer at us excitedly with cautious smiles and a reserved dignity. We are a sight for them, too. We wear bright-red life jackets and hold our yellow-and-blue paddles in our hands like cheerleaders' batons. In the village, behind the traditional "long houses," we fling out our purple paddling jackets, roll up our yellow boats, and erect our blue tents to dry. Our helicopter lands soon after. We have arrived with all the color and sound of an American expedition.

The Dayaks are a smart, fine-humored culture, with a rich, complicated history. Vestiges of a proud, fierce people remain. The elderly Dayak women still wear the heavy earrings that pull wide holes in their lobes. Older men have leather thongs on their wrists and ankles and, to our wonder, dowels of wood through their penises. The younger Dayaks, on the other hand, show the slow encroachment of a different world. The children wear clothes brought in by missionaries once or twice a year. The T-shirts have slogans that are decidedly secular and always misspelled: ITS THE RALE THING or SUPERMMANS. I am uncomfortable when I see them. Older siblings have already left for the logging towns on the perimeter of this wild island.

The Dayaks display no headhunter tendencies; they welcome us warmly. But they soon conclude that the West is full of bored, unspiritual people who foolishly risk their lives to "conquer" distant rivers. A few days after our arrival, we meet with the chief of the tribe. "Why do you want to go on this dangerous river?" he asks us, through a translator. "You might die on a river that you do not need to go down. Why?" He seems to be looking only at me when he says this.

*Character-building, life experience, challenge:* This is the way I explain it back home, and to myself. But these are inappropriate concepts to the Dayaks, who spend every day facing the possibility of death—through disease, weather, privation. The very words seem silly, naive.

It occurs to me at this moment that my manic search for adrenaline-producing danger is foolish. Perhaps it is not the experience itself that offers insight. Perhaps I am simply trying to induce a catastrophe, a head-bashing crash on a luge sled or a near drowning from a raft, that will wake me up. It may be that I am not, through adventures, trying to make my life important, but to see that it has been important all along, much as the person told she has a month to live suddenly savors every moment.

I stare back at the chief and nod my head. Why? Why run a river that means nothing to me and that I might easily die on? Perhaps I am looking in the wrong place for the "meaning" that I need. Perhaps it is to be found in smaller things. Where? And how? I want to ask him, this wise man, almost surreal in his warrior dress. But, facing him in my high-tech paddling gear, I find the language and the cultural barrier seem too vast. I do not answer his question except with a nervous laugh. But I do not forget it.

Meanwhile, the Boh Gorge is at flood level. It is impossible to run at this time. Daily helicopter flights bring back the same reports: The river is a torrent of rushing water, thick with trees it has torn down, brown with the soil it has overrun.

The team is called to speak again with the leading members of the Dayaks. The meeting is solemn and ceremonial. Again, the chief speaks; he tells us that he has seen Unanaga, an evil dragon-snake spirit. We have been forewarned. This river is not to be rafted; something terrible will happen if it is.

The production team, not Unanaga the spirit-snake, makes the final decision. It has been ten days, and it can wait no longer for the floodwaters to recede. We say good-bye to our Dayak friends and morosely take the helicopter out of the jungle.

We go to Australia and eventually run a river there. Still, I cannot get the words of the Dayak chief out of my mind. Why? he asked. Why am I risking my life like this, for things that do not matter in any real sense? Why?

It strikes me as ironic that I have not listened to my parents, to my college, to the ghosts of my upbringing. Instead, I am stopped dead in my tracks by a rain-forest chief. A white girl from Manhattan, a product of boarding schools and English riding lessons, a graduate of a good university, with a fairly expensive taste in cars and two caring parents, I am shaken by the warnings of an evil spirit-snake and the sage words of a Dayak headhunter chief with a wooden dowel in his penis. With the chief's question ringing in my head, I declare my search for the new and different officially over. I will go home, I will settle down. Perhaps fulfillment will come not from radical action, but from easing into the flow of life. Film is all I really know; I will enroll in film school. I will leave adventuring to someone else. It is time, I think, to become the person my upbringing has prepared me to be.

# THE TEST

At four in the morning the Bay Bridge is almost empty. I make this trip a few times a week and I drive fast, letting the lights of San Francisco slide away past my left shoulder. There is only an odd truck or car on the bridge with me. I wonder why they are up at this hour. Perhaps they wonder the same about me.

I like the mornings. I rowed crew in college and we practiced in the mornings, at five-thirty, when the water was especially still. For years I saw a sunrise almost every day and came to know the smooth, supple colors of dawn, and then the sudden burst of light when the sun crests the horizon. Dawn is different than dusk in this way. Dusk settles quietly, lowering itself like a blanket, slowly and carefully. Dawn creeps up like a small child and then explodes with sudden glowing laughter. I like the mornings; even when you know they are coming, they seem to arrive unexpectedly.

I let myself into the KPFA radio station. The door is thick wood, and at the top of a steep flight of stairs there is another door that a receptionist unlocks for you during normal office hours. She sits behind thick glass, with only a small half-moon of opening at the bottom, like at a movie ticket counter. All this security for a nonprofit, listener-supported radio station might seem excessive, but KPFA Radio features important guests, from Bishop Desmond Tutu to activist Cesar Chavez to mayors or members of Congress. And KPFA minces no words on-air. It is outspoken and often controversial and it makes enemies. Not to mention that its phones are believed to be tapped by federal agents. Some of the personnel have police records from political protests, including me.

I have the place all to myself at this hour, and all it takes now is a key to let myself in. I do the morning news here. For the past year, I have studied and taken the tests for graduate film school. Soon I will apply. I work odd jobs. But I volunteer my time twice a week to KPFA. As the morning news anchor, I get a ten- to fifteen-minute broadcast ready by seven o'clock in the morning.

To do this, I condense stories that other people have already written. I scan three or four newspapers. I listen to the national news on the radio. I "rip wire." Ripping wire is my favorite, because I get to read news as it happens over the teletype machine that brings in news reports from all the wire services, like AP and UPI. When Dan Quayle was chosen as Presidential candidate George Bush's running mate, I felt as if I were the first person in California to know. The news comes out in a long strand of paper that runs all over the floor in an exuberant display. Past and present curls in a matted mess at my feet, making a sound like the surf as I wade frantically through the room, preparing the broadcast.

This morning there is another story about the San Francisco Fire Department. *Doctored Photo,* it says, *New Racial Trouble.* I scan it: A black man is erased from a photo that ran in the San Francisco Firefighter's Local 798 newsletter. The union says it is because he is the only nonmember in the photograph; he is also the only black man, and he belongs to the opposing Black Firefighters Association.

I remember other stories in the recent past. Interracial fistfights in stations, a swastika near the desk of minority officers. Lawsuits involving racial discrimination, the first class of women coming into the department under duress. I am fuzzy on the details, the exact accusations and counter-accusations. Memory has a way of retaining the most dramatic parts of an account, sometimes dropping other essentials.

The San Francisco Fire Department is just a word game to me. I write a snappy story, but in my head I retain only a vague impression of a bigoted, unwieldy institution. I will not lead with this story, but I put it near the top. It will hold people's attention into minute three.

Later I drive home in morning commuter traffic. I am surrounded by men and women driving to their proper jobs in proper offices; my day ahead looms unstructured and unproductive. The year until I begin film school spreads out before me like thick, spilled paint.

As a prospective filmmaker, I once again find myself precipitously near to my twin sister, but in fact we have come at film from opposite angles. At seventeen, Alexandra landed a role in a television movie called *Paper Dolls*. She was cast opposite Daryl Hannah, whom neither of us had ever heard of. I fall into film with more cynicism, and I decide on the other end of the camera. I am attracted to film because it epitomizes detachment. I can observe through a lens, involved yet apart.

I work haphazardly with a small film company. My employer is Ann Silver, which is not her real name. But she likes the sound of it and Silver Productions, the company she decides to start in order to pursue her first love, power. She claims that her first love is film, but we are too similar to fool each other on this score. She knows little about film, but this in no way stops her. She has red hair that was once another color—brown, I guess—and she wears makeup so that her eyes appear to be rounder and more arresting than they really are. Men find her irresistible and she knows it. She conducts business with them brusquely. Always, there is an undercurrent of husky flirtation.

In her finely tailored skirt suits, with her Italian leather briefcase, she is the archetype of what I am supposed to be. Strong, independent woman, with sex appeal. Mysterious vixen with expense account.

Silver Productions and I have managed to make a decent training film for a software product. But yesterday Ann Silver declared that she is dissolving Silver Productions. "It's back to advertising for me," she breathed, smiling absently, fluttering her eyes. I was half relieved, half stunned. Now I make the left-turn exit off of the Bay Bridge and think, *I should not have chosen film school.* Medical school or law school would offer a more stable lifestyle.

I know that this sort of angst is typical, even accepted, for Generation X. But at twenty-five, do I even still qualify for Generation X? As I accelerate toward my gym, I feel even more disconsolate.

The gym is my solace. Here my goal is no longer the winter Olympics or the national crew team. It is only vanity; a diamond calf and a flat stomach. Luckily, years of swimming, rowing, and trying to outperfect my twin sister have kept me fit. But I am surprised when a wide-shouldered man with a hefty mustache stops in front of me at the lat pull-down machine.

"You are strong," he says, and he cocks his head to one side. This is the strangest pickup line I have heard in a while, I think. With a charming smile he says, "The San Francisco Fire Department is recruiting women. You look strong. How about applying?"

I stare at him, taken aback.

"The racist, sexist San Francisco Fire Department?" I say. "Thanks, but no."

The firefighter has clearly heard this before. He smiles politely and says, "Don't always listen to what the media says." He offers me an application card.

Since I am the media, I know what he means. After all, I do not research my data. I simply rip wire. My job is to catch the attention of the post-sleep, pre-coffee crowd. It is at once to simplify and to inflate. But the truth is never simple, and suddenly I feel something like shame. I reach out my hand and take the application card.

Later I twist the card in my hand. It becomes funnel shaped. I have no intention of becoming a firefighter—I have no idea what, precisely, a firefighter does. Still, maybe I should go see for myself what this department is up to.

What good copy this would make for KPFA, I think. An

undercover story. I will pretend to be interested in becoming a firefighter and go through the testing process. I will be alert for signs of discrimination. I will get a story.

I smooth out the application card and fill it in. A few days later, on the way to KPFA, I drop it into the mailbox.

The Moscone Center is a huge midtown complex designed for trade shows and conventions. I arrive in the early-morning gray, to take the test that begins the San Francisco Fire Department's entrance procedure. I am unprepared for the huge line that winds around the building and spreads out haphazardly near the front doors. Approximately five thousand people signed up for the test. Three thousand one hundred and fifty-nine show up to actually take it, spread out through the day in shifts. I eye the demography of the jumbled queue. I try to determine the ratio for my undercover story. Blacks? Hispanics? Whites? Women? It seems varied, though there are far fewer women than men in every category.

I am a terrible test-taker, but I feel competitiveness rise up in me and something else, too. Curiosity, perhaps. I want to do well on this test.

This day I do everything right. I make sure that my roommate Peter knocks on my door early to ensure that I am up on time. I go to the bathroom twice beforehand at home, once at the Moscone Center. I check my wallet for the correct identification the night before and once as I am driving here: I pull over on Howard Street when I begin to worry, irrationally, that I've left my driver's license on the kitchen counter. I take slow, deep breaths. I try to avoid distraction and talk to no one for very long.

I become momentarily confused—am I a reporter or a nervous, hopeful applicant? I am acting more like the latter, I think, as I allow myself to be gently pulled in through the big glass doors by the polite, nervous sway of strangers.

The test is a curious one. In the video portion, firefighters assemble a piece of machinery. They are of different ethnicities; one is a woman. The narrator speaks slowly, so slowly that snickers erupt from around the auditorium. Mid-snicker the video stops and the narrator asks a question (slowly, carefully) that we are to answer about the assemblage we have just seen. I realize that this test is trying to rid itself of all cultural, ethnic, class, or gender biases. There is no undercover story here, at least not one that is controversial and therefore interesting enough to pass the radio editor's scrutiny.

The test over, I quickly forget about the San Francisco Fire Department. I do not see the firefighter in the gym again, and no new stories about the department pass over my KPFA desk. Alexandra, who thinks anything that I do is cool and remembers everything, asks about it once or twice. No story, I tell her regretfully. Andy also thinks it is cool. However, we see each other less; he is tired of the ways in which I put distance between us. One of those ways is Mary, who is ten years my senior and has a dark, feral side that somehow attracts me.

I do not tell my parents about the test because any allusion to "undercover" activity would worry my father. My mother, on the other hand, would not worry at all, but she would not take much notice either, and that would be worse. My mother and I speak in formal small talk only, and sometimes I let that lapse, too, and would rather not speak at all.

Even if there is no single catalytic moment, no one action from which estrangement grows, there is a human tendency to want to pinpoint a source, a critical particle in time, and I hone in on the day my mother picked up Gail Sheehy's *Passages*. Halfway through the book, my mother seemed to go berserk. She went back to school. She filed for divorce. She no longer cried unexpectedly in corners anymore, as she had for years; we wanted the disheveled, weepy mother we were used to, not this new, hard-eyed whirlwind. As a young teenager, I was left openmouthed in the wake of her new-found fury, and for years we could not talk past a few stiff remarks about the weather. Now I am more polite and more adept at being distant, so our sentences are longer, but we have not reconciled. I am someone who allows even small scratches of betrayal to redden and swell under my scrutiny.

When the phone rings and a man who identifies himself as a lieutenant asks to speak to me, I am confused. He says I have scored high on the fire department test; the fog clears slightly. *I passed.* Not only did I pass, but I did well. I qualify, along with two hundred fifty others out of the original five thousand, to go on to the next phase of testing: the physical agility test.

"What?" I say.

"What?" the lieutenant repeats.

"I mean, okay. Neat. I passed. Thanks, thanks for calling."

"Yeah, Miss. But we need to confirm that you can go to your physical-test appointment."

I always do unexceptionally on tests; there is no reason that this test should have been any different. Unless this is not just a good test score, but a portent. Wait. Being a woman must have helped, the affirmative action thing. Oh yeah. It helped. But you'd get in one way or another on your test score, just some classes later. Oh. So one way or another, I'm in. If I want to be. I take a deep breath. My unusual test score, could it be a preternatural whisper of advice? I feel like coughing or laughing, I can't figure out which.

"I'll be there," I tell him in a voice that seems to be not my own. "To take the physical test." He hangs up hurriedly. Suddenly this is no longer about a radio story. It is about being a firefighter.

*Two*

# HEAT

# FIRE

San Francisco's first recorded fire was a grass fire. This grass fire spread into the western part of the city in 1847. The population of two hundred quickly recognized the threat to these dry, windy hills, and the first fire law went into effect: Anyone setting alight brush or garbage would be fined five dollars.

This is the first hint of San Francisco's incendiary past; two years later San Francisco suffered six big fires (called the Great Fires). It was 1849 and gold had been found to the east; the city's population had skyrocketed to twenty-five thousand people. For the next eighteen months the Great Fires devastated the city, tearing through the huts and temporary houses erected by gold seekers. The fires had a strange effect: Instead of cowering under the assault, San Franciscans rebuilt their homes within weeks of each razing. Each time the city emerged more beautiful and sturdier than before. Temporary wood and cotton-paper houses became permanent brick structures as people who came west seeking their fortune fell in love with San Francisco.

Fire took on a mystical side: Citizens boasted how many times they had been burnt out of their homes (four or five times was not uncommon), as if fire defined their character. Meanwhile, street preachers claimed that fire was "divine vengeance" wreaked on the rough, pagan drinkers and gamblers of this frontier town. Years later the official seal of San Francisco became a phoenix rising from flames in front of the Golden Gate Bridge.

By the third Great Fire, however, the citizens began to

think of forming a fire department. Benjamin Franklin had organized the first volunteers more than a half century earlier; on October 1, 1850, San Francisco followed suit, and its first official volunteer fire department was born.

How could I ever be a firefighter? The first firefighter looked so little like me; he was as mythical as the fires he fought. Documents claimed that "to be a fireman was to be a gentleman," but there are numerous accounts of brawls breaking out between fire engine crews. Sometimes at a fire one engine company would detach the hose of another engine company from the hydrant and substitute its own. Engine companies like Knickerbocker #5 and Monumental #6 were known to have actually shot at each other. At night crews did not work together but instead would creep furtively up to the fire, hoping to outwit other companies. At an opportune moment they would race past rival crews, hauling their hand-pumped engine. Fights would break out by the hydrant, sometimes only broken up by the chief of police. These first firefighters were rough frontier men. They *were* fire—unpredictable, with inflammatory tempers, and a capacity for both destruction and regrowth. It was volatile forces like these, as much as the later contributions of architects, politicians, and others, that made San Francisco the beautiful, charismatic city it is today.

But few of us are aware of it. On the surface, there is nothing that hints at San Francisco's charred, chaotic past. When we think of violent, temperamental forces in San Francisco, we think of earthquakes, with their monsterlike capacity to open up and swallow us whole. But in 1906, the real damage came not from the famous earthquake, but from the fire afterward. It lasted three days and devoured twenty-eight thousand buildings (twenty of them were firehouses). A hydrant painted gold on the spot where firefighters made their final successful stand remains at Twentieth and Church Streets, a small reminder of the inferno.

To me, everything about San Francisco feels clean and serene. I cannot imagine that the dirty, ashen hand of a firefighter shaped any of this. San Francisco's hills undulate softly; the wheels of its cable cars hum quietly; its amiable surf rustles gently. Its old Victorian houses are painted in lively colors; the one I live in is orange with yellow trim around the windows and the turret. San Francisco is surrounded by water and bridges, which gives the feeling that we live instead in a splendid castle surrounded by a moat, insulated and separate. Indeed, San Francisco calls itself Baghdad-by-the-Bay, and in more snobbish moments simply The City, as if none other exists. It seems the perfect place to live.

It is no surprise, then, that San Franciscans know little about their fire department. When it is accused of "institutional racism and sexism," many San Franciscans are able to distance themselves. But they forget that this is a city born from ashes and forged by flame, and that the predicaments of the fire department mirror the predicaments of the city.

These hills are a perfect place to train for the physical part of the fire department's test. I discover hidden neighborhood steps that run for two or more city blocks. They rear up the slopes and cut stealthily between houses and sidewalks, offering a good cardiovascular workout. I carry a bag full of weights to simulate the "hose carry" event, where I must, among other things, carry a sixty-pound hose bundle up four flights of stairs. Sometimes I carry two Cat Chow bags; this sets dogs barking, drawn by the smell of chow or sweat. People stare.

Practice sessions for the test are held in the huge cement space said to be fire academy grounds. The place looks instead disquietingly like a prison yard. Also on these grounds is an active fire station. It is here that I first catch a glimpse of on-duty firefighters. They stand at a distance, their arms folded on their chests. I hear rumors that the male firefighters claim that physical-test standards have been lowered to include women, so that now these men seem to be ominous and judgmental, waiting for a mistake to report back to the grapevine. Their dark blue uniforms give them the impression of being an entity instead of individual people.

It is 1988, and there are six women already in the department. They came in, under controversy, during the past two years. I have not met them, but at the test practices we whisper about them sometimes, wondering how it would be to have been one of the first. There is a secret relief that we are not treading a completely new path, that there is a slight trail through the thicket for us. "Slight" is an overstatement: There are six women out of approximately fifteen hundred men. The trail is barely visible.

A few days later the firefighters are gone. Someone higher up has told them that they cannot watch the test proceedings.

I feel an uneasiness that I blame on the strange physical test. Strange, because I know nothing about fire fighting. I pull up on a rope with a weight on the end. I have no idea what this has to do with the job, but I am assured that it is pertinent. I lift a ladder I have never climbed. I drag a hose toward a white line. At the white line I drop the hose. For a long time I wonder what that white line means—fire hydrant? Dead person? Kitten in a tree? Then I pick up the hose bundle that I simulated for so long with Cat Chow. After climbing four long flights of stairs, I drag an eighty-pound person across the floor. It is not really a person, but an understuffed, hairless, overused dummy whose arms look dangerously as though they are about to fall off. Then I push a large pole up and down for a minute. I push against seventy-five pounds on the vertical upstroke and pull ninety-five pounds on the vertical downstroke. I start to hear the sound—a loud, rhythmic clanging—in my sleep.

Even while I am working so hard at the test, I am convinced that I cannot be a firefighter. I have fierce prejudgments about the institution accused of fierce prejudgments, an irony I do not let myself look at. I begin to think along lines I never thought myself capable of: *A blue-collar job? What will I tell my friends?* The thoughts leap through my head with the long, quick gait of a greyhound, and leave a trail of matted dust behind.

Around the same time I pass the physical test with flying

colors, my acceptance to a graduate-school film program arrives in the mail. Instead of elation, I feel as if something large and ominous has just walked into my path.

The two separate worlds of fire fighting and film school offer an odd symmetry, anvil-shaped, as if to make a place on which to hammer my indecision into some definable form. At once I see the perfect crossroads in a heretofore jumbled lifestyle. Film represents my social background. Here rests responsibility, social status, and intellect. On the fire-fighting side of the anvil rests a darker, more primitive metal. It represents impulsiveness, rebellion, and instinct. There is a vision of a hammy, dirty hand grasping something rough. Its elemental force attracts me.

I shake my head; there is no crossroads, despite my lively imagination; being a firefighter is out of the question. I am on my way to film school in the fall. I send in my acceptance.

I go through with the last phase of the fire department's entrance procedure. I don't know why. I tell myself I don't like to quit, I like to see things through—why not finish it? But part of me knows that something more than momentum pulls me. I take a medical exam. Then I submit the information required for my background check: proof of residency, motor vehicles record, and police reports.

I have three speeding tickets and a long rap sheet, which I pull out crumpled from my bag. The investigating officer, a square-jawed firefighter with narrow, unsmiling eyes, smooths it out. He stares at the long list of misdemeanors.

"All, uh, protests," I say. He reads in silence.

"This is America, after all." I shift uncomfortably in my chair. He scowls; I shift again. Even my mother has been arrested for civil disobedience, for stepping onto government property in order to protest nuclear testing. I imagine her raising her arm defiantly and saying in her reedy, British voice, "No nukes" (which comes out *nyukes* in her upperclass accent) to an astonished police officer. The man in front of me continues scowling.

"We can't disqualify for misdemeanors," he says slowly.

It clearly bothers him that he can't disqualify for misdemeanors. "And slow down," he adds, shaking my driving record as he waves me away.

That's it, I think as I walk out. I blew it for myself. I'm off that list, for sure, once and for all. Perhaps I should have mentioned my mother, to add a bit of apple pie to the interview. Wait. I *don't want* this job. Nevertheless, I have a sinking sense of loss combined with the dull relief of someone who is pointed the way onto a flat, wide highway.

A few days later I am accepted into the San Francisco Fire Department, Academy Class Number 75, off the first recruit list under the 1988 United States Federal Court consent decree.

# IGNITED

*Now, therefore it is hereby ordered, adjudged and decreed,*
the Federal Court proclaims. With these words begins the
"consent decree" describing the court's plan for the next
seven years to combat the systemic racism and sexism of the
San Francisco Fire Department.

I am part of this plan.

If I choose to be, at least. Instead I panic. This process
started off so simply; now I am mid-step into a new world,
pulled toward it by something visceral. Perhaps fire itself
has a deeper hold on me than I realize. Perhaps all the
notions of honor and glory and bravery and adventure that
fire fighting represents have seeped into my psyche and
lodged there. The firefighter, or, until recently, the fire*man,*
is a cultural hero. He represents all that is courageous, self-
less, and strong. He alone deals with basic elements, fire and
water; he is privy to divine forces.

Now there is a chance for me, a woman, to be a fireman.
No wonder I hesitate, at once drawn to this mythic career
and pulled away by my background. My life has opened up
many options for me, but it has almost completely closed off
this one.

And the thought of telling my father scares me silly.

"Fire fighting," says Jonathan. "Seems cool." He runs a
hand over his long hair. We sit on the front stairs of my
house while he smokes a cigarette. "But what about all that
paramilitary bullshit?" He looks at the tree in front of us as

he speaks. The colors are a vibrant yellow and the slight breeze gives them a soft blur.

On the one hand, Jonathan worries, the fire department may be a secret arm of the government. On the other hand, this is about fire trucks. Fire trucks ignite the same excitement in him as when he was a boy, as they seem to do for many men. However, they did not mean much to girls of my generation. Firemen had no resonance at all, except for grade-school crushes and the understanding that marrying one was out of the question for reasons your father would not quite explain. The first distinct image I have of a firefighter is a photograph I saw in high school. A crowd of black protesters are scattering under the force of a fire hose held by a sharp-faced white man in uniform. The picture is famous and I have seen it many times since. It haunts me. I substitute my face for his and feel my stomach contract.

"And that is another good reason to turn this thing down flat out," I say.

"Yeah," says Jonathan, still staring at the tree. "But you haven't. You haven't turned it down at all."

He is right, I haven't.

Jonathan blows cigarette smoke out slowly, watching it pass in front of him and then disappear.

"Well, great, if you decide to be one—a fireman." He puts out his cigarette with soft bouncing movements. "Firefighter," he corrects.

"Glade, I just don't know," I say lamely, looking down at the sidewalk. Glade is a nickname that Jonathan obtained some years back, when he lived in a commune in Tennessee. There people were named according to their spiritual development; a glade, the commune explained, is where sunlight and animals gather, and indicates the small but beautiful space inside my brother that mills with love and hope. This space, however, is surrounded by the darker, thicker forest, representing the part of him still needing spiritual growth. When Jonathan announced his new name, Alexandra and I dutifully called him Glade, and even came to like it very much. However, he soon let us know that he had reached a new spiritual level and his old name was now obsolete. His new name, he informed us, was Mountain. This we found not so easy to use. Now, years after his short stint at the commune, he remains Glade.

"Besides, I'm in film school," I continue.

"Yeah."

"I could do both, but . . . It just seems so, I don't know, *unlikely.*"

"Yeah."

We sit in silence for a while.

"You know, Caroline, you've got to do what you want to do, to hell with everyone else," Jonathan finally says. "You can't worry about it. You'll never be normal anyway, if that's what you're looking for. Neither will I. You and me, we're not Dick and Jane."

He stares at the tree again and sighs. "Hell, this world is going to be unlivable in ten years anyway." My brother feels that the globe is heading fast toward environmental doom and never fails to add this to a conversation. "You have to follow your heart, follow your soul. Somebody has to." He drops the splayed cigarette nub into his pocket.

"Just don't tell Dad," he says.

It is hard to know exactly what Dad will say, because Dad at once conforms to and dislikes his background. Why should he mind if I shuck mine, in favor of—let's admit it—a blue-collar job?

We are a family that has not drawn a genealogical tree, nor would we ever want to. Our ancestors do not interest us much; there are no claims to famous or infamous bloodlines.

My mother comes from England, but gave up her passport with relief and became an American citizen. She shed everything British except her accent. Her war with her past leaves her a woman who believes in working hard and earning one's way, but who inherited most of her wealth. She was born into the British upper class, but now she represents the downtrodden in her small practice as a social worker.

My father talks little about the small town that he grew up

in. He told me once that he had never heard of Yale University before he went there; he only knew that it was the farthest from Middletown, Ohio, on his college list. Yet now, in Massachusetts, he still leads the reserved life of a Midwesterner. His only connection to the past is to one not his own: My father collects antiques of every sort and size. Among other things, he has a faded document from Leopold of Prussia that he has partly deciphered, a large seventeenth-century clock that stands like a sentinel at his dining-room door, and a pair of shelves so delicate that he points closely but never touches them. He understands the imprints on silver and the mint letters on coins. It is hard to figure him out or fit him neatly into any category. He is a man of high integrity, a peculiar product of what he has worked hard to forget and what he has worked hard to become. My parents are both at war with their past; as a result, the whole family is under the American illusion that we can constantly remake ourselves.

*Firefighter:* The word sticks to my lips, the syllables clumsy and strange. I can't possibly tell my father: He'll have a heart attack, a stroke, a fainting spell.

Alexandra points out that my father is in perfect health; it is I who looks pale and sweaty. She has just finished the film *Dragnet,* where in one scene she tackles a snake in a wide pit of water while in a wedding dress. She knows about adversity.

"What should I do?" I ask her.

"You should do what makes you happy," she says.

"Now, that," I sigh, "is a stupid answer." Happiness has never been part of the equation.

I call the San Francisco Fire Department. I ask if, instead of accepting or refusing the position, I can put off the decision a little longer. They have a nice neat word for this procrastination. "Deferring," the brusque man on the other end says and pauses to scratch my name on a formal piece of paper. "You are now deferred," he repeats, and the phone goes dead.

When the "quake of '89" strikes, I am on the top of the student union, on a break from a graduate film class. The building is a gray stone monolith made to look modern and architecturally daring by its strange angles and concrete hummocks. I sit on a chair in a balcony-like area, on top of one of the concrete protrusions, when the earth moves angrily. My coffee, which is on the ground next to me, topples over; I cannot stand up for the shaking. From my vantage point, however, I hear a collective moan from the campus and see students stream wildly out of buildings and from under trees as if they are insects under a rock that has just been violently turned over. Inside the buildings, cabinets have tipped over and the lights have gone out.

Later I watch the Marina neighborhood burn from a hilltop not far from my house. My housemates and I sit with our chins on our knees contemplating the strange orange haze.

The next day and for days afterward, the newspapers are full of the destruction and chaos. The Bay Bridge has lost a section to the tremors, closing it, so I must take the train across the bay to KPFA. I start out the night before and sleep in the office in order to get the news out on time.

As I scan the morning papers to collect my stories, I see a strange transformation. The San Francisco firefighters are now heroes. "The Firefighter Who Wouldn't Give Up," reads a headline, detailing how a firefighter named Shannon crawled into a building to get to a trapped woman. The building was leaking gas; it was in imminent danger of collapse or fire. He got to her, the account says, and reached for her hand. He promised that he would not leave without her. He cut her out with a chain saw while the building began to burn.

Later he said, "When someone holds your hand and you are a few feet away . . . I couldn't go no matter what was happening."

Another San Francisco firefighter crawled into the sprawling debris of the Nimitz freeway, with no certainty that it would not collapse further and sandwich him. Forty-two people and their Fords, Toyotas, and Hyundais were crushed or dying. Three other firefighters pulled a man from the remains of an apartment; two minutes later the burning building fell.

I stare at the printed stories. Life is complex, I think, and these are complex men. Men who, despite alleged racism or sexism, also reach in and hold hands with strangers at the risk of their own lives. What would the Dayak chief think of this way of life?

Now, *that,* he might say, is an *important* danger.

# THE FIRE ACADEMY

The San Francisco Fire Academy consists of a series of makeshift plywood houses, erected temporarily years ago and still unchanged. Neatly dressed men with mustaches stare sternly at new recruits. We in turn look back nervously, saluting and jogging on command. There are thirty of us in the seventy-seventh class. Six of us are women.

Inside the temporary houses, we sit in a large classroom with walls of faux wood. It is dark; there are not many windows. The room is designed to make its inhabitants feel encased but not comfortable.

The lieutenant draws a big triangle on the board.

"This is fire," he says sternly.

We stare.

Oxygen, fuel, heat. He points slowly to each corner of his drawing. "These elements make fire."

"In the right amounts, that is," he adds.

The three elements must combine precisely. It is a friendship of minute and fickle agreements. Too little oxygen, he says, and there will be no fire, despite the dry wood and the hot match. Too little heat and the perfect fuel in the perfect oxygenated environment will not burn. He intimates that this is a world with an infinite potential to burst wildly into flames. The elements are all there, constantly, but they must be in the right proportions. It is a delicate dance.

We wriggle and cough in disappointment. We want raging primal anger, the fight of a mythical beast. We want the legendary force with which Prometheus changed human-

kind. This "delicate dance" does not resemble the wild creature that we expect to encounter.

"And there is a fourth element," he says in a monotonous
drone. "There also has to be a chemical reaction." He taps in
the middle of the triangle and looks back at us blandly.

"That's a square," someone says, to snickering and shuffles.

The lieutenant shrugs. The chemical reaction has only
recently been pinpointed as a crucial aspect of fire. It is not
well understood. No one, he explains, has bothered to
change the diagram.

I glance at Ritch, a few seats to my right and behind me,
who taps his watch and rolls his eyes. I need to stretch my
legs. Lunch is soon, but we have only half an hour to buy the
burritos at the corner and eat them. I have learned to eat fast.
I eat as I have seen ravenous dogs do, with great concentration. I tap the yellow helmet on my desk absentmindedly.
Lieutenant Gibson, who barks orders in a deep Southern
drawl, warns me that my long hair with its shaggy bangs
does not meet regulations. In the mornings, the other women
help me braid it, but every morning he warns me again. An
ex–military man, he speaks in short bursts.

"Hair, Paul," he says. "Don't meet regulations."

Or he calls me by my number, 27.

"Don't meet regulations, 27," he says, and his deep-black
skin shines in the sunlight as he speaks. I nod silently, my
expression vacant. I nod silently a lot these days.

When I told my father, finally, he, too, was silent. "That's
fine, honey," he said suddenly, but I could hear puzzlement
in his voice. *Just a phase,* I imagined him thinking. After
another pause, he said, "Just be careful. I have enough gray
hairs as it is." He laughed hesitantly, and I thought I heard
sadness in the sound. *No more Jane Pauley,* he must be
thinking.

In the academy we all wear shiny yellow helmets and
blue overalls. I appreciate the way I can disappear into the
large shapeless material, and pull the rim of the plastic helmet so that it reaches out from just above my eye line.

Framed in a medium shot, as they say in the film biz, we all look alike—woman, man, black, white, Asian, Hispanic, American Indian. For moments, we are all just bluish shapes with lids like struck match heads bobbing nervously past hose lines and forcible-entry tools. My number is written on my helmet, my books, my desk, my locker, and the place where I stand at lineup and salute. I have never saluted before in my life.

Training at the San Francisco Fire Academy takes fourteen weeks. From 7:30 A.M. to 5:30 P.M. we attend lectures and then go out to the asphalt-covered "yard" and simulate fire scenes. We learn to couple and uncouple hoses, name extinguishers and their specific uses, recognize tools like the Chicago door opener and the ten-pound maul. We learn to "throw" ladders, the most menacing of which is the fifty-foot ladder. While most ladders require two people, or sometimes three, to raise, "the Fifty" needs six. We are told that it weighs three hundred and fifty pounds. At any given time in the raise, as few as two people may hold all the weight.

The Fifty is my introduction to the psychology of fire fighting. I never have any trouble with it, but I keep thinking that I might have trouble, and the words *three hundred and fifty, three hundred and fifty goshdarn pounds* crackle maliciously through my synapses.

My number falls between #26, quiet Tom Ellis, on my left in the lineup, and #28, Mark Fields, on my right. Number 28 is part of a family legacy of San Francisco firefighters. Accordingly, he looks like the quintessential firefighter, with a large, round physique and a vigorous brown mustache. Number 26 is a stocky man of mixed heritage that is hard to pinpoint. He doesn't say much; what he does say is carefully thought out and reliable.

We sit in uncomfortable folding chairs for the lectures. The lieutenants make me nervous; they chastise us loudly and unexpectedly. There are rules that seem to make no sense except as psychological conditioning: We must always have a hose spanner in our pocket, despite the fact that we seldom use it; we must run when we cross the grounds, as if alert and eager all the time. If we are seen walking, we are yelled at. I find myself at a half jog even at home, making my way across the kitchen or out the front door in the morning. Habits are ingrained quickly. That, too, makes me nervous.

We are shown videos of explosions, of firefighters on fire, of melting apparatuses. We scale a seven-story building using thin ladders called pompiers. These are fourteen-foot-long pieces of wood with small handles that run up either side; they resemble the vertebrae of some fragile, long-dead creature. At the top is a long metal piece with small teeth that grips the wooden sill of the window above you. Pompiers were once carried on fire trucks to climb to windows normal ladders could not reach, but they are no longer used in the field because they were deemed too dangerous. Instead, the academy uses them to test the mettle of recruits.

I start on the first floor and lean way out with the pompier in my hands. I flip its thin jaw to the window above. When it catches, I wrap myself around its threadlike frame and climb. It sways and bends mercilessly. As I get close to the next window, I can hear the sill creak and groan. The jagged edge of the pompier seems barely able to hold on to the wood, and each successive pompier splinters the sill so that it looks as if finally the window must give way. Up the side of the building each of us goes, like young, clumsy spiders uncertain of their web. At the sixth floor, we are told to belt ourselves to the ladder. Then comes the command: Lean back. Way back. Arms out, crucifix-like. More. People sweat and curse under their breath. Some let go only briefly, to be yelled at and told to do it again by the lieutenants below. One man throws up afterward, claiming he has the flu. To me it feels as glorious as flying.

I like all my classmates. They are pleasant and smart and funny. Still, the class quickly divides into quiet cliques. On the surface the groups are not about gender or race, but about which high school one went to, what sports were played, who has family in the department. However, this eventually stratifies into gender and color. Many of the people of color, for instance, have no family in the department, nor did they go to the predominantly white Catholic schools. The women, too, feel a lean, hard loyalty toward one another. Nothing direct has been said to us, but we all know that we are under scrutiny by our male classmates and our lieutenants.

Crammed in a small, makeshift locker room, we trade tips on ladders or on the weekly test. Wendy is a paramedic and Anne is on her way to being a nurse; they help the rest of us with the Emergency Medical Technician tests. Jackie is the only black woman. She is beautiful, and proud that her hair is shaved closer than any of the men's. When she is angry, her face is wildly animated. As the herd of recruits subtly begins to fall into groups, Jackie makes it clear that she regards herself as black first, and then as a woman. She believes that is the way the world regards her. Being black in a white man's world is harder than being a woman in a white man's world, she says.

Unlike Jackie, I am not used to being in the minority. As a white, I have taken my inclusion for granted. As a Paul, my popularity has come easily. Only as a woman have I time and again understood what it feels like to be excluded. But when it happened (and it did), it seemed like a game. Mostly, I ignored it. Now I no longer can.

In the Fire Academy, we drift to those who seem most similar to us. I have never noticed this tendency in myself before and see it now with trepidation. Of course, I have never interacted with such a diverse group of people. My social attitudes have never been so fully tested.

Fire fighting itself is a new and different culture. It is a community built solely on male codes. As a woman, I strain to understand each unfamiliar inflection in this new language. The fact that I have many male friends does not help me as much as I thought it would. This world is about men, not men and women.

The social codes remain murky for me while the weeks in

the academy slip by, but the job of a firefighter becomes clearer. To my surprise, our work involves not just fires, but lockouts, leaking roofs, and medical calls.

Medical calls are fast becoming the most common calls that San Francisco firefighters respond to. This is a city guarded by forty-one fire stations. Fire stations are three minutes from any emergency in the city. On the other hand, there are usually only fourteen ambulances on the streets at any one time. At night this can drop to seven. At times an ambulance cannot arrive for twenty minutes. It is the fire-fighter's job to keep the patient alive until the paramedics come.

As a result, Emergency Medical Technician (EMT) train-ing has come to the academy. EMTs administer basic lifesaving care. We learn to use defibrillators and do cardio-pulmonary resuscitation (CPR). We are taught to recognize a diabetic reaction, a neck injury, the last stages of labor, and post-seizure confusion. We are shown pictures of gross dis-figurations and massive burns.

By the time graduation rolls around, I still have more questions than answers about this new life. What *is* fire? All I have gotten so far is a triangle on a board, though the excitement that fire will have for me has taken root.

But the San Francisco Fire Academy has indirectly taught us about a different kind of fire: the smoldering social elements that bind and divide us. The Fire Academy, under the blunt tutelage of the federal courts, has become a testing ground of another kind, where the social problems of a nation will now face off. It is perhaps the perfect place to do this. For all the disrespect it has garnered over the past few years, the fire department is an institution that knows how to battle great dangers. It is a place where courage and loyalty and teamwork are stressed. Firefighters understand instinc-tively the primal dance of elements. Characteristics of fire mimic our own traits. We can combine to become something wholly new; we can smolder angrily, and then rage out of control. Or we may decide on a balance of elements where fire cannot start at all. A firefighter understands that under one circumstance we must come together: fighting fire.

Will I be a good firefighter? "Big fire, grab the big hose line," my academy friend Ritch says, shrugging. "Little fire, little line. That is all we've got to remember." It is graduation day and I do not wear a gown this time, but a stiffly pressed uniform with a cap. My father arrives from Massachusetts, but my mother does not bother to come. I imagine that she looks at this as a step down from my Stanford graduation, and not worth the flight. Alexandra puts on my cap and we stand in front of a fire engine while Dad takes the obligatory picture. "Good going, Mugsy," she whispers.

# THE FIREHOUSE

Station 53 is on the edge of San Francisco's warehouse district. Here, the buildings squat like old, tired barns. Tar spots stain the streets. There are few cars, and remnants of train tracks cut haphazardly across sidewalks—runes of a past age. On corners, hulls of buildings sag near cranes and bulldozers; the deep guttural sounds of destruction and reconstruction blend indistinguishably. It is a part of town neglected until recently, now gradually being patched by new buildings and streetlights.

I pull my bag out of the car and stand staring at the open station doors. In the bag are the trappings of my new life: Fire helmet, fire coat, turnout pants (called "bunkers" in some fire departments, presumably because you tumble from your bunk and put them on). A sleeping bag. Toothpaste, toothbrush, hairbrush. A handful of bobby pins. Shower slippers. Tampons. Extra blue T-shirts, like the one I am wearing under my wool uniform shirt. I take out my coat and helmet; I will come back for the rest. I want to walk in self-assuredly, not limping from a load of toiletries and bed accessories.

The fire engine and the fire truck (Station 53 is a "double house"; a single house has only an engine) face me, nose out, the shiny chrome momentarily intimidating. I glance at my pants. Not a wrinkle yet. These pants are made for men, and they were fitted by a man's tailor shop so that the hems are short, like I remember my father's pants to be, hitting my ankle bone. I put my free hand on my shiny belt buckle that says SFFD, feeling the imprint on my fingertips.

No sense in standing here. Just walk in.

I tell myself this twice, and then I start to move. The sunlight of the morning abruptly drops away as I step from the sidewalk (not a sidewalk really, but a platform for the rigs that drops slightly into a street spotted with holes and tar patches). The shadows adjust and I am inside. I take a deep breath.

It smells like a fire station should, of ash and of something sharp, a mixture of gasoline and wet leather, I think. On the floor lie turnout coats, gnarled and faded, with fire helmets nearby. Locker doors run the length of this huge garage, and an oil can sits off to one side. I think of what I will say—"Hello" will probably do. But it doesn't seem enough, as if I have to cram an explanation of myself into the length of handshake. Just then a door swings open, and a man walks toward me.

His shirt is untucked. An unlit cigar is clamped between his teeth. He is short and trim and intent on something in his hand, which turns out to be a match. When he sees me, he stops.

"So you're the new girl." He does not remove the cigar when he speaks, just steadies it as if it is a nail to be hammered.

He nods at me, and his thin gray hair, hanging in slabs on his forehead, swings with the motion. I introduce myself and he turns to his left and leans in, squinting. "Speak up. I'm deaf, like the rest of these jakeys," he says. "The sirens. You got to wear your ear protection, okay, or you'll end up like me." He laughs, understanding a new irony: In some ways I will never be like him; in other ways I will.

"I'm Tom," he says, sticking out his hand now. "Let me help you with your stuff." He stops and adds, "Well, um, ya know, I'd do it for a guy." He is momentarily embarrassed. I know that there have been specific instructions about how to act, what to say, what not to say.

A door slams and the tallest man I've ever seen approaches me.

"Firefighter Paul," he says in a booming voice. He has wide shoulders and the long lope of a man used to bending over to get under doorways. At six foot seven he is clearly not a man to be trifled with. "I'm your officer. Jim Leahy."

"Hello . . . Uh, hello, Captain. Nice to meet you,"

"Jim." He smiles. "Call me Jim."

Tom shuffles off to light his cigar; Captain Leahy leads me toward the kitchen. I follow him shyly. A dizziness washes over me. I have felt this vertigo before, on the first day of the academy.

*You won't fit in. You are not a fireman.*

Not that I know what a fireman is like. Fire Man, jakey, smoke-eater. There are many names. Fireman is no longer accurate for the new department, though it fits the old-timers in a curious, archetypal way—Fire Man. Jakey did not come from a guy named Jake, as I had once thought, but from the J-shaped keys that firefighters once used to open the corner fireboxes. Smoke-eater, self-explanatory, has a rough, tough edge that I do not relate to.

The little I do know about firefighters is mythical and was learned in childhood. They are knights in brown-and-yellow armor. They wield axes from roaring red steeds. They charge at fiery dragons and slay them with wild, piercing cries. As kids, we watched them gallop down the street. *"Fire Men!"* we whispered in awe, letting our ice cream melt down our hands; the name is at once an alleluia and an amen.

Then there is that other myth, the more adult one, laced with admiration and awe but tinged with a slight disdain, the condescension we reserve for what we do not understand or are excluded from. Because the firehouse is a home and the fire department a family, a culture in and of itself, a private domain, a secret world. This myth says that *Fire Men!* are chain-smoking, hard-drinking, *what the fuck do you think you are looking at, boy*–rugged, blue-collared men who save lives. Not just lives, but babies and homes as well. Babies and homes! What is more sacred than innocence and property?

You won't fit in. You are not a Fire Man!

Suddenly I want to turn around and leave. Was all this a dream? I am a woman, for God's sake. This is a man's world. I cannot picture myself here, in my new clean fire coat, treading with the easy relaxed roll of Captain Leahy. I know that I am quick and strong and that fear of shame will keep me brave. I know a little about hoses, knots, and ladders. But I have no myth of my own to follow, not even a stereotype. I have never pictured a woman as an axe-wielding hero. I have never seen one kick a door in or drive a big truck. I do not smoke, never had a beer.

Could I be a Fire Man?

Captain Leahy walks past a small sitting area and then enters a kitchen. He waves his hand for me to enter.

Utensils dangle above a large, squat oven. Massive pots and pans line shelves whose doors have been left casually open. In front of me is a long rectangular table, crowded with bread, jars of peanut butter and jelly, some coffee cups, and surrounded by people. The noise in the room suddenly pivots and stops as faces turn to stare at me.

I have never been the last to be picked for a team, never had my braids pulled in class, never felt the sting of high-pitched laughter as I walked past the "in crowd." I have never been a misfit, a dangling social appendage. But at once I imagine that this is what it feels like not to belong—this enveloping silence, this crush of stares, this heavy discomfort. My mouth feels tight, the rigid smile glued on haphazardly.

The quiet seems to go on forever.

"The Stanford grad," someone finally says.

"The vegetarian," someone else says, and laughs slightly.

"Welcome to Station 53." A short, disheveled man comes forward to shake my hand. "Johnny," he offers.

He is older, in his fifties, perhaps, with black-gray hair. "Come on in, come on in," he says, and brings his hand up in the air in a large wave motion.

I think that this man must be an angel in clever disguise: His pants are wrinkled, his hair is uncombed and sticks out at the back, and his collar has caught under itself, forming a curve under his ear. His shirt is half-buttoned and askew, as if a great wind has just passed through and tossed him about. A pair of glasses perches unevenly on his nose. He tilts his head to look up at me and then leans back further to look through his glasses.

Johnny suggests that I sit and read the paper—how about some coffee? A man with a double chin and a big belly—Al, I hear him called—moves over on the bench, nodding without looking at me directly. His handlebar mustache ends in two hard lines below his mouth. He wears a baseball cap to affect a casual look, but I know instinctively that his mustache is carefully groomed, his pride and joy. He yells across the table for the butter, which is spun at him at great speed, and he laughs loudly. Everything about Al takes up space, though there is something about his bluster that forms a fence around him.

Johnny squeezes past Al with the coffeepot. In the awkward space between introductions, I am grateful for the goodwill that accompanies the coffee.

The handshakes and nods begin now in earnest. A stocky man with hammy hands, fingers blunt like rivets and callused at the tips, introduces himself as Randy. He has long, bushy sideburns, and a bushier mustache. "So your sister is a movie star," he says, not unkindly, and glances around the room as he speaks.

Johnny offers me a tour of the fire station. It is old but comfortable. The furniture is worn, the tiles in the kitchen blur together, and the dorm is crowded and dark. Out back there is a small, carefully tended garden.

Johnny is a board member of the Firefighters Union. I know that the union has fought long and hard against women entering the department and against affirmative action. I remember that it is the union that erased the picture of the black (non-union) member that I had read about while at KPFA. It is also the union that is backing six white male members in their ongoing suit against the Federal Court's consent decree. They have even gone so far as to state that the entrance procedure has been simplified in order for minorities and women to pass. One man claimed in the local newspaper that "many of the minorities that they have hired and promoted are not competent."

Despite this, there are valid questions being asked. Can a woman handle the physical demands of fire fighting? Is it "fair" and "just" to institute a system of preference based on gender and color, to replace one that is maligned for its preference for the white male? These are delicate questions, questions that can be construed as sexist and racist. It seems to me that sometimes they are, but sometimes they are not.

From the moment the fire department entered my life, people who know little else about fire fighting are sure of one thing: Watch out for male firefighters. Watch out for the *fire men.* They are out to harass you.

KPFA staff members tried to talk me out of joining the SFFD, claiming that the monolith of bigotry would crush me. My mother's first comment was that men from the New York Fire Department defecated into the boots of female probationers. Even strangers looked at me incredulously and asked if I had been harassed yet.

How did an institution that stands for courage and self-sacrifice get such a terrible reputation? It would be easy to simplify the situation into the "good guys" and the "bad guys," as each opposing faction has done. And yet here is Johnny, a member of the "bad" union, showing me, his alleged enemy, around the dorm with casual waves. I make a mental note to keep an eye on my turnout boots.

Johnny points to a bed that I can use each shift with my sleeping bag. Nearby is a portable "privacy screen," behind which I can sleep or change my clothes, since I will have no locker or bathroom of my own. We work twenty-four-hour shifts, and at night I will also be in the same dorm as the men. This doesn't bother me a bit but, according to rumor, bothers many of the wives. However, it must be said that there should be nothing less threatening to a wife (or a husband) than a firehouse dormitory. It is controlled chaos, crammed with the remnants of previous shifts: reading lights left on to cast fatigued shadows, old coffee cups, ragged paperbacks still open on chairs, sports pages. On the other hand, there is a sterile regimentation to the long lines of beds and lockers. The room is dark, as if someone just shook out a dozen dirty blankets and the dust is still in the air. Dark so that sleep can come more easily, despite the snorers and the farters, between the emergencies that conspire to snatch you out of REM sleep as soon as you glide into it. The only wide spaces in the whole dorm are the pole holes that lead to the rigs on the ground floor. This is a functional place not made for leisure or pleasure of any kind. It is a place made to slip easily away from.

Alone in the dorm, I take a deep breath. Pushing aside a *Car and Driver* magazine, I carefully arrange my turnout pants like everyone else's next to the bed. The pants curl down along the boots, and the suspenders are untangled and free.

I sit on my bed and stare at the pole. I wonder if I will sleep tonight, and if I do, will I make it into my turnout pants and down to the truck without killing myself? I look around and step quietly into the boots, hoisting the suspenders onto my shoulders. I pace the steps to the pole—five and a half. I don't slide down the pole, nervous that someone will see me and ask what I am doing. I step out of the boots and arrange them again.

I am a "probationer," also known as a "probie" or "probie scum." For the next three months at Station 53, I will be assigned to the truck and therefore be "that probie scum truckie." This is better and more anonymous than *Ah, the Stanford grad,* or *Ah, the one with the sister who is a movie star.* To be "probie scum" is to be almost invisible. For once in my life this is what I prefer.

The truck is an awe-inspiring creature, snaking its way through crowded streets, its size and siren demanding attention and deference. It is ribbed with ladders and tools. Along the middle is its longest arm of rescue: a hundred-foot hydraulic-powered aerial ladder. The driver aims this ladder at the windows or roofs of burning buildings. People scramble down its massive length to safety. Sometimes they must be coaxed by a firefighter, as if the ladder itself is more intimidating than the fire. There are other uses for the aerial ladder: A nozzle is attached to the end for a high vantage of attack in big fires. It is also lowered against windows, breaking them to ventilate the hot smoke and gases. Some firefighters have been known to pin a suicidal "jumper" to the side of a building with the aerial ladder, locking them to the wall with the rungs.

When the alarm goes off I jump, though my body has been waiting for it. The alarm, called the Bee-Bop, is not an alarm at all, but a loudspeaker that begins with a series of tones. Then a voice from the dispatch center breaks into the room, indicating the address and type of call. *Street Box 2191*, the voice intones, *Brannan and Third. Street box only*.

I am on the rig before anyone else, bolt upright and breathing hard. My helmet and coat are on, and when the siren starts, I feel its sound resonate in my ribs. No wonder Tom is deaf.

I recite the steps I must take if it is a fire: belt, axe, air pack, Chicago door opener. When we reach the corner, I trip out of the seat, my truck belt cinched at the last hole—still too loose—squeezing my axe tightly. I looked at the axe earlier this morning while I inspected the truck, making sure where everything was. The axe head is deep gray and flecked with the spoor of past fires, small nicks and scratches. The axe handle is worn, the grain of the wood smooth and veined. This is the truck person's Excalibur.

"Get on board, rookie," someone says. "False alarm. Just some idiot pulling boxes."

I do not move. I look around. I steady my breath and readjust my axe.

"False alarm," someone says again. Leahy is motioning to me.

"Oh." I am embarrassed.

Leahy motions again, and points to the end of the truck.

"Go on up," he says. He points to the tiller, the legendary steering position of the ladder truck, the one the kids wave to when the long, thin rig goes tearing by like some sort of mad, weaving centipede. The seat perches on the back end like a grand throne, and the tiller operator helps the driver by steering the rear of the truck independently of the front, in order to gain wide berth around corners and cars. To do this the tiller must steer opposite from the driver, turning the back end away from the corners that the driver steers toward. The current tiller—was his name Doug?—stands up and leans over. He does not say anything as he settles into the training seat. I climb up and the truck slides out onto the street.

I grip the big oval steering wheel splayed like a tray in front of me. As tiller operator, I have no brakes, so I am effectively being pulled across the city like a cart. My only defense is to steer, and this can be a complicated affair. Steer opposite, I remind myself, *away from. Opposite, opposite.*

The only time I relax at all is at red lights. I let the corners of my eyes wander to the sidewalks. People stop, lean down to their kids and point. *Firemen!*

The kids notice first, mid-wave.

"It's a girl," they announce to their mothers. "Look, the back one. It's a girl." The mothers glance up again, poke their husbands' ribs. Whole families stand, catatonic. They don't know what to make of it; their world has shifted a little.

A few days later, Jackie calls. She has had her first fire. "It's black, blacker than me," she says. "The air is hot, and thick like stew." I try to imagine it, but I can't.

At my self-contained breathing apparatus (also known as an SCBA or air pack) drill, I reel off the numbers and parts I've learned. Three thousand psi of air, gauge on bottle, gauge at side. Open it up, lefty-loosey, righty-tighty. Pressure-release valve. Arm strap, hip strap. Regulator. Face mask, side straps, top strap. Captain Leahy nods quietly. He is a good teacher, patient and attentive.

Behind me, I hear the sound of laughter, and a high female voice. Randy introduces me to a woman in the neat white uniform shirt of a chief's driver. Tess is tall, Caucasian, and pretty. Her hands are huge; they seem much too big for her soft, high voice and the shining white shirt and perfectly pressed pants that make her look like a toy soldier. She extends one of them in welcome.

As I reach to take it, she pulls it back quickly. She lets out a loud guffaw. She looks at Randy and laughs again. I pull my hand back and let out a quick laugh, too. I want to pretend that I approve of her joke, but my high, squeaky laugh belies me.

I glance at her as Captain Leahy explains again that when there is a quarter of a tank of air left in the SCBA, an alarm will go off as a warning signal. "With ninety seconds left of air, the alarm will stop . . ."

Jesus Christ, I think, no one warned me that I might have to worry about the women, too.

"So when the alarm stops, you'd better be close to a door." I nod. What will I be like when I am in Tess's place, with a few years under my belt and a host of acquaintances I am intent on impressing?

To make things worse, today's my day to cook in the firehouse. Everyone is nervous about this. With good reason. I can't cook. I have rarely made a complete meal in my life. I eat only things that are unwrapped, unpeeled, or untied. To make matters even more grim, I am a vegetarian.

I have heard legends about these first times—how a probationer will bring in his wife to cook, how the meals can be so bad that they are launched across the room mercilessly, how the worst sin of all is when there is not enough food to go around. The meal is the symbolic center of firehouse culture; to cook a bad meal or, worse, a careless one is blasphemy.

At first it is surprising that such good meals can be produced by such big-armed and macho firefighters, seemingly too ham-handed and boisterous for the quiet concentration of a kitchen, the delicacy of thin slices, and the subtleties of herbs and sauces. But the legends are true: Firefighters are excellent cooks, and the Firehouse Meal is an affectionate worship of excess. The tall, steaming pots fill plates two or three times. There is also an urgency about the meal, as if the danger of the job lurks always in the background and the firefighter wants to get as much out of the moment as possible. To be at Station 53's dinner table is to be totally present, each moment highlighted at high volume. Passed words, passed food, passed laughter—even to watch as I do, shy and reserved, is an inclusion.

Lunch arrives late in one tall pot. "Vegetarian chili," I say, clearing my throat.

"Where's the beef?" someone murmurs jokingly as the crew starts to eat politely, glancing at each spoonful before raising it cautiously to their mouths. Afterward, Captain Leahy says, "That was excellent," but he is being kind. As we clear the dishes, I realize that my meal, no matter how terrible, will never be thrown against the wall or pitched to the ceiling to see if it will stick. I wonder if that is a good or a bad thing.

Just as the dishes are cleared and the leftover vegetarian chili is stored hesitantly in the refrigerator, the Bee-Bop sounds for a "body in the bay."

The body is not in the bay at all, but lying near the end of a cement pier. It is facedown and, judging by the lividity in the hands, the body is dead. I have never seen a dead body. I stare at the misshapen pile. To see a dead body, really see it, is a profound experience.

A crew is already there and a tall man with glasses shakes his head as we walk up. "Dead. Looks real bad." He glances at me. "You don't want to see it."

In fact, I do want to see it, as if death could provide a revelation I have long been waiting for. I stare at the corpse. "She was beaten," he continues as Captain Leahy leans down and rolls the body over.

Death, far from being revelatory, seems at first surprisingly brutish. If a passage into another world, it is one like a sewage pipe, dimly lit and reeking. Later I will see people who have died in compromising positions: during sex, on the toilet, while in the bath. They lose their bodily functions, and any secrets roll off, too; teeth, wigs, and hidden fat lie matter-of-factly around dead bodies. We seldom hear last words of any significance. Even less frequent is the presence of loved ones holding them in a last embrace. Today my first impression of death is that people die horribly alone and violently.

She is no older than forty, white and overweight, with a particularly cheap blond hair dye. Her face is beaten so badly that it looks like an oversized ball of putty. Her features are barely distinguishable. Her eyes are open; the rest of her face is a blur of reds where the blood pools beneath her swollen skin.

I step back just as Captain Leahy checks the pulse on her neck. It is an unnecessary move, but he is a conscientious man. Protocol demands that death be determined before we leave. I think it is his way of making sure that she gets the concern in death that she did not have in life. He stands up and coughs. "Let's go home," he says.

As I near the truck, I turn to look again. The dead body is still motionless. It is as if Death, before this, was only a concept, a story to be read and put away. But there is no easy place to stash this. I stare at the body one last time. My mouth is dry, but my neck starts to sweat.

# SWINGING AXES

The glass gives way easily to the axe. It is a satisfying feeling, and I stop after the first stroke, listening to the bluster as it leaves the frame, before it shatters to the ground. Leahy takes this for hesitation.

"Keep going," he says. "Clear it all out. Always hit the top of the pane, so the glass doesn't come down on your hand." These little tips are obvious, but I never think of them myself. I sweep the frame free, and the night air slides in, smelling of fish and salt.

The fire is confined to one room. At three in the morning, out by the bay, it is a miracle that anyone noticed the smoke at all. It is my first structure fire, in an old run-down diner by the water, a place for mariners that looks itself like an old rusty boat, ready to sink. Leahy motions for the thirty-five-foot extension ladder. It feels light in my hands, the adrenaline pumping. On the roof, which is flat, smoke seeps through unseen pores, drifts past my eyes, which water and tear. Leahy points to vents and chimneys. "Knock the tops off," he says.

An old-timer lights up a cigarette. He takes off his gloves and puts his hand on the tar, then exhales thoughtfully. "Ain't hot here," he says.

I want to swing an axe into the roof. "No, no," Captain Leahy says, palm out like a traffic cop. "No sense in making holes if we don't have to." He knows this fire is not big. Inside the engine crews spray water. When the steam rises I hold my breath, thinking that it is smoke. I don't yet know the semaphore of a fire. I look expectantly at Leahy, axe in hand.

"Steam," he says.

But now, at overhaul inside the diner, I have my chance.

Leahy points to a window frame, black and blistered. "Go ahead and take this down. Carefully now. Look at the way it is put together. Take it down that way."

I stare at it. I can swing an axe, but I know nothing about carpentry. Leahy, on the other hand, understands the intentions of the creator. I sense that he, like most firefighters, regards objects that have been built with a spiritual intensity, the process of deconstruction a communion, not a battle. I, on the other hand, just want to demolish it.

"No, no, no," Leahy says as I swing the axe into the middle of the left frame. He sounds offended.

The room quiets. Everyone likes to swing an axe, but here is something more amusing. *The girl's got an axe!*

Some have never seen this before. They doubt it can be done.

There are rumors about how a woman swings an axe— that it bounces right off the wood, that it can barely be lifted, that amazing high-pitched whines come out of them from the exertion. I come from New England, where even the most genteel families chop their own wood. Chopping firewood is part of being a Connecticut WASP; we like the self-sufficiency it implies. My mother, at fifty-four, still chops some of her winter store. But these men are not Connecticut WASPs; many of them have yet to see any of the few female firefighters at work.

Leahy steps back. I squint at the frame, trying to look intent, feeling the many stares at my back. *Not the sill, I tried that.* I feed the axe into a crack. How on earth do I know how this was put together?

I wonder if I can escape scrutiny if I work silently. I breathe quietly a few times and pull abruptly at the pick. The wood gives way somewhat with a rubbery feel, not the resounding crack it should have.

"One more time." Leahy doesn't seem to notice that the

whole room is watching. "Get the blade in and use the opposite side as a fulcrum."

The room has become so quiet that I imagine I can hear the soft wheeze of wood fibers slowly giving way from water and heat. I continue to stare intently at the frame. Okay, the top piece could go next. I bury the impulse to send the axe crashing into it, to overwhelm the audience with light and sound. I cock my head slowly and pretend I am puzzling out the best angle. Then, without further ado, I bring the axe crashing into it. Before Leahy can say anything else, I swing again, and again. The frame is in shambles on the floor.

It isn't pretty. It is not even a very good job. I can hear Leahy start to tell me again that I am using too much energy, that it can go down with finesse, to try again, slower this time—*look at how it is put together.* I kick the fallen wood out of the way. I nod slowly; we walk to a new window. The men turn back to their work; I hear the hum. *Okay. She can swing. Somewhat. Huh. Yeah.*

It is not until a few months later, on one of my last watches at Station 53, that I get my first "greater alarm." It is six in the morning, and our shift is almost done; the dorm lights snap on, and the Bee-Bop begins. *Fire in the building,* whines the loudspeaker. I am bolt upright in my bed and then into my boots before it can even repeat itself. Across the room Randy says, "This is it, probie." He knows: A call early in the morning for a fire probably means that it is a fire, and not a false alarm. Odds are that it is a good fire too, big enough to wake someone in these sleepy post–last call, pre-commute hours.

Everyone in the station except me recognizes the address. It is a large brick building, abandoned since the earthquake eight months before. The building's macabre past is vivid in the minds of Station 53 crews: In the earthquake, one of the brick walls gave way and fell on a car that was full of people. Station 53 responded to this call; they pulled the flattened bodies from the wreckage. It is not an address they would forget easily.

Smoke pours out from behind windows blocked by wooden panels. Since the building is condemned, Leahy does not let any of the crews go inside. The San Francisco Fire Department is fiercely proud of its "interior attack" strategy, and not to be allowed to attack this building, of all buildings, aggressively is an affront. But as the ladder we throw against the building quickly catches fire, Leahy waves us farther back. The brick walls heat and threaten to collapse. Large lines are set up to "surround and drown" the structure.

As for me, I do what I am told. As the fire goes from a single alarm to a second alarm, then a third, crews arrive from around the city. I know there is order to the chaos, but the textbooks do not wholly prepare me for this scene. Despite the seeming confusion, I see the veterans go to work with an ease and a calm that comes only with years of meeting fires head-on.

At the station, Leahy puts his hand awkwardly on my shoulder. It is our last time together. He clears his throat and congratulates me on being a hardworking, successful probationer. He quickly drops his hand and nods at me.

It is as close to a man-to-man talk as I will get. I am grateful for it.

# FIRST WOMAN IN

There is a method to fighting a fire, though a spectator would see only chaos and noise and great light. The methods are peculiar to each city and town, depending on the types of houses, the terrain, and the number of residents.

To most people, San Francisco is simply a quaint and beautiful city. But the firefighter doesn't see only that. The firefighter looks more closely and sees kindling in its historic wooden houses. The firefighter sees hydraulic power tools, like the Jaws of Life, in use as the steep hills claim yet another car; watches the deep blue Pacific surge on the long beaches and wonders who will drown and how; scans the high, majestic cliffs for a stranded tourist. Not out of morbidity: Firefighters love San Francisco. Most of them were born and raised here. When they give directions, they say things like: *Go down three blocks to where St. Peter's church was, hang a left at the furniture store that burned in that fifth alarm ten years ago, and past the old warehouse that was near Old Station 4—you know, the one that is now the supermarket.* For a firefighter, the characteristics of the city are the topography of the job.

When there is a reported fire in San Francisco, a "full box" goes over the loudspeaker. The city is divided into box numbers that correspond to those red metal containers at street corners—a method from the old days when there was no loudspeaker or computer and fires were reported in a series of bells that directed firefighters to the firebox and therefore to the general vicinity of the emergency. It meant listening to the bells and counting them and then checking a card system to see if your station was due at that box number. If not, the incident still had to be "pegged," or charted on a huge board, so that at any given time each station knew what the others were doing. This was important because your vehicle was responsible for a shifting area of the city, depending on what crews were busy. Your rig would be relied on if a new emergency arose in the district of an occupied crew. Now modern technology charts the responsibilities of each firehouse. The loudspeaker indicates the location of the incident, which fire vehicles should respond, and the exact address. But the old-timers are fond of reminding us how tough it used to be, and how easy we have it now.

When the full box comes in, the stations disgorge quickly and dramatically. A huge contingent of furious light and sound descends on the city and at the address of the alleged fire. Three engines, one or two trucks, chiefs' cars, and a Rescue Squad race through the streets. The rigs arrive in quick succession. The sirens piggyback and for one moment reach a crescendo, then fall silent as feet leave the siren button. The crews leap out. People stand around in shock as we arrive, as if troops have suddenly invaded.

Onlookers ring the fire with fingers outstretched at their sides and mouths open, as if communicating on another metaphysical plane. They stare at the leaping flames as we run into the building. They need to be there, to experience the deep primitive force of fire. It seems to awaken a profound response in them.

Of course, they are also gawkers, nuisances who bring their children to witness destruction and death. They get in the way of the fire engines, of the hoses. I understand, but only later, when the fire is over and I am back at the station. Afterward, they, too, are probably saying, "Jesus, there was this *fire*," and then they are speechless, knowing only that, fleetingly, fire grounded them at once to the moment and to the infinite.

My mother, on the rare occasions that we talk, asks me

perfunctorily how work is; I tell her we had a *great fire, a really good burner,* and I hear her gasp. There is a sense that what I have said is unfeminine and coarse.

"That's an awful thing to say. A fire is always terrible," she responds, her British accent lilting over *fire,* as if it has two syllables. *Fi-yer,* she says, and I hear the awe in her voice. Fire taps something ancient and vital in each of us, something both snarling and reverential. Fire harkens back to our wilder selves, the parts we let out only when we think no one is looking.

I do not try to explain this to my mother.

At a fire scene, there will be at least five fire vehicles. As each greater alarm is struck, five or so more vehicles will arrive. These range from the chief's car—known as "the buggy" from the days when horses were used—to engines, trucks, and a Rescue Squad.

The fire engine is the small, squat vehicle; the truck is the long, gangly one. The fire engine holds 500 gallons of water, 100 feet or so of one-inch hose line, 350 feet of one-and-three-quarter-inch small hose line, and 1,000 feet of three-inch large hose line. There are also various brooms, rakes, spanners, and couplings on board. Since the engine is the primary medical unit in the firehouse, unless a Rescue Squad is stationed there, it also carries oxygen, a defibrillator, and various other pieces of medical equipment.

The long, thin fire truck, with wooden ladders on the side and a huge hydraulic aerial ladder along its spine, is more noticeable. It blocks the street like a large cannon and shoots its ladder to the roof of a building for access and evacuation. Inside its compartments are chain saws and axes and crow bars and a battering ram—anything to help get at the fire as quickly as possible.

Each vehicle performs a different function. The trucks use their ladders to access the fire building and perform rescues. Also, they open the roof with axes or chain saws to ventilate the heat and smoke. Meanwhile the engine (the crews become their vehicle, so that you are not described as a "member of the engine" but as "the engine," or "the truck") is crawling inside with a hose. They battle darkness and heat to find the seat of the fire. "Did ya put water on it?" they are asked when they get home, meaning did they get there first, or did another engine company beat them to it—something you never want to have happen. *Putting water on the fire*—being way in there, and at the very bosom of danger—is the only place to be, for an engine.

According to legend, the truck people are big, hairy guys who are loud and reckless. They swing axes, haul chain saws, and throw ladders with gestures as rough as their personalities. Their hands are like the thick slabs of meat that they like to eat at dinner, and give the sense that they could enclose the neck of that cow with their fingers. But they are too busy laughing to kill anything, too busy slamming their fellow big-handed truckmates to care. Legend sometimes pans out—this describes my truckmates at Station 53 well. Loud, exuberant, proud of being big, and equally aggressive with a joke and an axe.

Engine people, on the other hand, are lithe and quick. Legend gives them intelligent, alert eyes constantly half-narrowed as if against smoke, with sinewy bodies to crawl through long hallways. They are easygoing and quieter in the firehouse, and never say a word when their ears singe and their knees get red-hot in a fire. Engine people love the hot, greasy breath of danger, and somewhere in their soul there is a leaping ferocity.

Firefighters identify themselves with one rig or another and, while I enjoy my time on Truck 53, within a few weeks at Station 91, my new house, I know that I am an engine person.

I have heard firefighters from other cities say that San Francisco fights its fires in a traditional way. By that they often mean "outdated." I don't know much about how other departments work, but we are proud of the way we fight our fires. We have concerns other cities do not and we tailor our tactics to the distinctive dimensions of our city.

The buildings in San Francisco are made mostly of wood,

and sit tightly, side by side, like people packed on a bus, shoulders touching. So when a house catches fire, there is always great concern that the surrounding houses, called "exposures," will catch as well. This means that San Francisco's firefighters must be more aggressive than in other cities. We rush inside buildings to meet the fire head on; we cannot afford to stand outside and merely point hoses (the "surround and drown" method used in the abandoned-brick-building fire). To rush inside a building convulsed in flame and smoke seems counterintuitive at best, foolhardy at worst. But I have seen photos of two or three firefighters staring belligerently into the camera with buildings in ruin and charred dismay on the streets around them; whole blocks are lost. The only way to assure that most of San Francisco withstands its virulent fires is a cunning and dangerous interior attack by aggressive firefighters.

There are other special conditions to watch out for in San Francisco: Her streets are steep and narrow. Engines have slipped down hills; a truck once tipped over when its aerial ladder was extended and the side anchors could not be pulled out and secured completely because the street was too narrow. There are alleys and one-way streets where common sense does not apply and only supreme nerve positions a fire vehicle accurately. Topography has always influenced the San Francisco Fire Department, which made sure that its fire stations were built at the tops of its hills. In this way the horses that drew the water pumpers could go downhill on the way to a fire; they could slog up the exhausting hills on the way back, when speed mattered less. Horses were often accompanied by Dalmatians, who ran ahead to clear traffic and keep other dogs away. Dalmatians were ideal firehouse dogs, unfazed by the loud bells and noise because of their genial manner and bad hearing. Though the horses and the Dalmatians are long gone, these old firehouses are still in use. They perch like sentinels at the apex of steep, narrow streets. Even now it is easy to imagine the large wood doors dragged open and the dogs leaping forward with the horses behind—more than twelve seconds to be harnessed and at the curb was considered too slow—dragging the water pump. Great noise and hullabaloo, not much different from today.

Smell of smoke, some yelling. Engine 91 is first on the scene with no other engines in sight. My officer is Lieutenant Doshkov. He is high-strung, a big change from the pensive, laid-back Captain Leahy. Doshkov is the quintessential engine person, small and lean and aggressive. He is known to suddenly lose his temper, but not in an emergency situation. As we pull up to the address and see smoke trickling out the left door, Doshkov is out of his seat and onto the street before the engine has even stopped.

Patricia is quicker than I am and has the nozzle in her hand while I am still putting on the SCBA. I met her this morning, my first day at Engine 91. She stood in front of me and looked me up and down as if I were a cow being sized up for flank steak. At almost six feet tall and solidly built, Patricia is intimidating.

I smiled sheepishly and cleared my throat to say something that would explain myself, but Patricia looked at me as if she was not at all interested in what I might have to say. I have already heard that she is quick and merciless with a slam—I know that she can clip me with one searing statement. I nod dumbly. After all, this is one of The First Women In.

Patricia seems unconcerned about what it looks like to be talking to probie scum, especially female probie scum. "As long as you're not a wimp," she says. She does not take time for any small talk—the how-are-you, where-are-you-from conversational mulch laid down for a friendship to grow. She does not seem especially concerned with making me feel comfortable. But then again, as one of The First Women In, she has quasi-immortal status in my eyes, and quasi-immortals can bestow rich mystical secrets in clipped, even rude, sentences.

"And don't, for God's sake, flirt. That looks bad for all of us." Her arms are folded and her green eyes scarcely blink.

Patricia would know what looks bad for us. Blue-collar life runs in her veins. Married to a sheriff, she was once a cement layer. She worked for years on an ambulance, picking up pieces of people in some of the toughest neighborhoods in the country. She is now a firefighter, something she has wanted since she was five years old. I have heard a lot of men say this, but she is the only woman I have ever met who has wanted to be a firefighter for so long.

The apartment is narrow and smoky. Patricia seems to know where to go, even though visibility drops to almost nothing halfway down the hall. I am right behind her when she stops suddenly and yells, "More line!" I stand there, not understanding, and she yells, "More line!" again. I turn and run out, past the engine driver, who stands on his heels with his arms crossed, a crooked cap on his head. "We need another line," I say, and he looks surprised. I am back into the building before anything more can be said, the nozzle of a second hose in my hand.

Afterward, Patricia explains that "More line" means to pull the existing hose around the corners, up the stairs, anything so that the nozzle person can advance easily. It does not mean to get another line, as I did.

"You sure are dumb, for a goddamn Stanford graduate," she says. "But you were fast," and there is approval in her voice.

It is this way with fighting fire: You learn on the job, mostly. A real fire is much more than a triangular diagram; it demands language honed for sudden, dangerous situations.

I am lucky that Patricia decides to take me under her wing. It is either that or be crushed by her seismic wit. She gives me the tips that she wished she had gotten two and a half years ago, when she first came in. These are not tips that come with drills, but unspoken codes that are played out at each fire. The first rule, Patricia says, is Never Give Up Your Equipment.

"To give up your equipment to someone else in a fire means that now you are empty-handed and frigging useless," she points out. "A goddamn maiden in distress. If someone asks for your axe or your ceiling hook, tell him, 'Hey, fella, I'll do it.' Have him point out what he needs the equipment for and, Jesus Christ, do it yourself."

She lifts her arms and then lets them fall to her side with a slap, as if frustration over this point has gotten the better of her. Patricia is hard on women, and to gain her respect means to work like a man. Still, I get the feeling that she wonders whether she will ever be fully a part of this blue-collar life. She may never be fully accepted, despite her own blue-collar lineage and her strong, aggressive competence.

"But, uh, that doesn't sound like *teamwork,* you know? What if, well, someone else is in a better position to swing the axe than I am?" I ask this quietly, unwilling to lose the tentative foothold on her esteem. Patricia shrugs. These are the rules. And there is a meaning behind them. To give up your equipment means that you do not want to do the work, and, even worse, that you might be a wimp. To be a wimp is a shameful thing—I know that well enough. Even the volunteer San Francisco firefighters I had read about would sabotage other crews in order to do the most work. Doing the work, being the first into the grit and the last out, is an old tradition. In 1850, two volunteer firefighters from different companies crawled into a burning hospital to check that no one was left inside. They became trapped from behind by flames. The two savvy firefighters, both officers, managed to chop a hole in the roof to safety. "You first," said the officer from the St. Francis Hook and Ladder. "No, I insist," replied the officer from Protection Engine #6, "you first." They stood their ground and each refused to exit before the other, knowing that the final honor is to leave last, even as the flames quickly caught up to them. I do not know how this was resolved. My guess is that they squeezed through the hole together.

Fine, I won't give up my equipment.

"Never say you are scared, either," Patricia continues. "If you want to process, process somewhere else." In fact, I have rarely heard a guy say he was scared and, though I know that fear is part of the job, I admire this reticence.

Other things are allowed: anger, inconsistency, stupidity. But fear is almost never discussed. It may be superstition—firefighters are notoriously superstitious. It is also a realization that fear can be corrosive, and to dwell on fear is more corrosive still. You can articulate your situation so much that you are wallowing in it.

I read an article some time ago in which a female firefighter from another department had made a brave rescue, pulling a child out from under a bed in a burning building. The insistent theme of the story was whether the female firefighter had been scared. I have read many stories of courageous male firefighters and their rescues; rarely did the question of fear come up. It is not consistent with the image of the chain-smoking, hard-drinking male firefighter.

"And if you don't know what to do, do something. Go forward. Don't just stand there like a deer in headlights," Patricia adds sharply.

Unlike Station 53, Station 91 is a single-engine company with a chief and a chief's aide. There are six people instead of eleven, and it is a busy station. I am happy to be here, ready for more work.

Thomas talks slowly and carefully with long pauses between sentences. He has been a San Francisco firefighter for more than twenty years, and his father was a San Francisco firefighter before him. He knows a lot about engines. To Thomas, the machine is sublime. Communication between people can be strained and uncertain, but working with tools accomplishes something tangible and satisfying. By his own admission words come slowly and reluctantly to him, but he can fix a car or find the weak places in walls with eloquence. I myself find tools and machinery awkward. Instead, I use words like pistons—they connect sparks of thought and feeling, they move reality in front of me where I can see it. Thomas and I become friends.

Our friendship is unlikely, even more so because Thomas, again by his own admission, was against women entering the department. But like any man who believes in machinery, he believes the test is if it works when put together. If he sees that it does, he is willing to change his mind.

Working with Patricia changed his mind.

"Look for rust at the joints," he says, and motions me under the behemoth of an engine. I lie flat on the creeper, a small wheeled board, and unconsciously take a deep breath. I slide clumsily under the metal belly. The tubes and pipes and canisters wind and twist and scurry, making little sense at first. But when Thomas carefully points, a pattern gradually takes shape. To be a good engine driver, words must give way; I must watch the drips, rust, paint chips closely. The groans, clanks, and squeals of metal in action or in protest are the only signals I must listen for.

An engine driver is the heart of the fire-fighting operation. In medical-speak, you are the "sinoatrial node," in charge of signals for the ornery heart called the pump. The pump resides in the engine, and to get to it means pulling, pushing, and twisting at dials on the side of the rig.

The primary blood for this heart is, of course, water. While there are five hundred gallons of water to draw from in the tank on an engine, this water will only last as little as a minute and a half if big lines are used; three and a half minutes if small lines are used. The primary water source is the hydrant. After attaching a hose (or the vein, following the analogy) from the hydrant to the engine, the engine driver then adjusts for pressure and volume, sending the water out through different hoses. While this might sound fairly straightforward, it must be done while a building is burning up in front of you. Little things, precise things, like locating the hydrant and making the small dial adjustments for water pressure, become major feats when flame and heat and the sounds of panicked residents are all around you. While the water pressure in a small hose is supposed to be a hundred and thirty pounds per square inch (psi), excited drivers have been known to accidentally dial two hundred pounds or more. This much pressure will throw down whoever is on the nozzle; the feeling is much like trying to hold a wild bronco by the neck. It can easily throw a firefighter off a ladder or off a roof.

*Water goes in, water goes out,* the old-timers shrug and say when I walk out to practice the pump one more time. While I know that it is true, it does not demystify the process for me, or make it any easier. Perhaps it is because to be an engine driver is to be a particular kind of firefighter. It is a job of steady and precise dance moves—step to the hydrant, swing left with the spanner, swing right with the hose coupling. I am not a dancer, I am better at barreling through circumstances and hoping that in the wake of my momentum nothing delicate gets crushed. What's more, the engine driver is the proverbial person behind the scenes, integral but ungloried: the gaffer, not the director; the roadie, not the rock star; the wife, not the great man in front of her.

A few firefighters become engine drivers after they have been badly burned in fires; to my knowledge, this has never happened to Thomas, but he has been shot. During the race problems in the seventies, the National Guard accompanied the fire crews, their guns drawn. Nevertheless, Thomas was shot on the way to a call. The scar is not visible, but I imagine it as he reaches for the outlet gate #3, patiently going through the procedure with me one more time.

The woman has a pulse, but it is weak. It is hard to tell how deeply she is breathing; her color is pale but not gray. Subtle hues, like the quiet hums and haws of an engine, tell a world of difference. It is her eyes that bother me the most. They stare, unblinking, and I have the unnerving sense that she sees me quite clearly.

"What is her name?" I ask the staff, who have gathered around, wide-eyed. Already, they have told me that their oxygen bottle is unaccountably empty. Now there is an uncomfortable shuffling, a shifting of eyes, shrugs all around. *No name. Name unknown. We don't know her name.*

We are at the Sunrise Terrace, which is not sunny at all. It is horizon-flat, stuck casually between two old Victorian houses. I have never been inside a home for the elderly before this, but I expect it to look like the one in the movie *Cocoon,* full of spry old folk lining the hallways and chatting amiably with one another. But there are no spry people in these hallways, and none sit up in bed to greet us. None of these people can sit up, far less read. Hospital beds are lined up in rows, four to a room. IV stands glint in the light from the hallway like stern nurses beside their charges, whom I cannot see, as if they have become part of the bed itself.

I am open-mouthed at the idea that the oxygen is empty; I am more disturbed that this woman is unknown. They cannot find her chart, either. Next to me, Mike shifts his feet angrily. He has a pugilist's face, and big square hands to go along with it. He does not say much to me beyond a polite hello in the mornings. I cannot tell if this is just the way he is, or if he does not like a woman in the house. I decide to assume the former. "This place is the pits," he says under his breath.

Both of us know that, despite their white coats, the staff here are not doctors. But the doctor on call, they tell me, does not answer his page.

The paramedics arrive, breathing heavily from the weight of their bags, which they drop with a loud thud. One paramedic, thin and pale with a thatch of black hair, leans over the bed.

"Huuu-nnney," he croons to the woman. "Can you hear me?" He flaps his hand in front of her face. He tries again, endearments said in the same singsong voice, as if he were speaking to a child. He reminds me suddenly of a Doberman pinscher, flattened and stretched from toe to head, as he chants "Honey," "Dear," and "My girl," slowly, loudly, and with fake good cheer, as if the patient were not only old but deaf and stupid, too. I want to grab him by his bony shoulder and hiss at him to show her respect. Remind him that he is a young numskull punk, one third her age. That we both are. I look down at my boots and say nothing.

An airway tube is inserted unceremoniously down her throat. With a practiced flourish, he tapes the tube in place; her cheeks bulge and her lips splay out at awkward angles. She is trussed for rescue.

Mike hands me the oxygen-bag valve mask and I start pushing oxygen into her. Her eyes are still open and they stare at me, seeing me, I am sure of it. I begin to talk to her—nothing very interesting, just a few questions to see whether she will respond, medical questions that we are supposed to ask. I know from the vast assortment of medical classes we firefighters take that hearing is the last sense to go. She can almost certainly hear everything going on in the room. What is your name? Can you hear me? I ask silly things like that. There are other things I want to say: *Are you scared? If you are, that's okay, too.* Or *Are you comfortable? Should I move the sheets?* Things like that.

Unable to say them, I glance at her hand, spotted, thin, and pale. It is delicate and the skin seems translucent, so that when I look at it I can see the intimate inner workings of her—the blue veins, the thin strands of bone, the pads of muscle. I imagine that at this moment she is trapped inside an immovable body, frightened of the tumult around her, unable to speak. If I hold her hand, or say something to those eyes, I can make it better. I imagine the seventy years of her life, and think how she deserves this, at least.

*Okay, okay* is all that I finally murmur. I lean in and say it as the paramedic pricks her arm for a vein and keeps an eye on the heart monitor. Just take her hand, my mind admonishes, while another part of me is acutely aware of Mike nearby and what he might think. I stare at her hand and say "Okay" again. The fact that she might have heard that this nursing-home attendant does not know her name offends me deeply, but I am too concerned about my professional image as a firefighter to do the things I want to do to help her move on. I want to appear calm and in control. I want Mike to see that I am a hard-edged, coolheaded firefighter; I do not want to appear "female" in any way. I am following medical protocol; anything else seems frivolous. I wonder what Patricia would do. I stare at the woman's hand and squeeze the oxygen bag instead.

When the cart starts to move, I tell myself that this is my chance, that no one will notice. The hand, which seems so frail that the slightest movement might float it off the bed, stays put on her hip. I stare at it, but I cannot move, except to rhythmically press the oxygen bag. I will say something instead. I will tell her where we are going, that she will be fine. That it is raining lightly, but tomorrow it is supposed to be sunny. That the staff does know her name, but they are just flustered and unused to all this commotion.

I never hold her hand. I don't say much of anything. I just pump oxygen into her, and she dies on the way to the hospital. I know when she dies, as if her soul brushed by my eyelids and patted my hair. I lean back on my heels and listen to the siren.

Later, when I am alone, I cry. It is a slow, quiet weep—a molting, more, of illusion. I have found, much to my surprise, that I am a mediocre person; that all my arrogant pluck—my ability to fly planes, raft the biggest white water, or crash relentlessly into ice walls—means nothing; that in a decisive moment, I lose my guts. In an extraordinary moment, I remained ordinary. I gave in easily to insecurity, to fear of emotion, to fear of death. As the Dayak chief probably understood, I remain less than average in braveries of different sorts.

In a fire, the crews work together in unison. There is a formula that we learn: where the first engine goes (in front and a little forward of the fire building), where the second engine goes (to a hydrant to supply water to the first engine), where the first truck goes (in front of the fire building, behind the first engine). We learn what the engine crew does (enter the fire building with a hose) and what the first truck crew does (help with rescue, ladder the fire escape, ventilate). But it is the individual acts of heroism and courage that really put out the fire, the small movements within the mandates. It is the savvy to adjust when the situation is not "text-book"—and it almost never is.

Tonight, I remembered all the medical protocol, but I forgot the most important thing—that once another firefighter found the courage to hold a woman's hand while a building burned.

# THE FIRE TRIANGLE

When the alarm comes in for Masonic and Grove, it is late afternoon. There is nothing faster than the speed with which firefighters dash to the rig when a full box comes in. Fire! we think. Fire! we hope. The pole holes open with a crash like thunder, and bodies speed down the filament as if from heaven. Doors swing wide and other bodies plunge past; they grab coats, fire helmets, flashlights as they go. Despite the rush and loud noise, there is nothing graceless about this united momentum. It is movement in iambs, a clarion of sound. Fire is the essence of our job. All our other duties— medical calls, lockouts, water leaks, car accidents—are merely kindling; it is fire that ignites our soul. This is not to say that we love the destruction that a fire wreaks, but that when a fire happens, we want to be there.

At my 1989 department graduation, the mayor of San Francisco gave a speech. At the time, he was determined to dismantle the "old" fire department; it was under his leadership that public pressure and constant media coverage plagued the institution. He heartily disliked the department, and his presence as a keynote speaker was a special affront. Number 28 sat next to me with his fists pressed together and his head bowed, apparently offended that this man who accused the department of racism and sexism was speaking on this special day.

The Caucasian mayor recalled a fire that had happened years before in which a child had died. The fire was in a black neighborhood, which, full of grief and loss, accused the white fire department of taking its time getting to the fire. This misunderstanding, he said, was only one example of why an integrated department was so important.

The mayor said that he himself was sure that firefighters had arrived at that tragic fire as fast as they could. Nevertheless, his speech opened a wound. Not many things are as painful to a firefighter as the death of a child at a fire. But the accusation that not enough was done may be one of them. A firefighter plunges willingly into a dangerous situation, risking his or her life for a stranger and a stranger's property. The accusation that more might have been done when in fact everything was done is a searing affront. The mayor's point that day had validity, but it was lost in what many firefighters perceived as the implication that perhaps, yes, not enough was done. That perhaps they had not responded quickly or bravely enough because the neighborhood was black and they were white.

But it takes only a few days in a firehouse to realize that this is virtually impossible. When the call for a fire comes in, there is no hesitation. No matter where it comes from, despite any prejudices that a firefighter might have, there is a fierce rush for the rigs.

Station 91 is half a minute away from Grove and Masonic. When we pull up, black smoke is already spewing from an open doorway. A man is doubled over and gasping. Later I will learn that he is an off-duty San Francisco firefighter who tried to rush in but was kept back by the intense heat and smoke. Near the doorway people are screaming and pointing, and one woman is being restrained from running back in. Someone else crouches on the sidewalk and wails.

Patricia lets me have the nozzle. The probationer is supposed to be given the nozzle for experience; in only a few months it will be up to me to fight for it. My probation will be over and so will the daily drills and underlying stress of not being fully hired. However, I suspect that Patricia's stern, occasionally sarcastic glances will not change. I will always be a lowly probie to her.

Lieutenant Doshkov is not working today; instead, Lieutenant Murphy is the officer. I have only met him a few times. He rarely looks me in the eye; he seems too high-strung to focus anywhere for very long. He speaks with a slight stutter, not the result of a speech impediment but because his words spill out so quickly between short breaths. His movements are jerky and charged, as if the tension in his body were a struggle between his ligaments and his tendons. The only thing loose about him is his skin, which hangs morosely from his cheeks and around his eyes.

Behind me on the stairs, he bumps into me when I kneel to put on my air mask. Only a couple of feet ahead, visibility narrows to a thread and then disappears; the smoke is thick, black, and hot before I am even around the bend to the main hallway.

*Blacker than me . . . and thick like stew,* I hear in my head.

At the top of the stairs, I cannot see my own hand pressed against my air mask. *Hell must be like this,* I think. The nozzle is cool and definite in my hand. There is little tension on it, and I know that Patricia is "pulling line" for us on the stairs below. I am first in, where every engine person wants to be, first in, with the nozzle. In front of me is a chasm of black and, somewhere, the seat of the fire.

My officer is saying something to me. I hear only a muffled yelling as he tries to tell me something from behind his air mask. "What? What?" I say, but it comes out an elongated, flattened sound that falls away into the dark. He presses his mask close to me, striking my helmet. This time I hear him a little better, and then he is gone, back down the stairs.

All this has taken seconds. Gone? Where could he go? Is this a test? Later I will find out that he forgot his flashlight and went down to get it. What he thinks a flashlight will do in such unpenetrably thick blackness is beyond me. Nevertheless, there is only one thing to do: I step forward into the smoke. I don't understand why I have been left here alone, but I know that if I do not move forward, that will somehow indicate that I am afraid. Perhaps they are waiting, clipboard and stopwatch in hand, for a panicked retreat.

I crouch and slide into the absolute black. There is a lone-liness peculiar to fire, the realization that ultimately all mis-takes will be yours. Fire itself makes no mistakes; it makes headway or not. I know that Patricia is pulling line some-where behind me, but there is no one near me. The utter dark is so thick that, thus separated, I feel that I, too, have disap-peared. The nozzle in my hand and the hose that leads out behind it are the only proof that I have not. And it is hot. It is a cloying, leaden heat that makes me feel that the very walls are moving inward. I know the numbers: three hundred degrees one foot above the floor, five hundred degrees five feet above the floor, twelve hundred degrees at the ceiling. I drop lower.

This is a black that is so black it starts to assume shapes, as if the brain cannot stand the nothingness any longer. While the only real shape here is the heat curving around my body (I open up the nozzle to cool the air), I begin to think that I can see.

In the coming years I will realize that the experienced firefighter must shed all preconceived images; they will only play tricks on her in the dark. Instead, her mind and body should remain supple and pliable. When she runs into some-thing, it does not have to be named (table? chair? bed?) so much as gotten around—a small point but an important one. If you think that you have bumped into a table, you will try to get around it as a table. But if instead it is a bed, you will be thwarted by this bigger, less movable object. Trying to circle it or push it over will not work. Every fire is a new experience.

Intent on finding the seat of the fire by myself, I run into something that hits my knees. For some reason, I decide that this must be a stairway, and I step up onto it. I try to step up again but I hit something ahead of me. Sure that this must be a small attic space, I step up and lunge forward as if to squeeze into a hole. Again I hit something and my foot finds no step. Insistent, I lunge again, and perhaps again, rapping my head, hard, each time. All this happens quickly, and then

I feel a hand on my coat, pulling. Someone is behind me. The hand, all-knowing and seemingly all-seeing (or, more likely, adjusted to non-seeing), guides me to the left and we crawl down what must (it must!) be a hallway. The heat heightens. Shafts of lightning streak out in front of us.

Heavy, unvented fire does not look like carved flame and color. Instead, the thick blanket of smoke allows only gradations of light, slivers of non-black that dart and disappear like hallucinations. The person behind me is yelling now, and I spray the nozzle above us, in wide circles and then at the streaks of light. This simultaneously cools us down and ensures that the fire does not sneak above us and then attack from behind, trapping us. We advance slowly, at a half crouch, sometimes bumping into things. Breathe slowly, I try to remind myself. Slowlyslowlyslowly. If the alarm on the air pack goes off too soon, signaling low air, I have to leave the building for a refill. *Scared,* they would say, *sucked all her air. Goddamn hyperventilated.*

The heat is worse now, and we lie down, bellies on the floor, air bottles like shells on our backs, hot water hitting the ears, the neck, soaking our pants, our gloves. The thick protective leather on our hands inhibits touch, the air masks narrow our sense of smell to the rubber lining and our own sweat, our mouths taste only the sour fumes of our excitement. Finally, the black smoke muffles sound and sight. Every sense is dulled, yet never do we feel so alive as when suddenly we turn and there, in a wide grin of light, is the fire full force. This is the room where it started, now "fully involved."

There are more people behind me now, yelling and pushing. Everyone wants to see the fire, face it head-on. With the water directly on it, it bends and drops quickly. At my side, I hear my alarm go off. I hand the nozzle reluctantly to someone behind me and follow the hose out.

The apartment clears quickly once windows are broken and the roof chopped open. By the time I return with a new bottle on my back, the apartment has taken form. The stairway where I knelt to put my mask on is covered with a thin green rug. A wooden banister climbs up one side. I walk around the bend and up to the landing.

One glance tells me that it is no attic staircase that I was on. Instead, in a far corner, a single chair is propped against the wall. A sharp breath escapes me. *Jesus, no.* I was there, *on the chair.* I was not getting into an attic, I was butting the wall. Momentarily, I was a disoriented cow. I was Quixote, mistaking a windmill for a knight; I was from the Middle Ages, sure that the line of the horizon was the edge of the flat world. A portrait of prejudgment, I think. Thank God for the pitch black. No one else, not even The Hand, could see me.

The Hand turns out to be the chief's aide, or "operator," a tall, lanky man with a long, lanky mustache to match. His job is to be the eyes and ears of the chief, who stands outside and directs the fire crews. Inside, the operator relays fire information: the seat of the fire, its extent, its special hazards. It can be an undemanding job, according to hardened firefighters. Often the operator stands outside with a clipboard, in effect a secretary for the chief. But the first chief on the scene sends the operator in, and then the operator's job is an important and exciting one. Without a hose or an axe, only a radio, the operator must be both savvy and brave. Today, the operator has plucked me from darkness (and humiliation) and led me with a seeming sixth sense to the fire.

As if I have summoned him with my thoughts, he suddenly materializes near me and I look away from the chair. Does he know? If he does, I see no sarcasm in his eyes; he simply asks me where the hell my officer went. I shrug.

"You should not have gone in there alone," he says.

The body is hard to find at first, until someone steps on her among the debris and ashes and her intestines surge up like an orchid trying to bud. Someone tells me to come see, and I do. She doesn't look like anything human, just an effort of color—white, red—against the black ash. The smell is distinctive, like sour barbecue. Later, I will find that the smell clings to my coat, and I wonder if flecks of skin are lodged there in the seams; if I crawled over her in the blackness. Afterward, they will find the fire extinguisher melted beside her, which means that she died conscious and fighting. The fire started from her cigarette: ash flicked in the wastepaper basket smoldered, silently igniting the curtains. From there the fire spread quickly and brutally. Asleep, perhaps, she noticed only when she was wakened by a burning chair. Or burning hair. By then, it was far too late.

Outside, a woman is being restrained as she is told the news. She screams at the chief and then swears at him, a stream of words that rises and widens until she runs out of breath. She is black and he is white, a scenario relived. "You came too slow!" she screams over and over.

I feel my body tighten at the accusation, my adrenaline resurge. I remember the seconds I lost suspended in my own prejudice, on the chair against the wall so certain that it was a stairway up to an attic. The grandmother was dead well before this, well before the smoke seeped down the stairs and made it impossible for the off-duty firefighter to fight his way in, but I feel a guilt along with anger.

An exact balance of elements started this fire. If the cigarette ash had been cold, or the curtain made of heavier material, it might have been different. If the woman had been able to stop the momentum of elements with the extinguisher, she might be alive. I want to shout at this woman that I did all I could, that it was already too late, and that I was sorry, too, but the deadly fire triangle was well on its way. But here was my own fire triangle: I want to yell back, but that would ignite a situation already too sad and hopeless.

I walk away wordless.

Patricia, who is recharged by a fire, goes into a repeated tirade about *how in the fucking world* could a probationer have been left by an experienced officer. "How in the fucking world?" she says again, and swings her axe. I know she is more relieved than angry—relieved that at least I did not leave as well, follow him down like a scared puppy. Instead, I went into the fire all alone. "Stupid thing to do," she murmurs to me, but she is glad.

Lieutenant Murphy told me to stay put, it turns out, but I did not hear him through his mask, and the dark, and the heat. I don't care, anyway. I am exhilarated that I had the nozzle.

The fire *belongs* to the person at the nozzle, who is First In. Those who are First In are the ones who face the real danger. The real danger is uncertainty. Those behind have the security of knowing that the person ahead is still alive, and they have that extra chance that the person ahead won't get if something goes wrong. Despite this, no one I know wants to be behind. To be First In is to be the bravest.

Patricia claps me on the back. "Good job," she says, "for an idiot."

# GETTING ALONG

I pick up my fire helmet. It's true, the paint is streaked in wide brush strokes and Billy says that it looks terrible, that he'll paint it for me himself. I agree, it does look pretty bad. But I did it on my own, and that is enough. We prize our helmets, and paint them carefully, if not skillfully: red and white if you are on the truck, black if you are on the engine, black and white if you are on the squad.

Helmets are not just the emblem of the firefighter, they are good protection. I have had a roof fall in on me, and once an explosion sent the crew just ahead of mine reeling back into us. Last year, when I was still on probation, I once forgot to put my helmet on (these mistakes can happen only when you are a probationer and then only once). My officer noticed it just as I was advancing the line down the hallway ahead of him, and the film of smoke was turning thick black. *Her head is covered by a hair net!* This "hair net" was the webbing of the air mask on my head where the helmet was supposed to be. He ordered me out of the building. In the commotion I pretended not to hear. To leave a fire would be sacrilege. It could also become a rumor that I had fled in fear. As a woman, I much preferred a charge of insubordination to an accusation of cowardice.

*Perhaps a spray gun,* Billy tries one more time, but I laugh again. I put my helmet back into the rig near my coat; he shrugs. I know what he means, though, and I am touched. There is superstition around the firehouse, and the helmet is an object of protection in more than the obvious way. Small tokens are affixed to them: green Irish clovers, American-flag stickers, a playing card. Fire has a curious way of instilling the mystical in us. These small offerings to luck are testament that, despite the fact that most of my colleagues are good Catholic men, we all hedge our bets when hell breaks loose. For me, a small gold angel, made of plastic and a gift from my godson, is pinned near a particularly crusty paint streak. In a good hot fire, this angel will probably melt into an almost imperceptible dribble, but I feel it can protect me nonetheless. When Billy is gone I peek curiously at the playing card on a nearby helmet: An ace? A queen of hearts? A jack?

Ah, a laminated prayer.

There are, I know, other things that my helmet cannot protect me from. Some men make it clear by their body language that they do not want to speak to me. It is a contorted, tense posture, as if they are holding in so much disgust that they might explode, much as carbons in a fire threaten to do when they become highly pressurized.

I hear early on that there is at least one station that has made a formal pact not to speak to women. Ironically, stories are told in the firehouse about men who, in the days when cocktail hours were openly condoned in the firehouse and many of the men drank, would pass out and have to be put to bed. There was no secret pact against them. There are men so out of shape that after they throw a ladder they must lean against it, breathing heavily. There is no secret pact against them. The women have been singled out by this station, even though some of them have never even met us.

I know that the exclusion is not always deliberate. Men have a "ritualized" interaction that differs strongly from the "ritualized" interaction of most women. According to some studies, men frequently interact with one another using oppositional tactics, such as jesting put-downs, as a result of the strict hierarchical social structure they grow up with. They learn quickly that it is important to maintain one's position by self-promotion and the putting down of others. This becomes obvious in the firehouse, where many conversations involve hair loss, belly girth, or sly comments about another man's wife. Sociologists call this a "ritual of opposition"; the firehouse calls it "slamming." Conversational rituals for women, on the other hand, concentrate on subtly maintaining an appearance of parity. Girls are not often rewarded for standing out. It is important to appear diffident and gracious.

One day Billy tells me about a "slam" that highlights the difference in our ritualized socializations. Billy says that he suspected that his wife was having an affair with a Mexican Spanish-language teacher. Extremely agitated, he asked his officer for permission to sneak home and check if his suspicions were justified. Sure enough, he walked in on his wife in bed with her lover. Billy returned to the firehouse in shock. He stumbled around in a daze, and soon the whole firehouse knew that Billy had caught his wife with the Mexican professor. That night when dinner was served, everyone got steak and potatoes. Except Billy. The chef made him a plate of burritos, rice, and refried beans.

"Are you serious?" I exclaimed when he finished telling me the story. He had a smile on his face, but I was beginning to sputter. "That is so—so—*cruel.*"

Billy looked at me in surprise. "Naah. They were just trying to make me feel better," he said. "It was funny; they made me laugh."

"I see," I said, not seeing at all.

Neither the male nor the female way of interacting is wrong or bad. As sociologist Deborah Tannen points out in her study on gender interaction in the workplace, "When everyone is familiar with the conventions things work well. But when ways of speaking are not recognized as conventions, they are taken literally, with negative results." Imagine how hard it is, for both men and women, when conversational rituals that they have taken for granted encounter a different ritual.

To make matters worse, it is hard for either sex to join in the other's rituals. If a woman tries to slam, she is regarded as "unladylike" by both men and women. Similarly, if a man is intent on making another man feel his equal, thus downplaying his own attributes, he risks being regarded as a "wimp" who lacks confidence. The uncertainties that a minority member can feel in an otherwise homogenous group, according to these theories, are not only the result of outright resentment, but also of not sharing important ritualized behavior. This cycle feeds on itself; as women and men, blacks and whites fail to communicate with each other, each blames the other for not trying hard enough to understand and connect. This is difficult to change. Interacting with people like oneself, who understand and use the same conversation ritual, is more fun. It is *easier.* I know: I begin to realize that this is what I, too, have done all my life.

Some stressful situations result from miscommunications, but other situations don't. There are people who purposely want to inflict hurt. While the law tries to deal with silent exclusion—"shunning" is the technical term and it is prohibited in the fire department—it is easy to interact in small, clipped sentences as if every word is an effort or, more commonly, to talk nonstop to the people nearby as if the outsider were invisible. The point is made loud and clear.

Meanwhile, those who do not fear the brunt of this exclusion have the luxury to laugh about shunning. "I'm in trouble if I say something, I'm in trouble if I don't," they groan. "Now, does that make sense?" People complain that their conversations are inhibited, that they must always "watch out." The firehouse, once a haven for the rituals of all-white male conversation, must now include women and people of color.

Change is the law of life, but it is sometimes very difficult. Singly, these are good, thoughtful men. Together, they can bolster each other's bitterness. I understand this to some degree; in their position I might do the same. And it is important to understand their position. These are able men, with families for whom they want to make a good life. Suddenly, promotional exams they have studied hard for are declared "culturally biased." In 1984, for example, an exam for the position of lieutenant was suspended when not enough minorities passed to ensure that the test be deemed fair. To those white men who had put in many hours a day preparing for this test, the statistical analysis that showed "disparities sufficient to establish a prima facie case of discriminatory hiring and promotion under Title VII" was empty semantics. It sounded like the whining of people who happened not to receive high scores. Even though the city admitted that the "tests used were not demonstrably job-related," the white male firefighter had studied hard and done well. Suddenly an outside institution, which didn't know how to chop a hole in the roof or run a pump panel, was telling him what makes a "job-related" test.

On the other hand, there are insidious facts that cannot be overlooked. By 1974, there were only four black firefighters among eighteen hundred whites. Women were not allowed to take the test until 1976, and none were hired until 1987. Since 1970, the courts have asked San Francisco's civil service unit on three separate occasions to justify their tests, which were repeatedly found not to be job-related. The city did little to change them; the courts declared themselves "fed up." In 1987, the U.S. District Court ruled that "this sorry history will come to an end." Lawyers armed with the consent decree were to manage the fire department; certain "goals" would now be met in the hiring and promotion of women and minorities.

How else could it have been done? The fire department was given at least three opportunities to change on its own. The department dragged its feet in the recruitment of minorities and women. The result was affirmative action.

As a woman, my experience in the SFFD is mine alone. Other women and minority members, here and in other departments, have experienced things that I have not. Some have had a really tough time; others say that they have never had an uncomfortable moment in a firehouse—all these experiences are valid. Mine happen to be somewhere in between.

I have been told by one officer that I cannot drive the truck until he sees me swing an axe. What does swinging an axe have to do with driving a fire truck? Meanwhile, he lets a man junior to me drive—whom he has also never seen swing an axe. In just two months, this driver gets into two accidents. Nevertheless, the officer keeps the junior man at the wheel, waving off my requests. I do not profess to be a good driver—in fact, I am a lousy one, but no worse, surely, than my hapless peer. Only when I take the officer aside to talk to him does he get nervous about his clear discrimination.

"Look, I am not going to sue," I begin. I begin all my complaints this way because the threat of lawsuits hangs heavily over such interactions. The officer sputters. I drive the next watch, though now my new burden is to "prove" that I am worthy.

Another time I am told that I am "turning the guys on" when I wear only the normal uniform T-shirt. In yet another instance, mild come-ons are whispered to me by a firefighter as he passes by.

But most of my encounters have been more subtle exclusions and discomforts, a kind of insidious interaction difficult to explain to anyone who has not experienced it. People want to hear about breasts tugged, lewd words spoken, drooling hyena laughs. But there are far less obvious manifestations of prejudice, and I know them when I see them.

Once, I stop by another station with a notice that needs to be posted on its bulletin board. The man who opens the door stands with his arms folded across a gigantic belly. His eyes are deliberately expressionless. There is not a trace of friendliness, not even of recognition, though he knows that I am a fellow firefighter. He blocks the door, legs spread wide, one shoulder against the doorjamb, hands in fists. The scene strikes me as ludicrous.

"I'll do it," he says, reaching for the piece of paper in my hand. His voice has an edge; he clearly does not like even having to talk to me. He acts as if each word is an effort. Sneering, he shifts to block the door further, so that I get the message loud and clear.

Get out. You are not welcome here.

Prejudice at its best is like this. It does not raise its voice or shout. It makes you doubt your own sense of reality. Afterward, if you try to explain it, the thrust and weight of its insult cannot be accurately conveyed. That is the point: Prejudice bypasses the verbal synapses, and makes its sly, slow, insidious crawl straight into the trenches of your confidence.

As a twin, I understand the use of body language. An identical twin knows instinctively that the minutest of words, the smallest of posture changes, differentiates one twin from the other. We are attuned to these because they define us, make us separate. We know their power, and when they are used by others, we recognize them. With identical twins, it is hard to actually pinpoint what the difference is—only that there is one; likewise, a person's prejudgment is obvious, but hard to describe. People who do not experience prejudice sometimes doubt those who do; they can see them as whining, overreacting, manipulative, humorless. But step into a room full of people where you are hopelessly different and you will understand immediately.

A few years ago, the red fire engine was briefly painted yellow in some cities. Studies had determined that this particular shade of yellow was easier to distinguish than any other color; it would be safer for civilian traffic and for the speeding fire crew. It was an odd hue, a glaring yellow-green that gave the impression of neon. It soon became apparent that although this yellow was easier to see, a citizenry accustomed to red fire engines did not react as expected. The new yellow color meant nothing to them or to their reflexes. The old red fire engine held a unique place in their minds, one not easily changed by studies or mere facts.

In the fire department, too, some firefighters hold fast to their prejudgments of color or gender no matter how much individual job performance proves them wrong. To be a black or an Asian or a woman means that you have gotten your job unfairly, that you are unqualified.

But this is not a matter of easy rights and wrongs. The fire department is both a product of the culture that employs it and a mirror of the country's problems. That the San Francisco Fire Department had hired only five blacks by 1975 is more a telling commentary on racism in America than on racism in the department. Even the achievements of the Civil Rights Act in 1964 could not erase inequities with the stroke of a pen. The fact that women were not allowed to apply to the fire department until 1976 is not surprising, either: Only one in twenty-five girls were encouraged to do high school sports at that time. If physical activity was not considered something a girl could do in our society, why would the fire department want to hire women to perform such intensely physical work?

This does not excuse the problems. I have felt the heat of them; sometimes I am bitter. But firefighters have always made us question ourselves. We watch them run into a burning building and wonder, *Could I do that? Am I that brave?* Forget the finger pointing—*that racist, sexist fire department!* There is a lot to learn from San Francisco's jakeys, and the first step is to admire, as I do, the way they have struggled to handle change and diversity. Really, few of us have had to encounter such an abrupt and uncomfortable shift in our daily life.

I ask, Could I do that? Am I that brave?

# STANFORD LIFE

Steve, a friend of mine from Stanford, turns thirty today. How fast time seems to travel! My friends and I are suddenly careening toward middle age; I have already been in the department two years; my cat looks bigger each time I come back from a short weekend away; slowly but surely, the fabric on the seats of my car lightens and frays. This is the way we measure time.

The afternoon is warm. As the autumn light begins to slant toward the end of the day, the breeze makes the rows of backyard trees and bushes sway gently. Blues and yellows from the lowering sun pinwheel by. Steve's backyard is filled with people. The cake has been cut, and various speeches made. Advice is given. The thirties are great if you make sure you do this. The thirties are terrible but make sure you do that. Wine corks pop.

I recognize almost everyone here. Most of them are Stanford people. Some I know quite well, others just look familiar. This is my group—we carry ourselves the same way, use the same vocabulary, share the same experiences. We belong to the same herd. Here I am not in the minority: I am easily accepted, easily recognized as something knowable, familiar. It is a nice, easy feeling, a change from the firehouse.

And then the pleasantries start.

"What are you doing these days?" is the common icebreaker. While this is said casually, its meaning is precise and serious. Reading a lot, pondering various political quandaries, or running five miles a day are not acceptable answers. The question means specifically: What Do You Do for a Living? If you do not answer right away, the question is rephrased until you do (believe me, I have tried everything). My acquaintances will not be aware of how important this question is to them until, like me, they do not want to answer it.

I find temporary refuge in saying that I am in graduate school for film. This seems respectable enough. I still have *potential*. Still, potential cannot be milked much longer. In one's thirties, one is supposed to be Doing Something. But I fall back on it now, to avoid talking about being a firefighter. I dread the initial silence, that space where surprise has not yet rearranged itself into interest. Into that space falls all the potential disappointment that I may be to my family, to my background.

There is idle talk about what films I have made, what films I like. There is mention of Hollywood—will I be joining Alexandra down there? Maybe I will direct her! Nods and laughs all around. Still the questioning look—or am I imagining it? Perhaps it is my own internal status meter that is measuring contempt in the eyes of the lawyer or doctor opposite me.

Finally it can be withheld no longer. After all, how do I support myself through film school? In truth, I am the only student there with a full-time job. I should be proud of that, and I am, mostly.

When it emerges—*I am a firefighter for San Francisco*— suddenly I am different again. Of course, there is a great deal of interest. The conversation veers sharply into fire-fighting matters: *Suspenders? Dalmatians? Do the men bother you?*

And everyone always wants to know about Death. They ask, swirling their olives, squeezing their tiny sandwiches, thin like lips with mayonnaise bleeding out the edges. Especially, they ask for details. How much blood, screams? *So what does a burned body look like?* I am as much to blame. I tell it slowly, like the porous spread of paint on canvas. They nod, widen their eyes, try to contain their voyeuristic glee. We forget our class refinements and sink into visceral excitement. For brief moments I am lost in the pure joy of recounting the wonders of the magnificent work I am involved in, and they are lost in the childlike self, where the firefighter is the eternal hero. But then it is over and the reality intrudes: I am a blue-collar worker and my acquaintance is not. Color and gender may be the obvious divisions in our society, but class is the insidious one.

My discomfort is only superficial—I am, after all, still undeniably a white Anglo-Saxon Protestant—but it is sobering. It is clear that we are a species that feels comfortable with similarities, not differences. Nowhere is this clearer than in my dual lives.

The man I'm talking to at Steve's party tries to reconcile the person in front of him with his idea of what a female firefighter should look like. He has never seen a female firefighter before, but he has a preconception. He is a stockbroker, and for my part, I have reflexively decided he must be boring, conservative, and spoiled, though all outward indications are that he is an engaging and interesting man.

"It looks like melting plastic, really, the skin hangs off in slabs," I say. "I saw a guy melted to a sofa a few weeks ago. Looked just like the paisley." I add this half jokingly, but it is true. Most gruesome things at the department are said with this edge of gallows humor, and I have picked up this bad habit even though I swore to myself that I would not. Just a few weeks ago a firefighter with a drinking problem committed suicide by hanging, and the talk around the firehouse dissolved into bets about which knot was tied. Was it the knot used to pull tools up the side of a building or the firefighter's hitch, used to keep large suction hoses in place? The firefighter was liked and the memorial well-attended; it is simply that humor is the result of traumatic events that are seen too often. Humor becomes the escape valve for downright depression.

The stockbroker, who has seen only the dead body of his grandfather in an open casket, a prim version of death, is nodding. He asks how I handle what I see. There is the smooth inference that it is unfeminine, not for girls. But for me, death has lost some of its shock, something I thought would never happen. I imagined it would always have an existential power over me, especially in its meaner versions.

At first I did the corny things when people died. I would lean in and slowly sweep my hand across their eyes to close them, as I had seen done in movies. But the eyes would always creep open, and after half a dozen times I gave up. Sometimes when they died right in front of me, I would look up at the moment of death to see if I could glimpse the soul as it wafted to heaven. It would be wispy and frail, I thought, perhaps leaving a faint trail of something like cigarette smoke. I would nod a surreptitious farewell, one that no fire-fighter could see. That was then. Now it is different. Death has become mundane. After only two years on the job people look in death as I imagine they did in life. Sometimes better.

I don't say all this to the stockbroker. It is hard to understand; sometimes I don't understand it myself. Steve sidles over, armed with an unopened bottle of wine. He is an artist who has managed to assimilate into the nine-to-five world with a business in graphic design. He also attends film school with me.

"*Vino,* anyone?" he asks, uncorking a bottle of wine by unceremoniously trapping it between his knees and grimacing as he pulls. I am glad that the talk of fire fighting is momentarily diverted.

"You're almost done with the editing." He nods to me as the cork pops. I nod. Steve was the cinematographer on the film I am making. The shoot is always over fast, but the editing can seem endless. Cutting a film is a laborious task, hypnotic in its monotony. But it involves a decision at every frame, which at this time is comforting to me. The process is mine from inception to completion, an exercise in complete control. When troubling instances at work sometimes occur at the whimsy of a social code I do not understand, I regain a sense of self in the small, hot, darkened editing room.

"Perfect," Steve says, raising the wine bottle to me. "It will be great."

"It will be great because you shot it," I reply. Steve pours wine into the stockbroker's plastic cup.

"So, aren't those firemen sort of, you know, bigoted?" a woman next to the stockbroker asks, veering the conversation back. She is a Ph.D. student in behavioral psychology. I knew her at Stanford only enough to wave and say hello to. There is a voyeuristic edge to her question. She is not the only one—everyone wants to know this with the same enthusiasm they show for stories about death.

"Oh, the fire department is like life," I say, taking the wine and moving away.

There is, after all, not a single black person at the party.

# FIREWOMEN

With two years in, I am no longer a probationer. I start to feel more comfortable when I go to work; the sharp smell of gasoline and ash is familiar, and the undercarriage of the engine, twisted with pipes and tubes, makes some sense. Firehouse life becomes easier.

On the first day at my new station, an old-timer pushes his hand out on the table in front of me. The skin is gnarled and twisted like the grain of an old tree. The old-timer, whose name is Bunker, stares at me. "This is how far I go in," he suddenly says. "Are you with me?" I stare at his burned hand.

"Of course," I answer quietly.

We have just come back from a call where a woman dialed 911 to complain of alien disturbance. When we arrived she pushed aside a heavily curtained window. She pointed to a nearby chimney. "Laser beams are coming from there," she said. "They don't think I know, but I do."

She claimed that it was causing a sticky, goo-like substance to seep through the walls, so I ran my hand along the paint. I nodded at her, though I could see or feel nothing out of the ordinary. We helped her fortify the tinfoil she had stuffed in the window cracks.

Bunker continues to stare at me, his burned hand forward as if to make sure that I understand its import. I stare back, unmoving. "Okay," he finally says.

"You are not at all like Elizabeth," my new lieutenant points out one day, soon after I begin my stay at this station. I shrug, but I say nothing. I hear the relief in his voice, as I have heard it before in others'. Just as you may be right or left of center, be fatter or skinnier than Cindy Crawford, have an IQ score above "genius" or below it, you are either similar or not similar to Elizabeth Sue Mandel. She has become the measuring stick by which each woman in the fire department is judged.

Elizabeth Mandel came in with the first class of women. She had been one of the plaintiffs in the court case that eventually led to the federal consent decree that mandated that San Francisco integrate the fire department. Once in the department, Elizabeth quickly gained a reputation for being difficult to get along with. The common refrain was that she had "a chip on her shoulder." Soon every firehouse had undeserved rumors about the things she had said, the way she had run away from this fire or that, the "monstrous" effect she had on people. By the time I came through the academy, Elizabeth Mandel had come to symbolize to opponents of the consent decree everything they objected to about affirmative action in general and women in particular.

When I first meet her I am struck by how pale and wan she looks—hardly the defiant rabble-rouser. Chipmunklike in expression, she nevertheless seems steeled as if for a blow. When she talks her voice is tight, and by the end of most conversations it has risen and tightened even more. I want to like her, if only because I admire the fact that she does not buckle under the strain of so much hostility. We are both women, both firefighters, our politics are similar. Mostly, we are both vegetarians. In everyone else's eyes, this makes us almost indistinguishable.

In some ways, Elizabeth is an unusual boon for women in the department. She is so vilified that the rest of us gain by contrast. Once we are seen to be less defensive or combative than Elizabeth—and rumors about her took on such grotesque proportions that it was impossible to come even close—the firefighter is so relieved that he is much friendlier than he might otherwise have been.

Elizabeth, though Caucasian, is a member of the Black Firefighters Association. She is respected by many of the blacks and by me for the way she stands up for what she believes. But in the firehouse, among many of the white men, she is either ignored or goaded: An open *Playboy* centerfold is placed on her bed, men do not speak to her, and recently she has said that someone tried to push her off a roof during a fire. This is a serious charge and I cannot say whether it is true or not; I do not like to think about it. The incident came a day after the United States Supreme Court rejected an appeal by the San Francisco Firefighter's Union to overturn the consent decree. Elizabeth symbolizes the court system to firefighters—intractable, temperamental, and uncommunicative—and she would have been a perfect target for a disturbed, angry, malicious person.

I never get to know her well, though I have a lot to thank her for. She has unwittingly made my first few years in the fire department easier than they might otherwise have been.

The smoke is thin and hangs like a fine veil in the air. I frown slightly. "Where there is smoke there is fire" is easy enough to say, but often fire is hard to find. It hides in walls and attic spaces. It builds slowly but erupts suddenly. Wendy, from my academy class, stands by the wall in front of me. She slides her hand down the paint. "Here," she suddenly says. "Here, it's hot." She sends her axe into the plaster. I am ready with the hose, coughing slightly. Beside me, someone stops and stares. He has heard. *Telephone, telegraph, tell a fireman,* the saying goes. By now, the whole department knows the news: Today there is an all-female crew.

By pure chance, Engine 60 has been estrogen-infiltrated. I am sent here because I have offered to take Bunker's "detail" today. A "detail" is when a crew member from a house that is overstaffed is sent to one that is understaffed. "Details" balance the workforce each day. When I walk into the station, hat in hand, tie in place, Captain Viviani has a large smile on his face. This is in itself not unusual. But he has a camera out and seems all ready to use it.

Later, when I understand—when Wendy and Susan walk in holding coffee—we take pictures with Viviani in the middle, still grinning wildly. "One more," he keeps saying. Though we have never worked together, Viviani had my academy friend Ritch as a probationer, and so he has always been very welcoming to me. I suspect that he thinks—incorrectly—that Ritch and I had an affair, so I am treated partly with the respect that a man has for a friend's girlfriend. But Viviani is also a genuinely nice man, a man who loves a good joke. He knows that today marks a milestone in the fire department and affirmative action, and it tickles him to death.

For me, it is more serious. I feel the pressure—more than usual—to do well. Better than well—excellently. For most, today is a day long awaited. For some, the wait has been with the held breath that will include a "See? I told you it would be a disaster" on exhale. For others, they are simply interested in seeing some questions answered. Can women do this job, or are they being compensated for by the men? And finally, there are those who call to laugh and joke and wish us fun and luck on our day together.

Only our officer is a man, and I feel vaguely sorry for him. He is handsome, with a bushy mustache and forearms like canoe paddles; perhaps a ladies' man, but *this* is not what he had in mind. He does not say this, but we know that by the end of the day he has endured ribbings from all over the department. Now it is almost seven at night. Wendy and I have kicked in every apartment door, searching for the source of the smoke. When the other crews begin to arrive, Wendy gestures me over. "Let's really bug them," she hisses under her breath. "Let's find this thing."

As I hit the flame, there is the satisfying feeling of knowing that Susan is at the pump. As a team we have worked well today. It has been busy. By noon, some of my tension has dropped away.

After the fire is out, Wendy, Susan, and I take turns slapping one another on the shoulder heartily. Mostly, we mimic and poke fun at the boisterousness we are usually not privy to at a fire. But partly we genuinely enjoy the male way of camaraderie. After a few years of watching the way men engage with one another, I have grown envious and admiring. There is nothing like watching the grudging respect men have for one another. The nods, the baritone greetings, the hearty handshakes and jokes hide an intricate language of esteem that a casual observer will miss but that these two years in the fire department have made plain to me. The chief walks by.

"Good job," he says, nodding at us.

The day I get the snapshot I am in the middle of sanding my helmet again. In the picture Susan and Wendy are smiling, and the officer is off to one side, looking uncertain. I look uncertain, too. Viviani is caught in a wide burst of laughter. The camera flash has given him red eyes. They make him look even more gleeful.

I continue to sand my helmet with short strokes. I sanded down my luge sled like this long ago, using each grain of sandpaper successively to get the perfect surface. Now I do not need a perfect surface, just one that will hold the new paint job for my transfer to Station 4, a temporary assignment that will last close to a year. Station 4 is a station with a reputation.

I do not pay much attention to "reputations." However, it is with some alarm that I notice that even the men are taking me aside and shaking their heads. "Watch yourself there," Thomas says. He doesn't say much else. Bunker shakes his burnt hand at me. "A lot of jerks," he says.

I paint my helmet carefully. It offers me protection: It is ribbed for strength and curved to deflect. But what can it do against attitudes?

# STATION 4

Station 4 is wedged between broken-down buildings and shoe-horned between two different worlds. On one side is one of the poorest, most vicious parts of the city, where prostitutes and drug dealers crowd the street corners; a few blocks the other way the sidewalks are clean and the buildings bright and manicured. The change is abrupt, as if a fence divides them. Emergency workers are probably among the few people who venture openly into both neighborhoods; otherwise there is little or no spillage, creating the bizarre feeling that one has not only turned onto the wrong block but somehow lost consciousness and awoken suddenly in a different world.

I walk into Station 4 expectantly. I remember my first hesitant walk into Station 53 three years before. I had heard stories then about the fire department, and they had been inaccurate. They no doubt had heard stories about me, and most of them had had the grace to see me as I presented myself. It is about time I drop the prejudgments, too. Stop listening to the stories. Everyone deserves a fresh chance, irrespective of niggling gossip. It is the same chance I want for myself. Besides, this is a busy house, and that is ultimately all I care about.

I am greeted with the same grunts and waves of a hand that any new person gets, so it is not until the middle of the morning, when Mike, another rookie, pulls me aside, that I begin to worry that the stories may be true after all. I do not know the rookie well, and I watch him shift anxiously from one foot to the other. Being seen talking to a woman can get a young guy embroiled in some heavy slamming from the regulars. But I know that Mike's best friend was in my academy class and respects me. This is a bond between us.

"Watch out for Todd Lane," Mike says quickly. "Last shift, at the dinner table, he said he was going to get you."

I am alarmed. "Get me? What does that mean? He doesn't even know me."

"He said he was going to cook an all-meat meal." Mike shuffles and puts his hands in his pockets.

My laughter comes out as a short bark, both derisive and hesitant. What? Ridiculous. Cooking an all-meat meal will not "get me." But I am on my guard.

"He deliberately switched into the cook chore today," Mike adds.

*Jesus Christ,* I think, as the pure malice strikes me. To cook for so many people is no easy chore; it consumes most of the day. The idea that someone would actually volunteer for the task, get no credit for it on the cook chart, and cook a meal intentionally designed to exclude a coworker is mindboggling. For Todd Lane to expend so much hostile energy on someone he has never met seems downright crazy.

That night, my first night at this new station, I stand in line for food. I realize that he "gets me" if I sit out from dinner. Dinner is the most social time of day, a time of friendship and bonding. The idea of breaking bread together is taken seriously. The meal is sacred. To be absent is close to sacrilege. It sets you apart. The last thing I need is to be further apart.

In case Lane's ill will extends beyond the dinner, I hid my coat so no one could take it and leave me looking ridiculous and unprepared when a call came in. I checked my turnout boots in case someone put something frightful in them, as my mother reported they did in New York. I spoke little the rest of the day. I said nothing at all to Todd Lane.

In the dinner line, I realize that Todd Lane has done his job well. There is not a single pot that does not contain meat.

The salad is full of shrimp and the beans are full of bacon. The steak is large and sullen, dripping lazily into the platter.

I do not care much about food. I have never expected others to accommodate my chosen diet. The fact that most stations have gone out of their way to make sure I have something to eat has always been a touching but extraordinary gesture, unexpected even when it occurred every shift. Tonight my stomach curls and my throat tightens. I could not have eaten if a vegetable garden suddenly appeared on my plate. The sheer malice of this move overwhelms me. Todd Lane means to humiliate me in front of a whole fire station, to indicate to everyone that I am purposely trying not to fit in.

Years later, I would crash my paraglider against a cliff, breaking an ankle badly. When I wake up the next morning, a large hunk of chocolate cake squats on the table by my hospital bed. A note explains that Chief Masters and Alberto had come by in the night. They left the fire station, armed with this massive talisman, when they heard about the accident. I am under the tender grip of Demerol and anesthesia when they arrive, so they leave their loyalty and concern wrapped carefully in foil. It is enough for three, and even its crumbs roll like dimes. I am moved by the sight of this hulking piece of cake, absurdly jaunty and excessive against the swabbed, solemn backdrop of the hospital. Food spans the place where words fail.

Todd Lane, then, knows what he is doing when he turns a meal against me. All this, *and he does not even know me*. He has never met me, not even this morning; he turned and walked away when I came into the communications room.

I sit at the table, my plate almost empty. I fill the plate and my mouth with bread, like a wallflower who needs a drink in her hand to look occupied. I look down at a space on the table, pretending to be absorbed. I pour water. Sip. More water. Pass the bread. Pass the butter. Cut it slow, spread it slower, to make the minutes go by.

I resolve, crumbs dropping nervously on my plate, never

to talk to Todd Lane at all. When he is not looking in my direction, I stare at him, half surprised that so much aggression can lie within one man.

Todd Lane has a red mustache that hangs over his mouth like the tail of a coyote. His eyebrows are thick, too, and they seem to shroud his small blue eyes. In other circumstances, he might appear to be handsome, but to me at this moment he looks menacing. His hands, big and able, look ready to crush something. His deep voice, sonorous in someone else, sounds harsh and aggressive. He has the long, slow laugh of someone who knows that he is listened to.

More bread, eaten intently, as if this is all I've ever wanted in the world. Everyone has noticed by now. I want to cover the bright white of my plate with my hand; I want to slink away.

My only consolation is the realization that the same emotion—call it hate?—that starts to consume me has already wrapped him in a brutal, suffocating embrace. My presence bothers him so much that he has unwittingly given me power at the very moment he most wants to strip it from me. So I have the last laugh, though laughing is the furthest thing from my mind.

Around this time, Alexandra lands a role on the television show *Baywatch*. *Baywatch* is a one-hour weekly drama. It features lifeguards on impeccably sunny California days making surf rescues. Also called *Babewatch*, *Bunwatch*, or *Titwatch*, the show is famous for its beautiful people with large smiles and larger mammaries. The script dispenses small moral tidbits about the environment and the importance of being nice. While it is frequently made fun of in the United States, it is the most popular television program in the world. In fact, it is the most watched show *ever*. I once saw a news clip that showed a tribe in the Amazon glued to a television set, riveted to the thong bikinis prancing around a bright yellow lifeguard truck.

Alexandra has been working steadily since she first started acting. The result is that people often seem to think they have met me before. Sometimes I catch them staring; at other times, there is a faraway look in their eyes when they talk to me, and I know that they are trying to puzzle out why I look so familiar. When Alexandra begins appearing weekly as *Baywatch*'s Lieutenant Stephanie Holden, the stares multiply. Every other day or so someone will say that I look uncannily like *that woman on Baywatch*. Or out of the corner of my eye I will see the unmistakable signs of someone mustering up the courage to ask for my autograph. First, the reflexive double take, then the refocus of the eyes as I am imagined into a slim red bathing suit. As Alexandra becomes more famous, the encounters become more comical: A fire drill that my crew conducts at a nearby grammar school is disrupted when kids break from the line to get my autograph; while flying to Canada, I am put in first class without a word of explanation, just a small wink by the flight attendant to indicate that *she* won't tell anyone else who I am. With the new *Baywatch* job, our twinship takes on a cartoonish similarity. Alexandra rescues people on television, while I rescue them in real life. How much more all-American can you get?

The photographer sent from England calls out enthusiastically, his camera fixed to his face, his body doing odd circles in the sand. "That's right, like that. More of that, more of that." Alexandra is hanging off the Malibu lifeguard tower, toes pointed, hair back on her shoulders. I am all that keeps her from falling to the sand below; my hands are around her wrists and I lean over the railing. Despite this awkward position, my head is up and I am smiling. A casual smile, I hope. Or a sexy one. I don't know which expression we are on, but there seems to be a list of them we have to get through. *Okay, give me a pout, a smile. Come hither, you're saying, yeah, that's right, big eyes, this way, yeah yeah, hither. . . .* I am glad that this is for a foreign magazine, and that no one in my department will see me like this, in acrobatic poses, in full fire-fighting gear, on the beach.

In a funny way, Alexandra and I each epitomize different

aspects of the American Dream. We are working women taking advantage of what America promises all of us. Alexandra is a glamorous Hollywood actress enjoying the jet-set life, a "star" of some magnitude. I, on the other hand, am a woman in a nontraditional job. It amuses me sometimes to see how far apart we can get—ash on my face, foundation and blush on hers—and how near we are, too.

"The rescue-me look," the photographer cries, lunging around us, clicking wildly. *"Now tougher, tougher, yeah, hands on hips, perfect, get the stance, no smiles. I'm dying, I'm drowning, great. . . ."*

On Christmas Day, I work at a station near Ocean Beach. Ocean Beach is on the northwest side of the city. It is a long, wide expanse of sand that invites slow, unguarded ambles through ankle-high water that seems deceptively manageable. In fact, the currents are strong and the waves can sweep unsuspecting waders off their feet. So it is no big surprise when the Bee-Bop interrupts our Christmas lunch, and we scramble for the Surf Rescue Truck, loaded with wet suits, kayaks, and life buoys. We swing out into the crisp, sunny day.

We grab red life buoys and scan the ocean. A park ranger points to dark dots in the water a hundred and fifty yards out; another ranger and some surfers have gotten to the man.

"He took off all his clothes at the edge. Then he went into the water and swam. Then he swam and swam and he kept on swimming. People onshore started yelling at him, but he kept on going." The ranger shrugs, as if such a thing on Christmas Day is not a big surprise. Suicides are common on holidays, after all. But swimming into the wide foreverness of the ocean momentarily gives me the chills.

My suit is not a sleek red outfit, but a bulky neoprene wet suit, designed for the fifty-degree ocean. Still, I think I hear the exuberant beat of the *Baywatch* theme song in the background; I wonder if suddenly I will start running in slow motion, sweatless, earnest, almost holy. I am momentarily Alexandra, momentarily a Rescue Babe, on the way to a swift and graceful lifesaving moment.

My reverie is broken when the beach truck gets stuck in the sand and I see the currents pulling the Park Service rescuers south. The wet suit makes every step graceless. I am squinting against the sun. The wind is up. This is reality.

There is a lot of shouting and cursing. Some firefighters try to push the truck out while others start down the beach without it. I want this rescue, so I leave the truck, too, and start to run. The current is taking the dark dots I saw earlier even farther down the beach. I jog faster and leave the others behind, and when I have passed the dots, too, I cut into the ocean, slipping on my fins. I have forgotten, however, that the water is only up to my calves for the first twenty yards or so. Unable to swim in the shallow water, but determined to make it out there first (first!), I shuffle and wallow and trip through the tide.

I look like a huge mammal hit by a stun gun but struggling to get away.

My urgent, inelegant waddles finally take me to the exhausted park ranger and surfers. They gladly hand over to me the man they have been dragging for a mile or so through the water.

Nearer to the beach, more hands reach out to help. The man never says a word, not even when we lay him on the sand. If this were *Baywatch* there would now be enthusiastic thank yous and quick speeches. Here, nothing is said except the stammer of voices shouting orders—*Get the blankets! Get the stretchers!* The man does not move, as if drained by some mysterious event even larger than hypothermia. He is a large man, Asian and in his mid-forties. He stares at the sky. The ranger takes off his cap and runs a stiff hand through his hair. He looks down at the man.

"Thanks for that," he says. "I was getting real tired out there." He stares down at the man. "He didn't struggle when we got to him. He just kept on swimming. Kept on, until we got to him and then he just stopped, just lay there trying to sink."

The wide, detached silence continues. This man wants not just to die, but to disintegrate slowly, to swim while feeling drops off into the cold—first the fingers, then the face, then the legs. Swim until he could feel nothing and then slowly sink. It is a gentle way to die—I have seen a lot worse—but this passionless agony seems even more terrible than a gunshot wound or an intentional overdose.

But still, I am exhilarated. A surf rescue!

Even when I realize, as I walk away, that I have put my surf suit on backward.

Meanwhile, Station 4 keeps me busy, and soon the potential that something can happen is almost as exciting as the happening itself. It is the same state of heightened awareness and tension we enjoy at a movie thriller. When the Bee-Bop goes off, I realize that I have been waiting for it. We jump onto the rig and careen into the dank streets of the poor neighborhood. The sirens whine, the lights flash, and now that "something" has happened, the call opens up wide with possible adventure.

I respect the crew I work with; individually they are good, hardworking, smart men. But in a group, they seem to change. A bullying quality takes over—the milling, braying quality of a herd. I learn from the first night and Todd Lane's meal that it is better to stay quiet. I retreat into a familiar place. I am the silent observer again.

When Jackie, my academy classmate, brings harassment charges against Captain John Wills, the case throws the department into a tizzy and me in particular into a depression.

Jackie is a friend of mine. I want to protect her, but I also want to assimilate. Secretly, I hope that I will not have to testify on her behalf. *Please, please, please.* This weakness surprises and embarrasses me; I always assumed that I would willingly stand up for a friend.

Captain Wills looks for a woman to testify as a character witness. I am relieved that I do not know him and will not be asked. Meanwhile, Jackie stops speaking to anyone. She takes time off for stress. She does not return my phone calls.

"Of course this crap happens," another classmate, Carl, says to me. Carl is a burly white man who told some of his crew members that he was looking for a house to buy for his family. He mentioned an area near the almost exclusively black Hunter's Point neighborhood. One of the lieutenants listening leaned forward.

"It is bad enough we have to work with them," he said. "Why do you want to live with them, too?"

Carl stared at the lieutenant.

"Just so you'll know, I am *married* to one of them." That ended the conversation.

When Carl tells me this story, he does not seem surprised or particularly outraged, as if his years in an interracial marriage have long shown him the worst in people.

I attend the fire department hearing on the Wills case. The meeting room is packed; many of the top brass and department administrators are present. Off-duty firefighters and union leaders whisper among themselves.

Jackie, usually animated, is slack-faced. When she takes the stand, her words are slow and precise, her inflections flat and emotionless. I am shocked by the change in her. She relates in a low voice how Captain Wills mimicked Homie the Clown behind her back. Homie the Clown is a character on *In Living Color;* he is a black clown prone to violence. Wills, in his imitation, stood behind her and pretended to hit her. Other comments were made, she said, including one on the size of her buttocks. One after another, each of the white firefighters present that day say that they do not remember this Homie the Clown act, nor any of the other comments Wills is alleged to have made throughout the shift. Jackie, the lone black and the lone woman, is outnumbered.

This sudden affliction of amnesia does not help Captain Wills. He is suspended. Jackie does not return to work for a long time.

# WILDFIRE

On the day of the Oakland firestorm, I am working. It is a normal day for Station 4. It seems to be a normal day for the city of Oakland as well, a large city within view across the bay, as firefighters there respond to a small brush fire on October 20, 1991. They leave after what they think is a small, successfully extinguished incident. Instead, embers remain. Fire lurks in the soil.

By noon, the fire is out of control in the exclusive Oakland hills. Mansions and large housing complexes heave and sigh once or twice before being engulfed in virulent flame. It is nothing that these firefighters have ever seen—part wildfire, part structure fire. Fire crews become tapped. A battalion chief dies. The conflagration jumps Highway 24. Oakland frantically radios surrounding cities for assistance.

San Francisco sends fire engines to help our neighbors across the bay, but my crew is not one of them. We pace the communications floor; already we sense that this is a once-in-a-lifetime inferno. The black cloud forming over the city is one hint, the mass mobilization of mutual aid another. The television shows a hysteria of flame and smoke as wide-eyed reporters point to exploding trees and evacuating cars.

As the fire gets bigger and the sky blacker, as off-duty firefighters start to pour in to pick up equipment, I get more and more depressed. I stare forlornly at the black disc of smoke that now creeps toward us while Richard leans over yet another drunk who is sleeping on the curb.

"Looks like we are going to miss all the fun," Richard

chuckles. He likes to joke and affects a high laugh that off-sets his muscular bulk. He is deep black and his head is shaven except for the nub of a ponytail; he looks like an exotic genie fresh out of a gigantic bottle. He is in many ways "one of the guys." This is surprising, not because he is black and nonunion—a member instead of the opposing Black Firefighters Association—but because he is married to a female firefighter.

Richard and Nancy met in the academy; their marriage was the first liaison that I knew of between firefighters, though there have been others since. The diameter of Richard's arms and the hillocks that form his traps probably discouraged any malicious comments.

"Maybe it will go until tomorrow," I say. I say "go" so I do not have to say "burn," which is what I really mean. I am embarrassed that I could actually want the devastation to last until I am free to volunteer. But Richard understands. He loves to fight fires. And it has become painfully clear that, with hundreds of structures already burned, this is the biggest firestorm any of us has ever seen.

By dinnertime, as the ashfall becomes heavy and smoke chokes the streets, there are warnings to watch out for fire in San Francisco. We remain glued to the television. Heaps of chicken parmigiana and vegetables with mashed potatoes (my portion) are served while the conflagration rages only a few miles away. It is a peculiarly despondent feeling we share. The few jokes we make about the fire are told wanly and greeted with wry grunts.

Most of the San Francisco firefighters are posted at the regal Claremont Hotel, which is the second-biggest wooden structure in the United States. There is fear that if it burns it may set all of downtown Berkeley on fire. But the fire doesn't reach it; it is faced down by the weary but stubborn San Francisco strike teams.

The statistics from the Firestorm, as the media begins to call it, tell a story of how mighty fire is. Cars exploding, engine beacons melting, fifty houses on one street all burn-ing at the same time. In all, 3,469 living units are destroyed,

2,843 of them single-family dwellings. Fifteen hundred and twenty acres burned. A 5.2-mile fire perimeter. Twenty-five deaths.

I am depressed. But I cheer up momentarily when I am told that Tess was arrested during the Firestorm for "impersonating a firefighter." While in full fire turnouts, she was stopped by a reserve police officer on the lookout for looters. Despite her uniform, he demanded identification. Because her mutual-aid team was given only a few minutes to get ready, she had no ID, and therefore no "proof" that she is a firefighter. The police officer handcuffed her and threw her in the back of his squad car. She was indignant; he laughed. She probably stole the uniform from her boyfriend, he claims. A surprised fire chief identified her after she convinced the police officer to drive to where the San Francisco Fire Department was making a stand. "Get out, bitch," the police officer said.

I have stayed clear of Tess since her withdrawn handshake, her lilting guffaw at my expense. But now I feel sorry for her. All her years in the fire department have not yet changed the Real World.

Otherwise my gloom is unremitting. In every firehouse, stories circulate about the Firestorm, the flames bigger and hotter at each retelling. I sulk quietly.

Life at Station 4 is not easy. I can't wait to leave.

The warehouse fire comes in around midnight. It is really going when we arrive, and since the warehouse is full of tea, a sweet, floral smell fills the air. I run into Patricia near a big line. She tells me excitedly that she and her crew had tried an interior attack but had retreated when the stairs they were on started to collapse and they heard the roof falling in. This is just the sort of thing that makes Patricia happy. She keeps explaining the feel of the stairs underneath them, soft and pliant like sponge. She repeats that they almost "lost it." There is amazement in her voice and a smile on her face.

From then on we are ordered to "surround and drown,"

which is mostly boring, except that it gives you a chance to stare, hypnotized, at the roiling, brutal beauty of the flames.

For a few hours I hold various hoses, but soon I take my turn at the top of an aerial ladder to use the ladder pipe. The ladder pipe is a nozzle at the end of the aerial ladder, which is supplied by a hose running up the rungs. Ladder pipes are effective for large fires where "master streams" are essential; the aerial is stretched high above the fire and angled at its optimal climbing position of seventy-five degrees. It looms past the warehouse, eighty feet of ladder (the maximum extension allowed with a ladder pipe), over flames and water.

The smoke and steam are so thick that my climb is like stepping into heaven. Near the top of the ladder, seven building floors up, the smoke and steam clears and the whole city spreads out around me in small, precise lights.

My job from this high vantage point is to direct the water, which shoots out forcefully from the tip in a concentrated stream and then loosens and falls. There is a quietness at the apex of the scene, despite the rush of water near me, but soon the three-story warehouse below becomes so hot that the cement walls split, and the sudden sound is angry and sharp. Steam and smoke waft up from the new rift. They cover me, a soft billow that blocks out everything but the nozzle in front of me so that I feel oddly as if I am nowhere at all, suspended in nothingness. After an hour I am soaking wet and very cold, but I do not want to come down. I am alone; it is peaceful, and stunningly beautiful.

I descend when my own shivering threatens to topple me off the ladder. Steam continues to rise from the building; it looks like a simple by-product of fire fighting, but it is actually, in and of itself, a potent fire-fighting tool. Vapor absorbs heat as much as six times more efficiently than liquid. But right now I do not think about relative absorbtion or efficiency. The smell of tea is everywhere, and the view is beautiful. I descend slowly, to savor the pungent, potent night. For a while I am away from the petty discomfort of

Station 4. When I reluctantly reach the ladder's turntable, I nod to the firefighter waiting there to go up and take my place above the world. Dawn breaks over the smoldering building.

# THE BRIDGE

One foot in front of the other, slowly, carefully. Deep breath.
Hands out as if grasping thin air. Not thin air exactly, but
close enough: only a cartilage of wire on each side of me.
The wind picks up now, and I think that if I stop I might get
blown off. More steps, slowly, carefully. Beneath my feet, a
three-foot-in-diameter cable. Below that, nothing, for 746
feet.

I am on the Golden Gate. Not the bridge itself, but the
suspension cable. The suspension cable above the bridge,
that leads up to the north tower. If this were a skyscraper, I
would be the window-washer outside the sixty-third floor.

The ocean hits the cliffs below with a long *hussssssh.* I
make myself look; the surf peels into white, blinking in the
dark. From so high up it seems as if the earth unzips a layer
momentarily and then zips it back up. *Hussshhhh.*

To the left is the city. Always a beautiful skyline, tonight
it is framed by the long cables of the easterly suspension so
that it stands out like a prized painting. Or is that my adrenaline? In the foreground is Alcatraz Island, once a notorious
prison, now lit to look like a small castle. Behind that is the
long, spidery stretch of the Bay Bridge. Why didn't we pick
that bridge to climb? I wonder. It is a low, squat bridge with
none of the high, lean, dizzying aspects of the Golden Gate.

*Why am I up here?* It is the third time I ask myself.
Behind me are four other slim, dark silhouettes, moving
slowly, bent in concentration like monks. At this point, the
question is simply rhetorical; turning around and going back

down would be as bad as continuing up. Anyway, we each know why we are here: We have dared ourselves to do it.

*A dare is a STUPID reason to be up here,* I think. *STEW–PID.* My hands are getting cold. The cable rears up now at a sharper angle; I walk on my toes to stay balanced. But even as the traffic grows smaller far below me, I know that the dare *is* very important. It is an ancient rite of passage, a demonstration of will and courage, of the "stuff" one is made of. Each of us is here in a private initiation, a self-inflicted hazing, and though right now, from this great height, with the ground dropping away from me on all sides, it seems crazy, I know that this is an important moment.

Because I just got a permanent spot on Rescue Squad 3.

This is the first time a woman has been an assigned as a member of a squad. Some have worked there temporarily but then have moved on to different stations when their seniority permitted them to request a permanent assignment. "Floaters," as unassigned firefighters are called, go from station to station at the whim of headquarters, just as I "floated" into Station 4 for nine months and then out again. It has come as a surprise to some that a woman would even want a permanent place on the Rescue Squad. Perhaps to me as well.

The wind picks up even more. Behind me, it is silent except for Ellie's lilting soprano singing of "Waltzing Mathilda," torn away in whole pieces by the wind, so that I hear only snatches. It is Ellie's idea to do this. *Come on, it'll be fun, it'll be crazy, what the hell.* She is an Olympic swimmer who has just been diagnosed with chronic fatigue syndrome. With a better understanding of what has hindered her swimming for years, she is determined to beat it. Beth thinks this is a fine idea, too. My longtime rafting teammate and close friend, Beth is never one to balk at an adventure. This time, however, there is another reason she is here. A close friend of hers has just drowned in his kayak on a river like the ones she paddles on. She hasn't been doing much these days. She can't sleep. She can't eat. She can't get into her kayak; she doesn't know if she ever will again.

Melea and Jane round out the group. They were both easy to convince. Jane has just finished writing a book; she is going through the usual postpartum anxieties. Melea, on the other hand, is locked into a job as a lawyer and is feeling stale and bored. Born and raised in Hawaii, she is steeped in the kahuna tradition; she understands the inherent power of ritual. Disturbingly beautiful, her face rarely indicates what she is thinking, which will be helpful if panic grips any of us.

We all think that if we can climb this bridge, we can do anything.

The official color of the Golden Gate Bridge is not golden. It is "international orange," the color judged to be the easiest to see in fog (next to black-and-white checks, which is what the Coast Guard originally argued for), and there is some debate before we start about what color clothing to wear. We dig in our closets for international-orange possibilities. Black, an easier color to find, is our eventual choice. We decide to see the late show of Sylvester Stallone's movie *Cliffhanger*. A climbing movie set in the Rockies, it will kill time before we set out at midnight, and it will psyche us up for our urban mountain. The choice is a mistake; the first scene throws an unfortunate climber down a chasm after the unlikely mechanical failure of a buckle. Now we are here, and it runs through my mind that the wires I hold on to could snap, the cable I walk on could sever, the bridge itself collapse.

The red light is just ahead. Ellie has warned us about this; she claims that it is a video camera and that we are to duck by it. From my vantage point I can see that there is nowhere to "duck" unless we execute some strange maneuver that would entail hanging from the underside of our already precarious foothold. I stop and slowly turn to confer with the group. Melea is behind me, quiet and pensive. Then Ellie, singing, and Beth. I have not heard a peep from Beth; I can tell by the stiff way she puts each foot down that she is in a private conversation with her doubt and anxiety. Far behind her is Jane, who wears full climbing gear. She slides a carabiner along one side of her, unhooking every now and then to get past a cross wire. All five of us have climbed before, but only Jane opts for this safety gear. The rest of us do not want to have to unhook like she does, and take our hands off of the flimsy wire. Her technique has slowed her down, but Jane is a top wall-climber. We are not worried about her nerve.

The five of us would easily pass as sorority sisters, and if we are caught, our story is that this is a sorority hazing. We are unlikely to be believed—we have picked a ritual of manhood to prove ourselves. Men, in my view, have always understood that walking the thin meridian of bravery will show them where they are in the cartography of the soul. High on this cable, a longitude over the city below, we, too, are trying to orient ourselves by mastering our fears.

*Master your fear.* I have just made my dream spot in the fire department, Rescue 3, and these words have never been so relevant. Fire fighting is all about conquering fear, and the squad—pronounced *skwwwaaaadd* by most firefighters, the middle syllables elongated to emphasize sarcastically the machismo associated with it—combines a precise amount of technical expertise with a loose dose of reckless What-the-Fuck. While every firefighter is asked to go into dangerous, uncertain situations, "skwwwaaaaddies" tote large amounts of expensive, complicated machinery in with them, adding a false veneer of control. The Rescue Squads are expected to shore up the chaos and mayhem as a last resort. Everyone but Batman has already been summoned.

Rescue Squads are called in to perform rescues of every type, in all kinds of conditions: the surf, the cliffs, confined spaces—you name it. This year is a special year for them—the first year that a woman has gotten a permanent assignment, I to Rescue 3 and Mimi to Rescue 5.

Mimi and I are very different women. A construction worker before she was a firefighter, Mimi herself reminds me of a power tool: solidly built, silent unless it serves a purpose to talk, and prone to loud, angry outbursts capable of ripping an ego apart as though it were a thin piece of wood. She speaks little; everything she says is said in the time a nail needs to go through wood. She rarely says a word to me, though I see her sometimes at my gym, where she easily presses almost twice my body weight, so I can imagine what she would do to me if I ever incurred the wrath that seems to seethe behind her long bangs. But I respect her; she is an excellent, aggressive firefighter.

She spoke a full sentence to me once. I had trouble starting a power tool. She walked over soundlessly, waved me aside wordlessly, pulled the cord contemptuously, and the engine roared to life so fast it sounded as if it were trying to back away from her.

"Put your foot here," she said suddenly, without looking at me. "And your left hand, not your right, on the cord. Now you are right over it and it'll pull straight and nicely." A few months later, a saw needed to open a roof on a fire building would not start. I offered to try; using Mimi's technique, it started easily.

Women on the squads!

Permanent squaddies must be formally certified in all types of rescues. I have to take many classes, including a confined-space class, and get my rappelling and climbing skills tuned up. I must get my fire service scuba-diver certificate, my Coast Guard boat driving license, my tunnel-rescue certification, my surf-rescue certification, and my Heavy Rescue 1 certification. Heavy Rescue means that I will know how to rig up pulley systems with ropes and carabiners and move large objects with anything else available (from telephone poles to cut-up parking meters) in case of earthquake, building collapse, tunnel explosion, train accident—you name it.

*You name it* explains the Rescue Squad better than any of these certificates ever will. For all the skills I am taught, how prepared can I be for a rescue on, say, the Golden Gate Bridge?

Rescues on the local bridges are not uncommon. Recently, Rescue 5 pulled a jumper off of the Bay Bridge.

He had climbed over the railing to jump and then lost his nerve. Squaddies rappelled to him and brought him back up. Once a firefighter on the way to work saw a man climb over the side of the Golden Gate Bridge and disappear. The firefighter jumped out of his car and climbed out after him. The man sat on an undergirder getting up the guts to jump while the off-duty firefighter shimmied toward him. They sat talking high over the bay, the large ribs of the mammoth structure above them. Perhaps they talked about beer and football and the meaning of life. Eventually, the suicidal man changed his mind. A firefighter can do that, talk seamlessly and charismatically even as hundreds of feet of thin air yawn beneath him.

Where I am now, however, the wind would wrench away any calm words I might have to say. We are still contemplating the red light, and I can see that the cable now gleams with a thick dusting of dew. We decide to run. "Run" is a relative term when you are on a slick suspension cable and the wind is blowing and your fear threatens to seep into your muscles and force you to stop. We each move as fast as possible past the video camera. I am stiff-legged and stiff-armed, Frankensteinesque in my hurry. We are near the top now, and the shadow of the bridge, reflected off the clouds, is strewn across the sky. I am glad for the purplish ceiling peculiar to city nights, even though the long dark lines above me look eerie. I could not have handled a clear night, which would have offered a look into the infinite. Now the cable rears to meet the tower at such a steep angle that my hands seem to be at eye level. The top is bathed in spotlights. And then suddenly it is there. The top! The pinnacle! The zenith! I shimmy from the suspension to the girder. I sprawl on the wide, damp, steel surface and stare at the rivulets that the braided wire has left in my palm. I laugh because this has been so stupid and so important, all at once.

*Three*

# FIRE

# RESCUE 3

On a cool day, you can catch the faint smell of ash and anti-septic. The mild stink of wet neoprene clings to the scuba tanks in the corner. A sting of rubbing alcohol hits the nose. Perhaps the timid hint of blood.

Today it has rained, so we have tracked crooked lines of mud on the metal floor. Stacks of ropes in blue bags take up the left top shelves like large sleeping cats. Helmets to one side. Then the gibs, the pulleys, the carabiners. Below are the bulky trauma bags, soft and heavy with tape and bandages and face masks. Bottles of distilled water stand like stout soldiers.

On the right are the wet suits, folded and piled on top of one another. The fins and masks. The thick gloves and hoods. Sometimes, if the driver takes a corner too fast, a fin flies out at you. Other things have fallen on me, too—the defibrillator, the burn kit, a flashlight. I sometimes wonder how they will find me if we ever have an accident—smothered, decapitated, gashed in a thousand places—brutally, spectacularly killed by the vast array of equipment that we use to rescue people.

This is Rescue 3. Sometimes it is simply called *the rig,* as are most of the other vehicles of the San Francisco Fire Department. "What rig are you on today?" you might be asked. "That rig," you say. You point, because there are many rigs and they are all red and seem larger than life. *That rig.*

Alberto stands near the hazardous-material clothing cabinets. He runs a bakery on his off days; perhaps this accounts for his customary calm. Even in the midst of chaos, he is thoughtful and centered. It is as if fighting a fire is somehow like baking bread and he is used to it—the heat, the stress, the firm grip on the axe handle not much different than on the rolling pin. He has a thick black mustache and short black hair. He assures me that once he had a beard and long hair, but it is hard to believe.

Alberto worries about me because I am a woman. It is in his upbringing, he says. He apologizes for it sometimes.

There are only two windows in the rig, and they are small and impossible to see out of, so that there is the odd sensation of traveling wildly and fast, but with very little sense of where one is heading. Time does not seem to move forward, but from side to side in angular, jerky movements. Even if Alberto and I cannot see where we are going, we recognize the roll and sway of the streets in our dispatch area. I hear the engine accelerate down wide South Van Ness Avenue. In narrow alleys, with double-parked cars and errant garbage cans, we slow down. But not much. This is the Mission District, full of old wooden houses and crowded, noisy intersections.

For many years, Rescue Squad 3 did little work: It was stationed in the city's wealthy Pacific Heights area. Rescue 5, on the other hand, was in one of the most haggard and crime-ridden parts of San Francisco and was busy all the time. As a result, they called themselves the Real Squad. They called us the Other Squad, or, in kinder moments, the U-Turn Squad, because we were often canceled from the emergency before we got there.

But Rescue 3 was quietly removed from the mansions of Pacific Heights and placed in its new home at Station 64. Here, there is more work. The Mission District is crowded and poor. Crack and heroin are the drugs of choice. Molotov cocktails or .22s are the weapons of choice, or sometimes machetes. Fires start easily in the thin, pinched houses. Rescue 3 is no longer a U-turn rig.

Now the brakes hiss and catch. We smell the smoke before we are even out of the rig. The air packs are lifted from their compartment and held high above our heads so that they drop onto our backs easily. It is a small silent game here, though Alberto doesn't notice. He is slow and careful in his movements and not in any race. But the rest of us want to be the first with the air pack on, the first to get to the building.

Horace Miller plays this game grimly. He would hate to get beaten by a woman. He does not talk to me, but if he did, he might well say that he is glad that he is not my partner today. Miller himself is short and pudgy, soft enough to look like a woman from behind. Sometimes I am curious at his silent vehemence, but not now. The only thing that matters now is the fire.

Someone is being carried out and laid on the sidewalk. The smoke is black and angry and pours out of the side windows. An engine hose runs up the steps and into the blackness. The Rescue Squad goes in without water. Our purpose is to rescue, not to put the fire out. Sometimes it seems crazy, to run in without water. But only when someone asks me about it—"How can you go in like that, without protection, without water?"—do I take a minute and think about it, and it does seem crazy. But it is not something you can ponder too much. The mind is not built for it.

"Does anyone else live over there?" I ask a neighbor as Alberto and I charge through his house. He stammers and shakes, overwhelmed by the sight of these helmeted, clanging, sooty firefighters running on his tan carpet, through his neat hallway. In the garden I get ready to jump the back fence to gain access to the rear entrance of the burning building. I have more than fifty pounds of gear on, but I have gotten over a lot of fences. The neighbor has clung to us, followed us past his flower vases and through his geraniums. Now he waves me off the fence hurriedly, worriedly. He points to a missing plank we can squeeze through.

At the house I turn to kick in the back door. I miss the wood and my foot crashes through a pane of glass. I bend and unlock the door from the inside. I make a mental note to practice my aim.

We kneel, knocking our helmets back. We fit our air masks against our faces. The respirator kicks in. Breath fills our ears like loud whispers.

Inside, it is pitch black. Tables, clocks, a phone. Books, a couch. All these things shift in and out of sight, materializing through touch and the weak, unreliable light of my flashlight. The light is thin and fragments wildly so that the beam looks like a long, narrow sieve through which darkness falls easily. But I am looking for something else: a hand, the print of a dress, the curve of a chin. Anything can start to look like these, so I must not let my mind jog ahead into the smoke. Instead, each moment must be allowed to sit and reveal what it will in its own time. Nothing can be missed. It is an odd discipline for a firefighter intent on rushing ahead to divert the future. I listen to the surf of my breath to keep me centered—in, out, and then it swirls within the closed mask like the rush of a wave.

We break windows to ventilate the smoke and heat. I crawl over chairs and around a side table. A stereo materializes in the blackness only when my face mask is pressed close to it. We pat the floor and make wide sweeps with our hands as if to smooth bedsheets; this is the only way to be sure we don't miss a body overcome with smoke. Slowly the smoke seeps out past the broken edges of window. As we round a corner on our knees, there is the blur of orange, delicate and lacelike in the murky black. We are drawn to it—it is Fire!—but we have no hose and possible victims are our only concern. There are voices nearby, so we know that the engine company will get to the fire soon enough.

I hear Joe's voice, and the sound of water. The smoke clears fast now. To the left a window is broken and through it I can see dusk gently outlining the skyscrapers of downtown. To the right is the Bay Bridge. The lights that line the span are beginning to turn on, making the water below it purple. A tanker with a red belly seems to shine momentarily, and then loses the last rays of the day.

"They were goddamn lucky," Joe says, and his silhouette gestures to Alberto and me. The hiss of steam and the loud voices of men take up the space where the silence and the thick, hot darkness had once been.

We head back to the rig, walking slowly to let the adrenaline seep back from the crevices and corners of our bodies. The clatter of broken wood and the soft, whooshing sound of wet, burnt belongings thrown on concrete begin their familiar rhythm behind me. The insides of the house will be raked onto the sidewalk. They will be separated with the pick of an axe and hosed down. This is the hardest part of a fire, when the small moments of someone's life are thrown in misshapen black heaps on the curb. No one else seems to notice, not even Alberto.

There is a moment of my own I want to hold on to. It is the deep, swaying continuum between me and my crew, as if our turnout coats and helmets were attached by some invisible filament. Even Miller cannot ruin this; it is the beauty of fire to hold us for a while simply as firefighters, without gender or color or any other distinction. For a moment, in the pitch dark, we are nothing but silhouettes of one another. We mimic each other's movements. We watch each other's backs. There is nothing but the communion of putting out fire.

Now no one else looks back at the house, so I don't either. Then the moment is over, and I hear the long, thin wail of the owner as the last of the belongings are soaked down with the hose.

"See ya at the Big One," someone from another crew says as he walks by on his way back to his rig. "Yeah," laughs Joe, and the man laughs back.

Rescue 3 resides at Station 64, in the dilapidated Mission District, named for the church that stands on its edge. Mission Dolores, the oldest structure in the city, was one of twenty-one missions established by Franciscan Jesuits, who used it to convert the local Cosanoan Indian tribe back in 1776. San Francisco grew outward from this Mission, but in the process seemed to leave the old district behind. Its tired, shabby Victorian houses, dense population, and crime-filled streets overshadow the proud heritage. But it makes Rescue 3 a busy, adventurous assignment.

The old shift talks about the calls they had over the past twenty-four hours as the new shift wanders in and prepares for the new day. Cabinets slam. Sports pages are unfurled and cracked loudly. Someone polishes his boots in rhythmic arcs. From the television there is the drone of newscasters. The clink of coffee cups. Loud voices, getting louder.

The coffee is weak, as usual, but I pour a cup anyway. It is a habit from four years ago, back when Johnny poured me my first cup at Station 53. As I sip it, I listen to the clangor around me. It is almost eight o'clock in the morning.

Yesterday's game is debated, dissected, debunked. With hindsight everyone throws, passes, strategizes differently and better. I sit down next to Tim and Hal, tight in conversation about the 49ers. I am amazed at their intensity and seriousness as they hunch over each play, as if they are speaking about death or family problems. Tim has long hair pinned untidily behind his head. One hand is on his suspenders, which he pulls when making a point.

The fire last shift is mentioned, but only briefly. Did the person who was carried out and laid on the sidewalk die? "I don't think so," someone says. Shrugs, nods. We are privy to small sentences of other people's lives, their intimate, tragic moments, but not the whole story. It ends at the sidewalk or at the emergency-room door.

"A climbing drill today," Joe says as he walks by. He walks at a slant, leaning forward and a little sideways as if to compensate for some gravitational pull no one else feels. We know it is because of back muscles worn down by the job, but people speak to him with their feet wide and their arms crossed, as if whatever force is pulling on him might suddenly affect them as well.

I like Joe. He speaks slowly and is calm and clear in an emergency. Not anxious, like some officers. Despite experience, their voices rise in pitch and they move with jerky indecision. Not Joe. And though he is not tall or big, I would rather have him with me in a burning building than almost anyone else. He is a great example of how brute size and strength is not in and of itself vital—smarts and bravery make a great firefighter. If Joe does not have the strength to throw a big victim on his shoulder, he will simply wrap webbing under the man's arms and drag him.

Joe is back with a bowl of ice cream. He leans over to tell Alberto about the climbing drill.

But before the drill, or anything else, the station must be cleaned. The station is huge. It is home to as many as twenty of us each twenty-four-hour shift. We clean it every day, which at first seems excessive. But when I remember a news article that I read which said that most dust is made up of skin particles, I know that it would not take long to cover the desks and floors with a thin, snowy layer of exfoliation. With the fire department divided into three shifts, that is sixty people who flake quietly around this three-story building.

My assignment for the morning cleanup is to sweep and mop the apparatus floor. I like the apparatus floor, where all the rigs park in calm, silent repose. There is a wide quiet in this huge hangar, and a solemn order. The lockers are lined neatly along the walls. Boxes of supplies are stacked tightly on one another. Each rescue vehicle stretches out next to another and offers its own precise geometry: the square Rescue Squad vehicle; two long, thin trucks; one short, lithe engine; the short chief's "buggy." As if to break up this linear harmony, brass poles drop here and there, like long, thick threads, providing quick access from the dormitory above. The apparatus floor is calm, but there is a sense of potential power.

Suddenly the emergency tone will echo across the tiled floor and high ceilings, shattering the silence and order. Engines will roar to life, shards of red-and-white lights thrown from their beacon. The rigs will wail and uncoil and thrust themselves out into the city quickly and ferociously to deal with the new emergency. It is the eternal illusion that chaos can be managed that gives the apparatus floor some of its magic, but mostly it is the chaos itself, the explosion of sound and light and movement, that leaves everyone spellbound.

I bring the mop down on the floor, through the various oil patches, ashen boot marks and mud flecks that are more eloquent than words about the daily life here. Outside, a chain saw starts and horns are honked. My neatly pressed pant legs lose part of their sharp crease as I splash hot, soapy water on the floors and myself. By the end of the shift my uniform will resemble the floor, the day's adventures spilling across in butter marks, grease, blood drops, sweat stains, and ash.

Alberto walks up to help me finish. He pauses at the large apparatus door, open to the day. It is a typical morning in San Francisco. The fog was thick and heavy for a while, but now it is rolling away. From the front of the fire station, where we look toward the hills and beyond, to the ocean, it pulls itself back like a thick horse's neck, wisps fanning out like a white mane. You cannot see the ocean but you can feel it—a cold thick wind that smells like fish.

Alberto strokes his black mustache and I let my fingers tap the seam of each pant leg. The sky is beautiful. As the fog recedes further, the light takes on a silvery glow and starts to throw streaks of sunlight through the sky. Because he wants to stay and watch, Alberto fidgets and murmurs something about how the shift is likely to go. There is something unseemly about this, this standing in the street and staring, just staring. Someone turns the radio on in the workroom. The hulking apparatus floor sends the sounds of the football game floating past us and into the street. I shift and take a step away. Alberto looks down at the asphalt and kicks softly with one boot. We are wary of beautiful things. Perhaps we think that they will make us soft. We turn and walk in.

"Lucky socks on?" he asks, nodding complicitly at me. I nod back—yes, of course I have my lucky socks on. My lucky socks are bright pink. They are against regulation, and once the deputy chief noticed them and gave me a dismayed reprimand. But they are lucky, so I wear them anyway, taking care to keep the rim of my pants down low on my heel. Lucky socks, clean pants, just-polished boots—these are all ways we try to coax a fire into our shift. Alberto pushes open the door to the communications room and we walk on into the kitchen. "I can feel it," Alberto says to Miller. "I can feel it, a busy day. It's the way the back of my throat feels. It always knows."

"That's thirst," I say, sitting down at the kitchen table. Miller says nothing. He chops at the center of the sports page to fold it. The crackle envelops him. He reads while fishing into a round tin of chewing tobacco with one hand.

Joe slaps at his newspaper from behind. "Miller, defibrillator class. Nick will take your place until you get back."

We are constantly going to class to be recertified for something or other. We are updated often on new equipment or medical and fire techniques, though fire techniques change in this department much less often than the medical ones.

Our newest medical device is modeled after a toilet plunger. It is used on chest compressions during cardiopulmonary resuscitation. After a man collapsed from a massive heart attack, his son saved his life by using a real toilet plunger. Doctors, amazed at the man's recovery, found that the suction ability of the toilet plunger drew much more blood into the heart than ordinary CPR. Now we have modified toilet plungers on some of the rigs on a trial basis.

This is only the latest effort to substitute for the work of the heart, and it is no less comical than earlier ones. In the eighteenth century I would have thrown the patient over a horse and clucked it to a trot. Some people built fires on the chests of dead people, hoping to connect with some inner fire of life. Later, the Navy hung a still-warm body on a barrel and rolled it back and forth.

"And we've got to have a drill," Joe adds. "Scuba or climbing. You guys pick."

"Nick wants to shake for it," Nick says. He runs a hand

through his short hair and grins. He speaks about himself in the third person loudly and with his whole body, thrusting his hips out and sitting back on his heels to take up more space. His eyes never stop moving. They give the impression that they do not see much of what is before them but are constantly looking for something else.

"Nick's up for a dive on such a beautiful day," he says.

None of us care, but we like to shake. The dice roll around like small hiccups in the brown cup.

Before Nick can continue a monologue, the Bee-Bop begins. We recognize it instinctively, stopping before we consciously know why, realizing we have been waiting for it all along. Sometimes in department stores, the tone that signals a sale will go off and it is not until the voice begins, *Smart shoppers, in aisle 5 . . .,* that I realize that my arms are stiff, my breathing has stopped, and I feel as if I am about to take off running.

*Fire in the building,* bellows the loudspeaker.

The poles rattle and squeak as people appear from the ceiling like dark glinting angels and fall to the floor. Engines roar and brakes hiss in release. The Rescue Squad is out the door first—there is always a race for this. Behind us the engine and a truck roll out like fingers on an opening fist.

My coat is still damp from the fire the shift before. I pull it on as we hurtle around a corner. Its grip is cold and heavy on my arms. My helmet slides out of reach on the shelf, and I wait until we turn the other way, which we do with a squeal and a blast of the air horn. I catch my helmet mid-slide, and flip it on my head, moving to avoid Nick. He is flailing his arms to stay balanced. He is saying something, as usual.

The building is old and brown, and crowded with windows that look lopsided. These are the buildings to watch out for, the cheap hotels that have escaped newer safety laws. They have empty hose boxes on each floor, their hoses recently pawned by heroin addicts; their stairways are narrow; and their hallways are crowded with garbage and people sliding into their highs. These buildings are lonely and sad; they are also lethal. Now people stream out of the narrow doorway. I smell something but I see no smoke.

"No smoke," Nick says.

We pound up the stairs, driven by adrenaline. I am third behind Joe and Nick, because I fiddled too long with the air pack, which lately has been catching on my right shoulder. I swear under my breath. It is a race to be first at the fire, too, and I have lost, unless I can push past them at the landing, which is definitely not good teamwork.

On the first floor people point up, skinny fingers of all colors poke the air; I have no time to notice their faces. The stairwell is thin and steep. My legs begin to tighten and for a moment I think that I should get rid of the batteries in my pocket and the extra ropes I carry. But there will be a time when I will reach for the batteries to throw against a window pane, to ventilate a burning building. And who knows when the ropes might come in handy. That is the nature of readiness, and sometimes what you are ready for never comes. And sometimes it does.

Then I see the smoke. But it is not thick, or heavy. It fills the hall with a gauzy haze. A police officer who arrived first is at a doorway, an extinguisher in his hand. We run into the room.

A man is curled in the corner, a dark shadow except for a sprinkle of white from the fire extinguisher. Then I see the orange embers on his neck, the way his shirt hangs from his body in shreds.

Nick is a paramedic. The horror does not slow his hands. Instantly, fingers on the neck. "Jesus Christ, he's got a pulse," he says. He pats the neck furiously, and then he pulls the man away from the wall and lays him down to begin emergency treatment.

The whole body is burned.

The man does not lie down, but remains curiously tangled in himself. His arms are bent in front of him, his hands curved and fingers gone. I reach to push them down but they are rigid. Joe is already opening the oxygen bag and I grab the mask. Nick is pale and keeps saying, "Jesus Christ, Jesus Fucking Christ," until Joe tells him sharply to shut up.

I am surprised. Nick, losing it? Nick the paramedic who once proudly ran down his list of medical experience to me: the twelve-year-old girl who had been sodomized; a mother shot by her son; legless, headless humans, all of which accounted for why he was so hard, "so unfeeling," he'd said with a shrug, his eyes darting about. "That is why Nick's so fucking fucked up," he had said, laughing in that weird way of his.

It is impossible to tell how old the man is. I think he is African-American until his pants are cut away. Only his legs are not burned; they are pale and thin. Everything else is charred and flaking like the side of an old building. I have the oxygen mask, so I must now look at his face.

He has no face. It is as if it blurred and sank into itself. Eyes welded shut, nose gone, mouth a small hole that he cannot move. I have an oral airway in my hand—a small plastic device to keep the tongue from blocking the throat— but I think I might tear a long gash if I try to get it into the mouth. I have a sudden vision of all the skin sliding away, revealing only a grinning skull.

"It'll fit," Joe says, as if reading my mind. He takes the oral airway and twists and pushes. He is right. It is in place and the skin is still intact. It did not break or give way. I let my breath out, unaware I had even held it in. I place the mask on the undulating hues of black and red, where I sense it should go, wonder momentarily whether his skin is soldering to the plastic rim, and reach down to get a seal. I must curl my fingers around his chin to lock the mask to him. I have my fire-fighting gloves on, and I am glad. The rubber gloves we usually wear for medicals would not have been enough. I want the thick barrier of leather. I do not look down as I make contact, but whisper to myself *please*. I do not know who I am talking to or what I mean, but it is enough. My hand is there and the place does not feel soft or gooey or as if it will break apart under me. I press the first few liters of oxygen into his lungs. His arms, seared into place, reach up past my shoulder. He cannot speak, but his body says enough; he is locked in an agonizing beseechment.

The engine crew is at the stairwell, breathing heavily, the hose in their hand. Joe waves them back. Off to the side I see the truck crew, holding axes and ceiling hooks like limbs askew. They are silent.

"Are you sure you got a pulse?" I ask Nick.

"Fucking positive," he almost screams, tearing at the clothes with scissors.

Then the man's legs move. They scrape across the floor as the legs of an insect half-stepped-on might. They trace a jerky circle, and the effort is immense. He is trying to move other parts of himself, but they will not budge. He is cemented in place by his burns. Everything is seared closed.

A noise comes from his throat.

I wonder what he is thinking. Locked in darkness with only agonizing pain and great heat—this is hell, his mind must be screaming. I want to lean in and say, *No, this is not hell, you are burned—someone set you on fire, and I am the firefighter in charge of your breathing, so stay calm, maybe go to sleep, and the ambulance will be here soon,* but it sounds dumb, it sounds corny, so I say nothing and keep clenching my teeth and squeezing the bag. I remember the old woman so long ago, whom I could not comfort either, and I think, *What the hell have I learned?* Joe asks me if I want a break and I shake my head.

"Where is the fucking ambulance?" Nick asks. Joe gets on the radio, and the hum of his voice takes my attention away from the noise in the man's throat.

Miller stands by the banister. I can tell by the way his jaw is held that he has chew in and has not spit in a while. He has forgotten all about it, and a brown line seeps from the curve of his mouth. I lean toward the burned man.

"The ambulance is coming soon," I begin quietly. "Real soon." I squeeze the bag into that melted face. "You've been burned, and we're the fire department, so just relax. The ambulance will be here soon." I close my eyes. I can hear the rhythmic squeal of the rubber bag.

The man is burned from his thighs on upward. A police officer holds up a bottle of vodka; they whisper that this is the ignition fuel. We do not say much; we see ourselves in the twisted man on the floor. The possibility of burning alive is very real to each of us, something so real that we don't even let ourselves think about it except in nightmares. I had a nightmare like that once. In it, the flames engulfed me, but there was no pain. Here, there is pain. Nick swears under his breath again. "Nick hates this, man, just fucking hates this," he murmurs.

The truck crew parts and two paramedics push through. Nick gives a quick report. "He was on fire next to the window. Trying to jump out, I think," he says, voice tight. "Partial thickness burns all down his back and buttocks. You see the goddamn face. The whole chest. It's bad."

The female paramedic works fast. She puts her bag down. Her eyes flicker over the body and she makes a sound somewhere deep in her throat. "Board," she says. "Load and go. No messing around."

Her partner throws out the burn sheets; hands wrap the man in it. Faceless, voiceless, bodiless, he is given shape and form by our imaginations only. And so embodies our worst fears. We describe it in culinary terms, but that is only to hide how unpalatable, how unfathomable, it really is. *You're toast. Baked. Grilled. A crispy critter.* We grimace and look away. Fire wins viciously, gleefully.

Nick whispers swearwords under his breath, sweat sliding down his neck from his hairline. We slip and slide quickly down the stairs with the backboard and the body, pushing the spectators aside. We scrape along the hallway and then down the last flight into the street. The ambulance slides away with a wail. Nick is pacing. Alberto fiddles with the oxygen bag. I look up at the sky, where broken clouds stretch over to the horizon, and only look away when Joe calls out that we are leaving.

"Two things," Nick says, once we are in the rig. "Two fucking things that scare the shit out of Nick, man." He is paler than usual and shaking. His manic eyes are wider and more bulbous than ever. "Sharks and burns, man," he says. "Those are the ways Nick just doesn't want to die. Sharks and burns."

I don't say anything. I fixate on the paint streaks on my helmet. Images are something that a helmet cannot protect your brain from. Images; twisted, coiled images. Nick puts his head in his hands and says "sharks and burns" to himself again.

# FIRE STORIES

By the time we get to the station, Nick has stopped wringing his hands. He recounts the story to Alan, but this time he grins. I think momentarily of phoning someone, but I decide against it. What would I say? *There was this burned man, see, just melted. And there was nothing I could do, you know? I just let him melt.*

It is hard for friends to understand. It is hard to look at the gore and horror, at the shock of how swift and relentless the end can be. The only person who will understand is Eric. But Eric is somewhere on Alaska's Denali, also known as Mount McKinley, at fourteen thousand feet. When he is off the mountain, there is a phone at the ranger station where he works as a paramedic rescue climber. He is one of my closest friends, and we talk often. He tells me the way dead bodies freeze into such contorted positions that they do not fit into normal body bags. "So we get these huge ones," he says, "huge body bags, because the corpses are stuck into giant pretzels." He does not say this with a laugh or to impress. He says it with awe, with a poet's eye for all that is simultaneously terrible and banal and absurd. He says it to get the images out of his head and also because he wants the images to stay, stored someplace between nightmares and waking conversation. He is a writer and he knows the beauty and poignancy in the place where life meets death. He describes fatal incidents with the care of a housepainter at a difficult place on a sill. He knows that I will understand.

If I can't call Eric, I won't phone anyone, not right now.

Instead, I walk to the kitchen. Hal is the cook today. He is a prime example of why firehouse meals have such legendary status. Everything Hal cooks is great-tasting and plentiful. No wonder it is easy to gain weight in the firehouse. Even the resident pets gain weight. One station had a twenty-five-pound cat. None of my cats weighs over twelve pounds; Tom Cat looked like a large blowfish with fur. One day a crew member found a huge rat in the boiler room. The fire-fighter beckoned Tom Cat over to it, but Tom Cat just stared awhile and then ambled away. Like firefighters, Tom Cat liked his meals large, but he was no dummy. Just because the rat lived in the firehouse did not mean it would taste like a firehouse meal. Tom Cat was much loved, and when he died, he was given a formal burial. The members dressed in their uniform jackets and ties and saluted while the department chaplain read a few final words. Taps was played, and the flag was flown at half mast.

Hal is a big man with a big belly and a voice that precede him. But his paunch is misleading: He is strong and athletic. I have seen him rip a roof apart as he sat on its peak, his legs awkwardly spread. He brought the axe neatly into the steep, thick shingles as if he were halving a sandwich.

Hal is from Truck 72 and, like the rest of his station-mates, he is not happy about being here. Station 72 is in Noe Valley, the next neighborhood over. But Station 72 has been temporarily closed for earthquake retrofitting, and the members dispersed to other stations. The crew from the engine has been sent to join a small station house in Bernal Heights. The crew from the truck now resides with us. They are miserable; Noe Valley is a quiet yuppie neighborhood with four cafés and two ice-cream shops in a two-block area, while the Mission District has three seedy hotels on one street and countless crack smokers.

I like the new crew. The captain is Trent Lee. He is a small, stout man with a way of edging small, teasing comments into his sentences. But when he is serious, he is straightforward and sincere. He knows when to joke and when not to. When Trent Lee respects you, you know that you have a loyal friend for life. Then there is John Benoit, who believes that the world is going to end on September 9. He is on a mission to let people know of this impending doom and wants us to be ready. This means that it is of the utmost importance that we convert to Christianity. Only then will we be among the chosen who will not perish in the coming Armageddon.

I wait impatiently for him to come and convert me. "Phew," I say when he finally approaches me. "I thought you didn't think I was worth it."

"Of course not," he replies emphatically, not hearing my joking tone, which makes me like him even more, even though others in the firehouse are tired of his crusade. We wonder: Will he retire on September 6 and blow all his money before the end? Will he take off sick the day of doom or stay to fight the biggest inferno we will ever see?

Station 64 already has fifteen and sometimes sixteen crew members per shift. With this extra truck, the station is packed with more than twenty people. That is a lot of people to cook for.

"Under control," Hal says when I ask if I can help. His voice is deep and rolls across the counter. He almost always smiles when he talks, as if about to say something amusing that he can't quite contain. Big, round brown eyes are set into his round brown face; a mustache loops his mouth. Everything moves when he speaks, especially his hands, which he swipes in the air for emphasis. Bits of onion fly. Nearby is Paul, who watches cooking shows on television as relentlessly as others watch sports. He is getting the hamburger ready with eager pulls and pats. Just because I don't eat hamburger and I am far from a competent chef, it doesn't mean that I can't do *something*. Helping in the kitchen is part of the firehouse day.

"Garlic?" I insist.

"Yeah, sure, garlic." Hal pushes onions to Paul, who sweeps them into his bowl. "Never too much garlic."

"Messy," says Paul, looking at me, squeezing the hamburger so that it oozes between his short, strong fingers. "The guy, I mean."

"Hmm," I say, nodding. "Yeah. Bad." I flatten the edge of the knife and lay it on a bulb of garlic. I bring the side of my hand down. It makes a satisfying *thwump,* and garlic seeps from its shell.

"What about the Bayshore Freeway thing? That was probably worse." Paul eyes my garlic. I know he wants to do it, because he does it better. I am notoriously clumsy in the kitchen and stick to what I do best. What I do best is chopping, which I do not do particularly well at all. Usually, the cook eyes me and says something like "Leave this to the men!" or "Off the terrazzo!" in a mock growl. I can be more help if I just stay out of the way.

"Those decapitations?" I say, even though I remember right away. It was hard to forget. A large car going eighty miles per hour ran into a truck. The car almost came out the other side. Instead, it remained wedged under the belly. Everywhere we moved we stepped on pieces of skull and brain. Later, small images would come to me—the way the top of a skull sat neatly on the upholstery like a hat, or the stiff, still angle of the unlucky passenger's long black hair down the backseat. The metal of the truck rested where her head used to be. When I told Eric, I could only describe the neat round circles of chalk around each fragmented body part on the street.

"They were just beside themselves over that accident, weren't they?" Paul says, chuckling. "They were in a little over their heads."

"Very funny," I answer sarcastically, but I smile. Paul can't stand it any longer and separates a few bulbs to do himself. He pauses, looking at the garlic intently. Unconsciously, he tosses the knife, catching it casually by the handle as it wheels over in the air. Then he dices the bulbs easily. •

To me, cooking is a dangerous occupation. Most of my burns have come from the kitchen, except one that left a small triangle on my forehead and another that seared my finger after an ember burned through my glove. In the kitchen, I have burned both forearms, my wrist, the palm of my hand (twice), and my thumb (countless times). In addition, I have diced off ends of my fingers, and reshaped knuckles.

It remains my least favorite part of the job, but I am no longer so anxious. I am still fairly useless, and stick to a painfully narrow list of tried-and-true meals. If I am particularly stressed, I have no qualms about taking shortcuts that Paul would find blasphemous. Instead of making sauces or salad dressings, I buy them. If I feel energetic, I may try to hide the cans or bottles. I pour the product into a bowl and place it on the counter as if it were my own. One day, with time running out before dinner, I took the thirteen heads of lettuce I needed for salad and, after running water over them, threw them into the washing machine.

They were spun dry in no time. The tart, tingly taste of fabric softener was only barely discernible. People do not expect much from my meals, so they did not mention it.

"It's gonna be sloppy joes for lunch," Hal says absently. We do not talk again about the burnt man. The men in my station rarely talk openly about how a bad call affects them. Feelings are instead directed into jokes and loud voices. Despite the surface vigor, it is a subtle communication. What remains unsaid is heard, loud and clear.

The outgrowth of this communication method is the Fire Story, and the Fire Story is a wonderful thing, at once colorful and loud and very funny. I love Fire Stories, though I am not good at telling them. Instead, I listen raptly as the Fire Story is woven, often at the dinner table, around the deep smells and rich tastes of the firehouse meal. A Fire Story is such that even if you were there, you do not remember the event, because it is transformed, reworked, blown up. There are no lies, per se. Circumstances simply expand or contract like putty. Long-lost quotations emerge from places deep in memory. Events from other stories are mysteriously patched in.

But the key to the Fire Story is the speaker, who re-creates the event with sprawling and excited words, adds humor liberally, and coats it all with a light overlay of cuss words. The Fire Story rarely gives insight into the deeper emotions of the speaker; it is not expected to. If it did, it would not be a Fire Story. When Nick shapes the burnt man into a Fire Story, he will not mention sharks and burns.

My favorite tale is one that Lieutenant Tom Donald told me a few months back. I began by telling him one of my own: I had just gotten back from a four-alarm fire on Pine Street. That house was really blazing, *really blowing out the back, really screaming black smoke when we pulled up*. . . . By the time Rescue 3 arrived, there were already other fire crews inside. The interior of the house was pitch-black, and we crawled down the hallway toward the heat belly-down. Sometimes—when the heat allowed—we rocked back on our knees if we hit a wall or an apparent piece of furniture. Our masks were on and were scraping the floor as we made our way deeper into the blackness. There was something bizarre about the house, but in the smoke and excitement it was not until the fire was over that we realized what it was. The entire apartment was covered in litter.

Not just covered: caked, carpeted, layered in garbage. The garbage was so high that a firefighter, in the dark and confusion, had fallen out of a window. He had fallen fifteen feet to concrete below because there was no sill to protect him—the garbage was flush with the bottom of all the windows. Newspapers and beer cans were wedged in a soggy, burnt mat along the hallway. Someone opened a closet and down rained a hodgepodge of cardboard boxes. After a few minutes we realized that these were used take-out food containers, thrown there until the closet was full. In the back room, where the fire had originated, it took a little time before we saw that among the cat food and ice-cream boxes and still more beer cans, lay the body of a man. In death, the garbage and he looked the same, until someone ran a shovel across him accidentally and his rib jutted suddenly through the mess.

Tom Donald is a veteran lieutenant on Truck 64. He listened politely to my own astonishing tale and then, in true Fire Story fashion, proceeded to amiably one-up me.

"We once had this three-hundred-fifty-pound woman," he begins.

"Get out," I say.

" . . . with one leg."

"No way," I answer.

"And a house full of garbage so deep that we had to crawl the whole way . . ."

To get into any of the rooms meant squeezing through the upper half of the doorway. The woman, a recluse, had not been seen in a while, and neighbors were angry about the putrid smell emanating from the house. The fire department was called to do a "well-being check."

"We half-crouched, half-crawled through this place, all garbage. And we couldn't find her anywhere. And we're thinking, *How in the hell do you lose a three-hundred-fifty-pound, one-legged woman?*"

Small, slanted depressions like runways in the garbage allowed them to slip into this room or that. No luck. After several hours, they were forced to give up. They threw away their fetid uniforms.

"Where was the woman?" I asked, disbelieving, completely drawn into the Fire Story. "Three hundred and fifty pounds and one-legged? Where could she have gone?" Here, Tom smiled triumphantly and delivered his coup de grâce.

The woman's body was found two days later. It seems that she had dug tunnels through the garbage in her home. She had created a whole new home as the garbage grew up around her, so that there was an elaborate room and hallway system underneath Tom and his crew while they had been crawling, like the corridors of King Tut's tomb. Unfortunately, the garbage had betrayed its owner. A tunnel had collapsed on the woman, suffocating her in her world of Styrofoam and cake tins and newspapers and cat food.

I repeat this story to Paul, but I do not have the story-telling skills of a veteran. Paul laughs anyway, wiping his hands on a towel, and then reaching for a long whip of scallions.

Miller comes back from his medical class mid-afternoon and it is decided, with little time left in the day for a dive or a climb, that we look instead at the air bags. They are inconspicuous cushions that inflate with an air bottle. The smallest, just five and a half inches square, can lift more than three tons. Slid under an offending weight—a building pillar, a train, an elephant, who knows?—the air bag is filled with air, raising the tonnage from the victim. It seems absurd that this small piece of equipment—if you could get a suitable purchase—could literally move mountains. Not as absurd, though, as the loudspeaker that cuts through Joe's lecture and informs us that the hospital needs Rescue 3's assistance in its emergency room.

There is only one reason that an emergency room needs a firefighter more than a doctor.

"I'll bring in the chain saw," Alberto says in a rare foray into crass humor. The compartment doors are wide open and equipment is being dropped onto the pavement. Air hose, regulator, air bottle. Miller is, as usual, expressionless behind his mustache. The beginnings of a double chin push against his collar. His small, plump hands close around a small red toolbox.

The emergency-room doors are held open for us by a bland-faced security guard. He stares at us, suddenly interested; it is not often that firefighters are summoned to the emergency room, where everything has stopped until they arrive, like highly paid doctors flown in from out of town.

Another fire engine crew is there, shuffling from one foot to the other, sheepish half smiles on their faces. When they are dismissed by the chief, they walk away visibly relieved. "Good luck, skwaaaaad," someone says, with a grin. "Yeah, man," someone else sniggers, "good luck."

The chief looks at us. "Keep it professional, okay?" he

says. Joe nods and we walk in, greeted by two nurses and our patient, lying on the emergency-room table.

The cock ring has been on him for two days, explains a nurse, handing operating-room gowns and masks to Miller, Alberto, and me. As I put mine on, I glance over at the man on the table. He is groaning. His hands are spread protectively over his groin, and his eyes are wide with panic. The nurse looks tired and slightly perplexed.

I have never seen a cock ring before. It is a simple device used to maintain erections. The ring is slid to the base of the penis, behind the scrotum. This allows blood to fill the penis for erection, but by constricting the now-swollen penis, inhibits the ebb. Sometimes men wear more than one ring— once the squad was called to a man who wore six rings, all stuck. Another time, the cock ring was so strong that even our pneumatic saw could not handle it and a dentist had to be called in with a diamond bit drill. Since that incident, General Hospital retains a dentist permanently on call in case of other such emergencies. But many hospitals, like this one, are completely dumbfounded by a cock ring gone awry. If the ring is too small, the erection cannot drain, and the result is the painful and dangerous situation before us.

"It is going to have to get cut off," the nurse says.

"We are going to have to cut it off," Alberto repeats cheerfully to the groaning man. "The ring, I mean." The man on the table looks as if he doesn't care much what may have to go, as long as the pain subsides.

Miller begins to hook up our small pneumatic saw while I lean over the man—a boy really, pale and thin with blotchy skin and sandy hair. He looks like he is straight off a combine in some Kansas wheat field, but I know that instead he is probably a hustler from the Tenderloin. I see that the ring is not made of anything our saw cannot handle.

Miller accelerates the saw for kicks, and it spins with a loud, insistent whine. I can see that the mustache that usually sags below his mouth is tugged back in what must be a smile, almost a grin.

"You take the head and talk to this guy," I say to Alberto. "And I'll pour the water."

"I'm not sure I want to take the head," Alberto chuckles.

"This might hurt a bit," I say. Miller, leaning forward, accelerates the saw again.

"I don't care," our patient replies. "Just get the motherfucker off." Then, as if he realizes it is best to keep us on his side, he says, "I'm sorry, I'm not mad at you, I'm just dying here. I'm dying." He pants heavily. "This goddamn hurts."

"Hey, hey, no swearing in here. It will just make things harder—uh, I mean more difficult," Alberto says, smirking.

In fact the penis looks anything but erect. It is swollen and limp, like a thumb recently caught in a door. The cock ring, the young man says, was for his girlfriend. "She wanted it on."

"It didn't work for the Dayaks," I murmur.

"What?" someone says.

"Nothing." I smile. There is an odd symmetry in this moment. In some ways this man could not be more different from the wise Dayak chief. On the other hand, they had this propensity to decorate their penises in common.

"You're a good man, Charlie Brown," Alberto says, positioning himself with a piece of cardboard.

I hold a cup of water, and a nurse stands near the sink ready to hand me more. A second nurse leans in and forces a tongue depressor under the cock ring, during which time the man screams and pants even more. Miller pulls his surgical mask and glasses on and revs up the saw again.

The saw has a small circular blade that I mistakenly think is similar to the saws that doctors use to cut casts off and will not cut skin. Nothing could be further from the truth, as Alberto points out: The tongue depressor is all that lies between the blade and a few notes higher on the musical scale.

"Ready?" the nurse asks.

"Ready," Alberto and I say. Miller just leans in, saw screaming, and begins.

The saw immediately throws a high arc of sparks. Anyone passing by, seeing us in the hospital gowns that cover our thick turnout coats, would wonder why these doctors are welding in an emergency room. The water I pour is all that keeps the ring from superheating. The man is screaming, perhaps more from apprehension than anything else, but he remains perfectly still, understanding that any movement could change his life forever. We, for all our joking, do not want a mishap either. A slip would send blood everywhere and, despite our emergency-room protection, we know how dangerous that could be.

Every so often, Miller stops the saw to rest and assess the cut. Meanwhile, the nurse at the sink is frantically passing me cups of water, which I pour with all the precision I can manage in this cramped space. Alberto looks on cheerfully as he places his cardboard at an angle to ward the hot sparks away from Miller. We are an odd emergency team, smelling of old smoke and sterile paper.

When the saw splits the tongue depressor, Miller stops. I reflect that his laconic personality at least makes him cool under pressure. I am glad that I did not have to make the cut. "That wasn't so bad, now, was it?" Alberto says politely. The man reaches for the cock ring to pull it off.

Unfortunately, one cut is not enough to slip the ring off. There will have to be another one.

"Caroline will do it," says Miller.

"Ha," I say, thinking that he is simply joking. The idea of a woman with a saw near a penis seems to amuse him.

"Go ahead, Caroline," Miller says again, mockingly.

"You can do it, Caroline," Alberto says. There is a defiant look in Miller's small eyes. *Wassamatta?* they seem to say. *No guts? Scared? Can't take the heat?*

"Okay, okay," I say, as nonchalantly as I can. I take the saw and press the trigger thoughtfully. "You guys are both perverts."

What I am really worried about is the fact that I have a lazy eye. It does not get in the way much, except that when I am tired or under stress it wanders slightly toward my nose. As a result, all my life I have had to overcome problems in depth perception. So far, they have never amounted to more than a softball in the nose, or a wheel against the curb. Today, however, a small problem in depth perception is all that it would take to make a very big problem.

"Ready, buster?" I lean in as close as possible without seeming positively prurient. I squint. I push the plastic surgical glasses closer to my head. I begin to sweat.

*Fuck you, Miller,* I say to myself.

The saw hits the ring decisively, and from there I cannot see anything but a brilliant array of sparks. "Jesus," I say. I stop the saw and back away. I expect the penis to be lopped in two, but it remains intact. There is a small new nick in the ring.

"Just getting that starting cut," I say with a nervous laugh. I should stop right here and hand the blade back to Miller. But I can't give the saw back. To do so would concede defeat. It would admit that I am less able, less agile, less courageous. Of course, the idea that the ability to cut a cock ring off is a measure of success would, in a more lucid moment, be ludicrous. Right now it seems of the utmost importance.

I lean in and squint again, aim and press the trigger once more. At a certain angle, I can just place where the blade is. I fix my eyes on the spot and try to focus my lazy eye. I could close it, but my right eye is farsighted. The lazy eye, however, is nearsighted, so that my vision is the culmination of a curious partnership—two local unions doing separate but closely related jobs.

"Whoa!" yells the nurse.

"Whoa!" yells Alberto.

"Whoa!" yells the man on the table.

The saw is off, and I look around casually. "I was on it," I say, picking up the tongue depressor. It is split through. Jesus, that was close. "How's the penis?" I ask, as if this were a social nicety.

"Wow," says the young man, panting and holding his traumatized member. "Thank you so fucking much. I thought I was going to die."

"Get one with a latch next time," I suggest.

"I think he likes you," Alberto says under his breath, just loud enough for me to hear.

# NODDING OUT

The woman is dead. They swear that she had just been talking, got up to go to the bathroom and then said something or other to them that no one can remember. "Kicking the H," says another woman. "She was kicking it." I have seen her somewhere but cannot place where. Of course, she looks a little like me. Young, female, white.

I am the driver today but do not stand outside with the vehicle because on a resuscitation everyone comes in to help. She is still warm, and if what the people standing around say is true, she has been down about three minutes. We take her off the bed and lay her on the floor.

Her body is pale and limp. She gazes upward in a blank stare, and her mouth falls open to cut a sharp triangle into her face. She is missing teeth, and I wonder about that, though I know that few teeth survive the streets. They are torn out by punches, broken by the concrete of the sidewalk, or simply loosened and lost by lack of care. Other, more fragile things survive, like a sense of self, and even self-respect. My teeth would probably do okay, I think, looking at the body. I have naturally strong, white teeth. That is what the dentists say: "Hmm, naturally strong, white teeth." But as for the other things, they would have fallen away long ago.

A woman sits in the chair next to a cardboard sign that says FIVE DOLLARS TO SLEEP HERE. Her hair is dry and thin and forced into unnatural angles by hair spray. Though she is not very old, her face is deeply wrinkled—lines where the skin seems to have given out. She is the matron of the apartment, a longtime heroin addict who lets people into her home to shoot up for a fee. As the sign says, if they want to nod out here, they have to pay more.

Hard living is a disease. There is a lot of it in the Mission District; it eats you, collapses your cells, sucks your energy. It tightens your mouth into a thin line, crumples your skin. Hard living does not fortify your character, it crushes you. You die at thirty-six on a brown, ragged couch, in a dirty sleeping bag that you've pissed on, with no one around who knows anything much about you except that you are *kicking the H*.

"A little late to kick it," says Joe, stepping around the wet sleeping bag. His scissors ply easily through the thin, dirty cloth of her shirt. Alan has the defibrillator machine open and hands Joe the pads. Joe pushes them onto her bony chest and then Alan snaps the electrode cords onto them—*white to right, red to ribs*. Sometimes we say it aloud to remind ourselves or just move our lips silently as if in prayer.

I shuffle to her head to give her oxygen—resuscitations are done at a half crouch and I am sweating already. It is hard to get a fit with the oxygen mask; the air blurts out past her cheeks.

One breast is bruised. I look closer, wondering whether some blunt trauma to the heart may have killed her, until I notice that the skin is pecked with needle marks. Who shoots up in their breast? The left breast, too, right over the heart. Did she pick that place in particular, some mean joke on herself?

From where I am kneeling, I see that the earlobe is scabbed and bent. The ankles, freckled with remnant blood. The arm, of course, long not an option anymore, is unnaturally white, as if the veins underneath have retreated deep under the dense plain of skin like hunted animals. When the paramedics come, they stick her with more needles but the veins slip away. Eventually, they decide to use her neck vein, a last resort. We watch and grimace.

Joe stops chest compressions to do paperwork, and Alan

takes over just as they put epinephrine down the IV and her heartbeat comes back with a bang. We joke that Alan has the doctor's touch and more, that he has a way with the ladies, that he makes their hearts beat faster. We are crude because we have seen all this before, and because there is no family to be worried about. I feel bad sometimes, because I remember that perhaps the body can hear us, or maybe the soul, as it waits for release. The paramedic grunts and shakes his head and says how most of the hospital people think these medical drugs are just a cruel way to force life back into a body that is already brain dead.

"Put enough epinephrine in," he says, "and a rock will get a heartbeat."

They cart the woman away; her heart is pounding hard, and Alan is beet-red from the teasing. He blushes easily, a tall, lanky guy with a quiet, polite demeanor when you first meet him. Soon he becomes less quiet, less polite, a mix of good heart and good humor. I like Alan; we have been friends for several years. We are rumored to be having an affair, or at the very least a serious flirtation. But then, I have been linked to a couple of firemen. Mostly, they have been linked to me, and I suspect that when I leave the room one or two endure a great amount of ribbing. Alan does, and he suffers this foolishness quietly. But I hear about it from other people, and occasionally I wonder if the friendship—all this teasing—is worth it to him.

It is no longer so hard to be a woman in the department; the male firefighters encourage their daughters, their nieces, their sisters to take the test. We have a few father-daughter combinations, a few cousins, a few in-laws. Richard's marriage to Nancy was the first union to come from the department; two longtime firefighters' wives have now joined. The four years since I entered have gone by quickly, but there have been substantial changes.

I pull the rig away from the curb and, lights flashing, do a U-turn in the street. We will head back to the station because the lieutenant's "list" is coming out today. Everyone wants to know who passed the lieutenant's test, who didn't, who the top people will be. I do not look forward to this. It will be a day of bitching and moaning against affirmative action.

Joe walks to his desk to fill out the report and I go into the kitchen. There is a crowd around the communications desk, so I know that the list is being passed around and discussed. I can wait to see who did well and who didn't; frankly, it doesn't interest me.

When the last lieutenant's list came out two years ago, four women were appointed officers. All of them tested in the top forty (nineteenth, twenty-seventh, thirty-third, and thirty-ninth), out of more than three hundred test-takers. All the women had a tough time. One got threatening phone calls at home. She considered turning down her appointment. Another was openly disobeyed. Another was bad-mouthed before she even arrived at her station. Elizabeth Mandel, the first woman to become a lieutenant, has not survived the department. She is going to sue for sexual harassment and discrimination—some people insinuate that this was her goal all along. I wonder what we will do without Mandel, whose demonization became a convenient way to avoid real issues.

Nick the paramedic has scored high, and despite the fact that he has only about two years on the job, there is no overt anger, just mild joking about how such an inexperienced guy could become a lieutenant. When Mandel scored well on the lieutenant's list with about two years in the department, the words "Someone is going to get killed" appeared next to her name. While she took this to be a direct threat on her life, I think it simply meant that someone with so little experience could endanger her entire crew. Still, Nick-with-the-shifting-eyes will get no malicious scribblings, no threatening phone calls—just some ribbing. Behind his back the men will shake their heads, but partly out of admiration, because they feel he must be smart to have done so well.

Interesting things have happened since the courts mandated in the 1980s that the San Francisco Fire Department

organize a hiring-and-promotion process to quickly integrate the fire department along ethnic and gender lines.
Some men searched their family trees and (legitimately and
otherwise) have come up with roots in protected classes.
They have tried to move ahead based on the new classifica-
tion. Others have angrily claimed that affirmative action is
unfair and has disastrous results.

Actually, a system of patronage like affirmative action is
not new to fire departments. In the late 1800s, a huge wave
of Irish and Italian immigrants came to the United States—a
wave that continued until the First World War. Local mayors, in order to win the immigrant vote, had them hired to
local fire and police departments if they promised their support. At the time, these immigrant Irish and Italians faced
heavy discrimination and disdain. NO IRISH NEED APPLY signs
hung in shop windows. Irish- and Italian-Americans knew
that, because of the prejudice they faced, this job-for-vote
exchange was a good deal for them.

Other people say that police and firefighter jobs are heavily Irish and Italian because city jobs were the only ones that
were open to everyone fairly. In the thirties, the "civil service" department was established to counter high-level cor-
ruption. Supposedly, you could no longer pay a high official
for a job, nor could he pull strings to get you one; now the
civil service sector administered objective tests. This made it
possible for people who were discriminated against to get
jobs through them. Of course, this did not include blacks or
women, so I do not know what to think of this explanation.
One way or the other, it remains ironic that almost a hundred
years later, these Irish- and Italian-Americans would angrily
denounce affirmative action.

Furthermore, for a long time military veterans automati-
cally got "points" in hiring and seniority in the fire department even if their service had nothing to do with fire. Can it
be a surprise that, for many women and minorities, the
grumblings of their Caucasian brothers seems hollow and
hypocritical?

To make it even more confusing, many firefighters understand that tests, even when they are unaffected by affirmative action, are problematic. We realize that if someone does well on a test, it does not necessarily make him or her a good lieutenant. Rather, it makes him or her a good test-taker. Going strictly by the numbers has its problems; experience is imperative. However, the length and the kind of experience that make a good leader are almost impossible to quantify.

Since the advent of the consent decree, San Francisco uses "banding" to rank its tests. This allows latitude to promote men of color and women, as well as a paradigm in which a strict test-taking aptitude is not always rewarded with a job. Banding is a process in which people within a certain range of scores are considered equal, just as a student who gets a 99 on a test and a student who gets a 94 on a test will both be given an A. Detractors claim that the band range is not related to ability, but is widened or narrowed according to how many minorities are needed to fulfill promotional and hiring goals. Supporters claim that tests are fallible and that a strict numerical ranking only favors the better educated, and thus the white, test-taker. They also point out that years of not hiring or promoting minorities has in effect "banded" whites for a long time; now it's somebody else's turn. To make matters more controversial, the test results are shrouded in secrecy. None of the test-takers are given an assessment of what they did right or wrong to deserve their score, so that rumors abound of favoritism and false scores. A few years after Nick passed the test, a black woman with nine years in the department will score third on the lieutenant's test and there will be murmurs that skulduggery got her there, as if there was no chance that she could have gotten there on her own.

The laughs and snickers around the communications desk increase. Maybe I will go read, hope for a call. As if I have summoned it, the Bee-Bop suddenly sounds.

*Rescue 3 to Capp Street. Well-being check.*

The address is just around the corner. By now, light is

fading from the sky. The windows are dark, the thick oak door locked.

We hate well-being checks. We never know what we will find.

"When did you last see him?" Joe asks the neighbor.

The neighbor thinks a little while.

"December," he says.

"December? December, as in two months ago?"

The neighbor nods and shrugs.

We are not pleased. Joe shimmies up to a window. It opens easily.

"No smell," he says as he slides into the apartment. That is a good sign. Maybe the guy just up and left. Retired, moved to Florida. The narrow beam of Joe's flashlight hits the window briefly and then disappears.

Seconds later, Joe speaks.

"I found him," he says in a calm voice.

The cold weather has kept the man from smelling too much, but the decay is unmistakable. A soft fuzz of mold coats the body, giving it a creepy, hairy look. Blood has congealed underneath it and spread from there like a wrinkled blanket. The fingers and toes have rotted off, leaving clumsy stumps. Most horrific of all is the face, which has fallen in on itself with the weight of time. It looks like a grinning skeleton. It glistens with what I first think is the beam of my flashlight playing funny tricks. I look again. The body is teeming with maggots.

I go back to see the body four times in the twenty minutes it takes for the paramedics to arrive. The first time is duty. The second is to see if I have the stomach to look at it again. But the third and the fourth times are for the pure unadulterated thrill of realizing how alive I am compared to how dead I could be.

Alberto says it is disrespectful to keep staring. Joe just shrugs. It is as if stumbling over a decaying body in the dark is an everyday occurrence for him. In the kitchen, we stop.

Incredibly, one burner is on; the blue flame still on its medium setting, burning heartily.

"Wow," says Joe. He shakes his head. "Now, that could have been a good one."

He leans in and switches the burner off. We stare at the greasy, blackened stove, and I think of all the ways in which that one flame, in two months' time, could have played out each moment. I imagine a fire, where I crawl over the rotting man and the maggots stick to my coat. Instead, by some act of grace, or mercy, it stayed there, looking over its long-gone owner like a small halo.

# FORCIBLE ENTRY TOOLS

Smell of smoke, shouts. Engine 64 hisses to a stop just a little ahead of the front door. Flames, and a man gesturing wildly. He is barefoot.

I am on the engine today, just for this shift. It is an assignment that I do not mind, especially when there is a fire. Today I can have the hose. First In, At the Nozzle.

I throw the air pack on, flashlight shoved under a strap, and go for the hose bed. From the corner of my eye I see that the front door is open. Fire runs up the thin stairwell in speckles. Something tells me this is bizarre; the staircase seems to leak flames, long teardrops instead of the robust, full fists of color and heat. As I round the rear of the rig, I see that Don Harris already has a hose line off the engine.

I murmur under my breath. "Darn. Kerplooey. Gee Whillikers." Nicer versions of my real feelings.

But in Harris's hurry to be At the Nozzle, he has not yet gotten his air pack. He is an old-timer, so it makes sense that he would prefer to *eat the smoke* rather than lose the nozzle. Old-timers have tricks for surviving in the thick, poisonous air; they put their noses right up to the water stream at the nozzle and breathe from invisible air pockets. In the early days of fire service, a fireman grew a long beard that he pushed to his mouth and breathed through—a crude filter. (Too many firefighters died early, cruel deaths of lung cancer and heart attacks. The average age at death of a firefighter is currently fifty-eight.)

I realize that Harris is going for his air pack now. He puts the nozzle on the ground.

*First In*, I think. *At the Nozzle.*

I reach in and grab.

If being At the Nozzle is the high point of engine work, losing that position is the most humiliating. To put the nozzle down like that, unprotected, is a cardinal sin. When I have had the nozzle, I have wedged it firmly between my knees. I crouch over it protectively while I quickly jam my air mask on. Now Harris sees me coming. But for once, being a woman is an advantage. He underestimates me.

The second I pull it from under him he jerks around. "What the goddamn fuck!" he yells. "What the goddamn fuck do you think you are doing?"

Don Harris has almost thirty years in the department. He is Caucasian, with long blond sideburns and a slow voice. He is a loner, talking to people rarely, never eating a meal with the group, never joining social functions outside the firehouse. He stays up in the dorm by his bed. He watches religious television with the sound turned down on a small black-and-white television set. He cooks his meals on a portable hot plate. "Don's Diner," they call the corner he partitions off with privacy screens meant to be dressed behind. In this odd igloo, surrounded by rows of beds, he stays all day, a quiet, private man.

Firefighters are an incurably social group, loud and fun-loving for the most part, and Harris's unsocial attitude is an affront. So, while being a woman may be a disadvantage in the fire department, being a loner is completely unforgivable. But Harris is always decent to me. He says good morning when I greet him and never ignores me more than he ignores anyone else. I like him and, more important, I respect him, because he does exactly what he wants, despite the backlash. And he is a good firefighter.

He yells "Fuck" another time. I drop the nozzle. Partly it is out of shock, partly it is out of respect for his thirty years of experience. Harris grabs it and immediately his anger evaporates; he knows that he would have done the same thing if the situation had been reversed. He heads for the stairs. I sigh; I will not be At the Nozzle.

Truck 64 pulls in behind the engine. I hear the motor whine as it strains to lift the hydraulic aerial ladder. It will sweep across the sky, expertly missing any overhead wires. Other ladders will be raised; sometimes buildings look as if they are propped up by them.

Onlookers are often confused by the sight of truck crews going to the roof. Are they running away? Don't they realize that the fire is *in* the building, not *on* it? Windowpanes are shattered, and they wince. They wonder, Are these truck crews here to help or to destroy? Chain saws start, a fire-fighter wielding an axe is silhouetted against the smoke. The sound of splintering wood gets loud, louder. Unknown to the onlooker, this roof must come open. It is all part of the plan.

Tiny flames are everywhere, like small stars in an early night sky. At the top of the stairs it abruptly becomes midnight, and the short streaks of fire converge into a broader aurora of orange that fades into the blackness. It is hot. I drop as low as I can to the floor while still "pulling line"— hauling the heavy hose line so that Harris will not have to stop. He seems to have a sixth sense about where to go; together we twist, turn, thread our way down a hallway. Time is like a long, drawn-out yawn now, but I know that afterward it will suddenly be crushed into one compact moment. Everything that happens will be shortened, fused. Adrenaline solders memory, past moments become statues allowed only one frozen pose.

Afterward, Harris nods at me. "Good on the line," he says. "I didn't feel it at all." We walk through the charred rooms, picking up a shriveled picture frame, pointing to a melted kettle, marveling at the iron bedposts, now twisted like candles from the heat. It can be a few hundred degrees on the floor, and it will be more than a thousand at the ceiling. A thousand degrees, hovering above me as I crawl. I take off my air pack and wipe my face.

It was not the nozzle, but following an old-timer is the next best thing. I reach under my helmet to push back my hair and the barefoot man from outside pulls at my sleeve. He is big-eyed.

"My wife," he moans. "My wife, I tried to catch her." His hands run up and down his cheeks. "Is she gonna live?"

They had found his wife. She lay crumpled below her third-story window, and the ambulance had whisked her away. I put my hand on his shoulder. "I tried to catch her," he says again, and spreads his arms wide to show me. I make a sound in my throat. There are no words for this, just sounds to fill in the space.

A burly man in a blue helmet taps a clipboard and then his cheek with a pencil. Fire investigators ask the first crew what they saw in order to determine the origin of the fire. I describe the way the door was wide open, the way the fire freckled the staircase.

"Yuh," the fire investigator says, nodding. "Molotov cocktail all right."

Awfully fishy, he explains, that the front door was open. He tilts his chin toward the husband. It seems the husband woke up and left his wife sleeping to get some sugared doughnuts. "Sugared doughnuts," he repeats, shaking his head. "At two in the morning."

The husband says that when he returned with the dough-nuts the house was on fire. The door, adds the fire inspector, was already wide open, with no damage to the lock, nothing.

"Jump, jump," the husband had urged his wife from the ground. "Jump."

The police lead the husband away. I take off my gloves absently, then put them on again. I am anxious because I have given something to the husband. It was just a sound in my throat—but no, it was more. I have doled out precious emotion, and it was wasted. In the emergency-services business, feelings are finite. We guard them as if they might leak away completely if we permit any small opening.

I pick up an axe. It distracts me. The truck crew will be here for a while and if I am lucky I can stay and put the axe into some wood. I like the overhaul; I understand better what Captain Leahy told me so many years ago. *Look at the way that it is put together.* Picking apart the charred window frame is a way to mull over the fire itself.

There is a lot to pull apart; the walls are wrinkled black and look like they will crumble with a slight push. But that is not true; swinging an axe is hard, dirty business. If you are not in shape, it will tire you out within a few swings, and even if you are in shape, you learn not to fight the wood but to nurse it apart, peering carefully at its grooves and its hinges.

The lath and plaster give way easily, in snaps and pops like breaking ribs. Tile splits neatly if the edge goes in right. The burned material goes in a pile that will be pulled out later, dumped in the street, and sprayed down.

The bathroom wall is burnt underneath. I call Ralph over to show him. Ralph used to play with the 49ers. Not with the 49ers, he corrects, for the 49ers. He was hired to play in training against the team, but he was never part of the team itself.

"Okay, babe, we'll pull the wall down from the other side, too." Ralph calls everyone "babe" no matter what the sex; a big man is permitted this by other men.

Ralph yells to no one in particular that the closet behind the bathroom needs to be taken apart. Someone asks for an axe.

"Give him your axe, babe, will you?"

Yeah. Right. I step over the wreckage. Much as I like and respect Ralph, I am surprised he would ask this. And who is this person in the closet who thinks I will give up my axe? Who does he think I am?

I walk toward the closet. "I'll do it," I say cheerfully, and try to step in.

Miller steps to the opening. He reaches for the axe.

"I'm already here," he says, without looking at me directly.

"I'll do it," I repeat.

"Give me the fucking axe," he says, his voice low and menacing. He draws out each word, as if they are evenly weighted and all mean *fucking*. Miller rarely speaks loudly. His large, unwieldy mustache catches most of the sound that leaves his mouth.

"Get your own axe, I'll do it." I move forward, shielding the axe with my body. Ralph is behind me and says nothing. Miller does not move.

This is a standoff where the struggle between being a team player and being an individual comes to a head. It is hardly worth grousing over an axe if the wall should come down. But it is my axe, I went and got it for myself. And it is Miller who is challenging me, a man who I feel hates me. And he hardly ever takes any equipment into the fire building. This has always angered me; you are truly useless if you have nothing in your hand.

By now he looks uncomfortable. It is clear that he did not bring in anything, and he oversteps the code by insisting that I give him an axe after I have refused, once, twice, three times. No one else says anything.

Miller does not step aside. Do I push by him? Do I turn away so no one can bring down the wall? Do I stand here forever?

I hand him the axe.

"Get your own axe next time, Miller," I hiss.

"Eat shit, bitch," he says.

I am still seething when I walk outside toward the squad. Paul does not notice, waves from the engine panel.

"He gave me almost two hundred pounds—did you feel it?" Paul says with dismay and uncharacteristic frustration in his voice. I shake my head and half-smile in sympathy.

Paul is talking about the second engine, which is responsible for making sure that the first engine—in this case, Engine 64—gets a constant supply of water from a hydrant. This means parking in front of a hydrant and attaching to it. There, the driver adjusts the flow and sends it on through a hose to the first engine, which could now be almost out of water, with hose and people deep in the fire building.

I feel tired, but it is a weariness deeper than the tendons and muscles. The incident inside has reminded me that I am still very much an outsider—that all of us women are. Recently, there was a fire at which the crew of Rescue 3 became trapped in an apartment because the other crews did not "pull ceilings." They did not, in other words, look into the attic space to make sure there was no fire spread. The fire traveled from one apartment to another, quickly and quietly. I heard the story quite a few times, as usual in different versions. Only once, however, was the name of the male officer responsible for the mistake mentioned. Rescue 3 almost lost two of its members because of the error.

As it happened, just the day before, another tragedy had struck. A firefighter was given too much water pressure by the pump operator, a mistake that threw him to the ground. He was immediately transported to the hospital and into Intensive Care with traumatic head injuries. This story was also repeated to me, and it, too, had varying versions. The one constant aspect, however, was that the name of the pump operator—a woman—was added. She was vilified and scorned. The name of the officer—also a woman—was also included in each telling. The implication was clear: Being female was part of the reason for the mistake. In each case a mistake *was* made, and an egregious one. But I was struck by the different ways in which the mistakes were treated. When something bad happens, it will not be only because you are stupid, careless, or unlucky, but also because you are a woman.

There are still eighteen hours to go on my shift, and suddenly it seems too long.

# UNDERNEATH

The water is cold. From where I float in it, I concentrate on watching the two detectives standing on the dock, staring at the ground. They point to where the gun was found, and the drops of blood. They make a wide sweep with their hands. They adjust their ties, nod thoughtfully. Police gestures.

The wet suit is warmer now, and the detectives look at the water and say a word to my tender. My tender is Lieutenant Sean Green, and he is a highly excitable man, excited at the prospect of a body recovery, excited that his diving lessons are at work. He always wants to go into the water himself; he has been known to strip off his uniform and dive after a car in a lake in only his underwear, despite his own warnings that all of us are to follow all safety rules strictly. I like Sean Green; his passion is infectious. When he is really excited, he leans in close and yells, spit flying.

The body will probably not be here; the tides pull everything out to sea quickly and efficiently. The suicide note found on the man's bed was written two days before, and it directed the detectives to the gun and the blood and the narrow, empty dock. Still, I wonder if they suspect foul play. It is hard to shoot yourself and then fall into the water, leaving the gun neatly behind.

I suited up on the way to the incident, my back turned from Tim, who was suiting up as well. To put on a wet suit in a wildly careening vehicle takes a miracle of agility. There is a story about two Rescue 3 members who were changing in the back of the squad car on the way to an emergency.

Threading their feet into the tight neoprene, they were thrown to the ground at a sudden stop and lay momentarily hog-tied in each other and their suits. The woman in the car behind was aghast at the sight of these naked men entwined and struggling.

Tim is a large, 230-or-so-pounder and, for safety reasons alone, I did not want him to fall on me. Otherwise, the embarrassment of being seen in my underwear and T-shirt did not even occur to me.

Today is not my regular shift, so I feel lucky that I am working anyway and can do this body recovery. Still, a part of me loathes the prospect of what I could find. Diving is an exciting experience, but rescue dives are marred by the fact that the San Francisco Bay becomes pitch-black a few feet below the surface. The only way to search is by touch. This means that, as in a burning house, hands are outstretched and sweep through the few feet of pure, thick silt. You touch other things—bottles, cans, twisted metal slick with algae—but anything could be an arm, a grinning macabre face. A drowned body is not a pretty thing. Bloated, often eaten away by crabs, it is the Thing Under the Bed, the Noise in the Closet, anything you dreaded as a kid. It will soon be as black as any midnight, and I am reaching around for that green, foul-smelling monster that always lay in wait. *Shoot,* I think, *this job can be a bit much.* That understatement is all I allow myself as, at Green's dramatic signaling, I hold the rope in the correct hand and let myself sink below the surface.

A rope is essential—only pull signals communicate with the tender at the surface and keep the diver on a relatively certain search pattern. For the diver, the world has suddenly turned heavy and black. You have to get not only to the bottom, but to the bottom of the bottom, settling below the layer of soft, thick mud. Even with all the wet-suit equipment on, I will feel the ooze gather up around me.

The bay is not a pleasant place, and the press of its mud and the unrelenting blackness can be terrifying to people less comfortable in water. In more than one drill someone comes up panicking, insisting that he cannot clear his ears. Another may get agitated when the big, bulky communications mask goes on. This mask, which looks like the helmet that *Lost in Space* characters wore, allows voice communication to the surface. It is comforting to have a voice in your ear as you make your way through the muck, as if a god is looking out for you, but the mask can be claustrophobic.

I don't use a communications mask today, just the tentacle of rope. I will do my search with my left arm perpendicular to my body, keeping the rope tight. In this way I will swing like a slow, earnest pendulum in a semi-circular area at the bottom of the bay.

I drop slowly. The light fades to brown and then suddenly, as if someone turned out the lights, to black. It is crucial not to try to see, but to accept the blackness. Any resistance can throw you into a panic, any effort at orientation into disorientation. Gravity and my body will do the work necessary for now.

I reach the silt. On rescue dives the main problem can be that the search is too high, sweeping lightly over the false bottom. I exhale deeply to penetrate the last three or so feet. I feel its sluggish grip, and then the hard, flat bottom. I sit here for a moment. One breath. Another. Okay. I am prepared for The Monster.

A tug on the rope signals to Green that I am ready. I slowly start my swim, which is more a body shuffle. You cannot go too fast lest something is missed, and too much fin movement can raise you too high off the bottom. Swimming too fast looks panicky, and while they cannot see my face, they can see my bubbles. The bubbles are the measurement of coolness and skill.

I admit it: I have gotten the shivers—that quick, involuntary body squirm when you think you have touched something horrific, something slimy. That is when I thank the darkness, because no one can see when my hands jerk back quickly as something wriggles, or I think something wriggles, out from under it. The ooey gooeys, I call them to myself. They are also called the icks, the creeps, or the willies by others. And this is in a drill, when there is really no dead body to be found. But the imagination runs wild, and whispers "what if" maliciously, and so you find yourself with the willies, the creeps, the icks anyway. Today there may really be a body somewhere in the silt with me.

Green tells us that we have to picture what we are looking for, picture it well, in order to recognize it when we touch it. I focus instead on a red-and-white plaid shirt—I don't even know if the man was wearing a red-and-white shirt—but it gets the hollow, crab-eaten face out of my mind.

Two tugs from the surface tell me to turn around. This is a major feat in heavy darkness, a different matter entirely from the usual casual twist in daylight. Here a sense of one's own body, something we usually take for granted, is essential. I switch the rope to my other hand. Then I extend that arm ninety degrees from my body. Ninety degrees from my body in total darkness is a peculiar thing. It is a feeling from the clavicle of a special tightness, and then a consciousness of the elbow being a certain distance away, of the knuckles at a particular tautness and the wrist extended. Having gained all this, I swim away from that hand, but keep it at that hard-earned ninety-degree angle. In this way I pull the rope, which has been let out a few feet by Green, taut, and my search pattern continues farther from the area I completed.

My physical being becomes highly tuned, just as in a fire, so that I almost think I can see. The roar of my own breath as it slides past my ears seems natural, the thick silt is soft on my cheek. The bottom takes form, its strange, tangled skin brownish green. I reach and pull at warts and bumps, bringing up old cans and bottles slick with algae. A fish here, there, and always the fine, misty mud. My arm sweeps as if unfurling a cape, and I see that my fingers are spread wide so as not to miss that red-and-white plaid shirt. . . .

. . . It's bullshit. I can't see a thing. It is still pure black, as I realize when two tugs from the surface signal me to turn around again.

There are two emergency calls that I hope never to experience: One is a dead or dying infant, the other is a body in the bay. Often the bodies of people who have jumped off the Golden Gate Bridge float to the surface, gaseous and bloated. The fire department fishes them out with its ropes and long ceiling hooks. I have been told stories of decayed, barely recognizable bodies that pop when touched, releasing a noxious smell and scurries of small sea animals.

But a dive recovery, that is something else. I like to dive, to sink into the quiet heavy darkness and swim. I am, like my twin, a water person, though in her job as a glamorous television lifeguard the water is always clear and the body is always found, alive and eventually smiling.

Green pulls on the line three times, indicating that I am to surface.

"It's gone," he yells, leaning down from the dock. "The sea has got him, no doubt about it." Spit flies. He puts up four fingers, indicating that this call is canceled. "We're going home." He grips my shoulder enthusiastically and then motions for us to head back to the station.

By Friday, I am in Spokane, Washington, where I have been once every month for the past three months. No scuba diving here; the rivers are frozen and as I doggedly pick up a megaphone and plant myself at the corner, it begins to snow. Behind me is the Spokane Federal Courthouse. Like many evangelists, I fix my gaze twenty or so feet in front of me, so that I can ignore any insults but engage with any willing onlookers. Alexandra has picked the middle of the sidewalk, and since we only have one megaphone between us, she passes out pamphlets. By this time, the citizens of Spokane know who we are. Some wave or nod congenially as they hurry by. Some stop and talk. We look harmless, if earnest. The newspapers have portrayed us as interesting specimens, at the very least. Besides, one of us is on TV.

"You're the ones whose brother is in jail," an elderly man says, the sides of his plaid cap swaying in the wind like an extra pair of ears. I nod. "Well, he's doing the right thing. Not that we are agreed on this animal-rights stuff. But he's doing the right thing, not saying anything." The man shuffles away, tugging at his cap. Alexandra and I look at each other. We go back to our positions on the sidewalk.

Jonathan is in jail here, though not considered a criminal; locked up but not under arrest. For the past three months my family and smatterings of his friends have come here to protest his incarceration. Spokane knows us. The taxi drivers yawn and ask, "How's your brother?" when we hail them from the airport upon arrival. "Tell him us taxi guys are behind him. Not on the political stuff. But this grand-jury thing. It's the government gone crazy."

The fire department knows nothing about my monthly evangelism. I don't tell them because I am sure that they will not understand. I myself hardly understand. The grand jury is a function of the government I have only read about briefly in connection with Oliver North. Until my brother is subpoenaed to appear in front of one, "grand jury" is just a vague legal term.

The grand jury wants to know about my brother's animal-rights friends. Jonathan refuses to talk and is thrown in jail. This is, we are told, not a punishment. He is guilty of nothing, they say, charged with no crime. He is not even considered a suspect in the case the grand jury is investigating. Jail time is to "persuade" him to speak.

How can I explain this to the fire department? They will write it off as another liberal scuffle and eccentric tic of the Paul family. I will once again be "different." Even my outside acquaintances, good liberals, good college-educated liberals, stare at me blankly and say, "Well, shoot, he should just talk if he hasn't done anything."

I have my litany down cold. "This is a democracy?" I shout to passing cars. "Where someone who has done nothing can be thrown in jail?" Pale faces peer at me from behind the blink of windshield wipers. "Not allowed a lawyer—

forced to answer every question." The light changes and the cars slide away. "Is this Turkey, or Russia, or Burma?" The street is empty now, but I continue anyway. I have felt much better, much safer in the hottest fires. There, I have my colleagues, whom I trust and admire. Here, the snow begins to fall with a vengeance.

# LAWYERS

"This department is like a broken marriage," Amy tells me, shaking her head. Amy has a degree in clinical psychology, which she constantly applies to her job as a firefighter. She pensively employs long professional terms in her heavy Brooklyn accent. Before she was a firefighter, Amy was a trucker. "Like a broken marriage," she repeats. "Too many lawyers." When she says "lawyers," she sighs to punctuate her unhappiness. Amy is rarely unhappy, but discontent in the firehouse upsets her because she is on friendly terms with everyone—black, white, male, female. Everyone loves Amy.

She came in around the same time I did, and though on the surface our careers parallel each other, in many ways they do not. "I want your defenses," Amy says to me often. "Maybe it is because you don't get along with your mother"—"muddah" is the way she says it—"but you have good protective mechanisms. Me, I'm an open book. I've got to learn to be more like you, you know?" She ends each sentence by throwing one hand in the air, as if throwing you the thought with the words.

In fact, Amy *is* an open book, which accounts for her popularity with everyone in the department. The most grizzled veteran firefighter will break into a grin when Amy enters the room. Even Miller smiles and blushes when she greets him with her characteristic enthusiasm. Perhaps even Todd Lane, the man who tried to ostracize me through his all-meat meal, would melt in her presence. Amy has the uncanny ability to make anyone feel comfortable, with a combination of humor, openness, and a genuine lack of cynicism. Unlike me, who consciously decides to maintain distance in an uncertain situation, Amy simply goes on being Amy, no matter whom she interacts with. My reserve is deep-seated, a mosaic of British stiff upper lip, Midwestern taciturnity, and life with a more precocious twin. I envy Amy's openness even though wholehearted public displays of emotion make me nervous. I reflexively think that there is an "appropriate" time for expressing a feeling. This despite the fact that I am completely intrigued by passionate forces like fire, which concede to no rules of appropriateness at all.

"Yeah, well, Caroline, you are always in control," Amy says. "It's your muddah, I am sure. She hurt that little girl in you."

Such analysis does not fit the image of firehouse banter. But Amy cares little about image. After breaking up with her girlfriend of three years, she shed some tears in the firehouse, whereupon the guys would pat her on the back.

"Firefighters don't cry," they said. "Especially not over a woman."

"Hey, guys," she answered, "I'm having a moment. Okay? I'm having a moment."

She would gesture with her hands as if she were signaling a taxi on a crowded New York street and unabashedly tell them that they repressed their feelings too much. They would shake their heads and smile indulgently and say that this was what the new fire department was coming to.

When I hand over the air pack to Patty Schecter, I think she may fall down; she is already breathing heavily under the combined weight of my turnout coat, turnout pants, and a helmet that sags dangerously on her head.

"About thirty pounds," I say, nodding at a Rescue Squad air pack. She grimaces. She is, after all, not a firefighter. She is a lawyer. I do not want her to back out of this before I have made my point. With a final flourish I hand her an axe, which she takes carefully. She shuffles over to look in the mirror, eyes shining despite the exertion. "Wow," she says quietly. Lost in a daydream of her own, she seems to forget I am there. I walk a few steps away and out of the corner of my eye I see her lift the axe for a surreptitious pose. *I am a firefighter!*

Patty Schecter is the federal court monitor, a lawyer assigned to oversee the implementation of the consent decree in the San Francisco Fire Department. She has a soft, even voice that belies her authority. Her neat, red hairstyle and pale, freckled skin give her a pleasant, unassuming look, though her precise diction indicates that she is not someone to be taken lightly. She has listened carefully to what I have to say, nodding at times, or taking notes. She has gamely put on my equipment; now she shuffles back to me ready to take it off.

"It is heavy," she says.

"And you've only had it on for a minute or so. Imagine being soaking wet, carrying hose—another sixty pounds—up a stairwell. Or swinging that axe—seven pounds—to get through a roof."

I have come to clarify to her the physical demands of the job. I want to make the lawyers understand how important it is that not just any women should be admitted to the department, but that strong women should be. There have been many lawyers involved in the fire department and its troubles since I entered the job. Things have improved under their watchful eye since I have been in—things that have helped everyone, male and female. There are separate bathrooms, better protective clothing, more specific management directives, an environment that strongly forbids certain harassments. But a major problem remains.

The lawyers are, after all, lawyers. They do not do heavy manual labor. They have no idea of the strength required for fire fighting.

"Why don't you put the mask on?" I open up the air tank on Patty's back. She is sweating, visibly uncomfortable. She may now begin to understand exactly how strenuous the job really is. Patty breathes through the regulator in honks and hums; her eyes widen with the exertion. She wants to get this over with. My point has been made: This job is tough, made for a certain type of person and definitely a certain type of woman.

No one has told me to come; I represent no one but myself today.

"What about the men? Aren't there weak men?" Patty says.

"Of course. This is not exclusively a gender thing."

"Or an affirmative-action thing," Patty adds.

"Look, at this point you lawyers have everyone so scared of lawsuits that no woman can get fired without everyone jumping to the conclusion it is somehow a sexist thing." I ease the air pack off Schecter's back and lay the axe on her clean rug.

Patty Schecter shrugs off the final layer of protective clothing. She glances at her watch—she needs to pick up her two-year-old daughter soon.

"Look," I continue quickly, "everyone has the same goal. Get qualified people in. And 'qualified' does inherently mean diverse. You and the union are not as far apart as either of you think."

The lawyers and the union have long approached each other combatively. The union has been—rightly or wrongly— demonized, its stance against the consent decree seen as racist and sexist.

The union states that it is not against women and minorities. They are against the consent decree's hiring and promotion goals, which mandate that certain numbers of women and minorities be hired. While I may disagree with the union's position, I do not think that it means that it is completely racist or sexist. The lawyers, however, approach it as if it is.

The president of Local 798 is a large man with a severe crew cut and light blue eyes that give the illusion of rarely blinking. He reminds me of a boat skipper, his soft, pale skin slightly shiny as if from a sudden spray. We have never spoken, but this is as much my fault as his. He is an imposing man, and I have subconsciously assigned to him all the epithets piled on the union over the years.

Jonathan Hunt, the secretary of the union, on the other hand, I find to be an approachable man with a firm handshake and a low, smooth voice. Early on in the union's fight against the consent decree, he must have realized that resolving the dispute with the usual take-it-out-into-the-alley attitude was inadequate. Firemen have always been proud of their independence and almost insolent individuality. But in thumbing their collective nose at the authority of the courts, the white male firefighters of San Francisco found themselves vilified.

Jonathan Hunt introduced himself to me when I was still a probationer and unsure of the union, though I had long been a supporter of unionized labor in general. Until I met him, no one had actually discussed with me seriously the pros and cons of being a female member of Local 798. A few men had talked loudly at me; one man shouted how "goddamn fucking selfish" I was. He then stalked away before I had time to say anything. I stood there and watched him leave. I thought how this behavior neatly typified all the complaints about this insulated union. It made me even more unsure.

One white woman stated that "change can only come from within." She said this over and over, like a mantra. She did not know what to say when I pointed out that this is not always true—the impetus for change in the fire department had come time and time again from factions outside the union. A neighborhood citizen group brought the first suit in the 1970s, and black firefighters completed the process in the eighties. She simply repeated her mantra and turned away.

However, when Jonathan Hunt approached me to discuss the reasons I was not yet a union member, the discussion was friendly and thoughtful. I carefully explained that I did not want to give my money to an organization that did not want me in the department, and I had already gotten the unmistakable feeling that there were people who disliked what I represented. Jonathan listened with his head tilted to one side. Later I realized that this was probably because, like many veteran firefighters who have given their bodies wholeheartedly to the job, he was hard of hearing. But at the time it offered an intent, pensive posture that impressed me. Pose or not, I sensed that Jonathan Hunt was a fair man. I soon signed up with the union. I also joined the Black Fire-fighters Association. Despite the fact that the pressures that blacks face are undeniably different from my own white, female experience, both of us are marginalized, and for me that was reason enough.

It is the lawyers who baffle me.

Their main goal is implementation of the consent decree. They are smart, with a passion for their work that seems to come from the satisfying realization that they are effecting quick and radical change. But their approach to implementing the consent decree gives them a single persona: "The Lawyers."

Patty Schecter is a recently appointed monitor who oversees the fire department changes—before her, my experience with The Lawyers has been brief but frustrating. It is somewhat my fault—I assume that we have a lot in common. We will get along, I am sure, because our liberal outlooks will easily mesh. Our feminist agenda will coincide; our mutual overeducation will ensure downright chumminess. Finally, these lawyers represent me as a constituent of the consent decree; they are, in effect, working for me.

I foresee no problems when I enter the office to talk to Jennifer Karl. I am a firm proponent of affirmative action, though I do not think it is a perfect system. Mostly, I am concerned over the physical entrance exam. It is too easy, and so it does women a great disservice.

I find Jennifer Karl surprisingly familiar, but not in the way I had expected: Her sentences are crisper and not flecked with swearwords, her job uniform is more colorful, and her biases are backed up by mounds of imposing paper instead of gossip. But otherwise she is astoundingly similar to the forces she claims to be fighting. While her philosophy is the polar opposite, it appears to me that she approaches her job of implementing the consent decree with a rigid and narrow prejudgment that she claims the San Francisco Fire Department is guilty of. As I talk, she remains seated at half profile, as if at any moment the phone might ring and she must snatch it up in a minimum amount of time. She sets her jaw as if to keep from interrupting.

The change in the physical entrance test that I propose is not radical. I explain my position carefully: I want women in. But this job is a physical one, and we need higher physical standards to ensure that we get the strongest women possible in this changing fire department.

She looks at me with a look reserved for people who need to be talked down to. She slows her sentences, as if our disagreement is simply a matter of my lesser intelligence. She repeats herself.

"The standards of that test have been approved by experts. Statistically, its pass-fail rate is such that it does not bias women or minorities."

Statistics! What about the real world? There is a real context that cannot be overlooked—that women are weaker than men, that nevertheless there are women who can do this job.

"And, by the way, those standards were set by firefighters in the department," she says. I know this; the standards were set by the scores of the lowest-performing firefighters in the department. The legal reason behind this is that a firefighter already in is assumed to be qualified for the job and therefore the lowest test scores reflect the minimum standard necessary to perform fire-fighting tasks.

"But those standards suck!" I am angry now, and dismayed at our growing antagonism. "Look, for all your statistics and your legal minimum standard this and that, all I can say is that this is a test that can be learned in such a way that it does not measure strength at all, it just measures an ability to learn a skill and perform it in a required time. This is going to backfire on all of us."

I sputter now; Jennifer Karl looks at me and then at her watch.

"Look," I go on, trying to smooth my voice and set a small, sweet smile on my face. "I don't understand why you are against a tougher standard. At least this test should be taken with the gear that we wear—helmet, coat, and air pack. That would make it very 'job related,' which has always been the major concern."

"A harder test would have an adverse impact on women," she says. "Adverse impact" is a legal term to describe a situation in which there is a "significant disparity" in the test scores of different classes. The exact disparity varies according to the case, but the "Uniform Guidelines on Employee Selection Procedures," a federal regulation, suggests that if one class's pass rate is less than 80 percent of the pass rate of the top scoring class, this strongly points to an unfair test. These are the guidelines that the San Francisco Fire Department is held to, and Jennifer Karl is suggesting that women would fail miserably if the test became harder.

If the test does have an adverse impact, this alone will not nullify the results. The fire department, however, must go on to prove that the test is job-related. This was where the San Francisco Fire Department fell short during the 1970s and eighties. It could not show that the physical or written tests were valid. The third time that the courts asked it to show them job-related test procedures, the city agreed that the tests were no good.

The current test was not put in place, as many people think, in order to lower standards for women and minorities. It is an attempt to improve on earlier, poorly designed tests. I am not a test expert, but I am a firefighter. The current physical test in the San Francisco Fire Department does not seem to me to be job-related either. It is only a compromise between two tired, angry, and frightened factions.

Jennifer Karl glances at her desk pointedly. She reaches for papers, but I do not take the hint.

"I came here on my own," I say. "I'm not doing this for anyone but myself." She lifts the stack of memos and does not answer. I almost plead, Look, can't we understand each other? She and I seem to have so much in common. But it is the fire department itself that has shown me that these allegiances are superficial. The men I work with, who are supposedly so prejudiced and narrow-minded, listen to me with much more interest and concern than this lawyer, who should be on my side.

I stare at her with a feeling close to disgust, and something else. Fear, perhaps. Shock. That I am here, arguing against someone who at one time I would have amiably interviewed on KPFA. Have my politics changed? Should I call my father and tell him the news, that I am finally the conservative Republican he has longed for? Or perhaps I have slowly gained a nonpartisan open mind, a realization that many issues are not as simple as we would like them to be.

Her voice becomes clipped. "There is a history of institutional racism and sexism . . ."

"Look, I know all that. But part of this is about people, not these vague institutions you talk about. You don't really know what day-to-day life in the firehouse is like. I appreciate all you have done, really, but there has to be room for the gray areas. There just has to be."

But there can't be, not for The Lawyers and Jennifer Karl, who stands up to shake my hand stiffly. I do not try to talk to The Lawyers again until I meet Patty Schecter and she obliges me by putting on full gear, which is the only means I can think of to drive my point home.

The man stands on the second-floor fire escape as we pull up, waving his arms and screaming "Fire!" and then he jumps. He writhes on his back, and the crowd that has gathered surges forward as if a bag of money has been dropped. A collective breath escapes in a long *whoosh*.

I turn on my air pack with one hand, grip my axe with the other. We can smell the smoke. People are streaming down the stairs. I beat Miller to the door—a private dig that I know he understands—and up the stairs. I push past people who hold hands to their faces and cough. On the second floor the engine crew turns left, dragging the hose down the hallway. It has filled with a thin gauze of smoke, but there is no visible fire yet. This is a tense time. Where is the fire? These hotels, old and run-down and unkempt, are dangerous firetraps. They are often deceptively large despite the narrow hallways and small ten-by-twelve-foot rooms. They wind around themselves like an Escher painting—the same brown doors and yellow walls forever.

I knock impatiently on each brown door. If it is locked, I turn my back to it and bring one leg forward. Then I crash it into the door, which gives way easily. The "mule kick" is the safest and most effective way to bring a door down—the dramatic front kicks one sees on television are only invitations for a twisted knee and a dented, unopened door.

Miller and I usually avoid being partners; when the squad splits up into two teams, I usually go with Joe. But today Joe is not the officer. Today's officer, Lieutenant Walden, is a nice man, but he is not aggressive. He seems unsure of what a squad member must do. Nevertheless, he insists that the least experienced firefighter go with him. John Fisher is the "unassigned" member today, so he works with Lieutenant Walden.

I tell Miller that I am going upstairs to search the next floor. He does not say that he will go with me, which does not surprise me, but he grins unexpectedly.

"Okay," he says. "I will be right here when you get back." When I get to the top of the next stairwell, I understand his sudden congeniality. The stairwell leads to the roof. He has just been up here; he knows this. I laugh in spite of myself—I should have realized from the outside how many stories high the hotel is. An old-timer will waggle his finger and tell you: Notice the exits! Notice the layout of the floor you are on! Where are the windows? Where do the stairwells meet? Do you have at least two paths of egress? It is important to see these things before you enter. One point for Miller.

I bound back down the stairs; the hallway has gotten darker and suddenly, down to the right, I see that telltale glow, as if the sun is setting gloriously through a window. By now, the engine crew and its hose have gone the other way, and I know that we must get another line up here, fast.

I shout down the stairwell, and someone yells back that a line is on the way. Both Miller and I are poised at the end of the banister, masks on, ready to intercept the nozzle—take it from whomever is coming up. The smoke gathers quickly now; a figure suddenly emerges from below.

It is John Fisher. He has the nozzle cradled in his arm like a football. One shoulder is dropped to ward us off—he knows his teammates well. He stares straight ahead and—because he has not stopped to put his mask on—I can see that his handsome, square jaw is set in an unusually determined line. Both Miller and I stop our sudden lunges—John, sweet, polite, choirboy John—looks as if he might bite our necks if we so much as reach for the hose. I decide not to fight for it—he has earned it—and Miller goes down the stairwell to pull hose. It is the only thing that Miller and I have ever agreed on.

Like me, John is friendly but reserved with everyone; like me, he is a person of manners, who believes that even if all hell is breaking loose, a polite hello and a handshake can somehow keep the chaos at bay. Otherwise the similarities fade—he comes from a long line of Irish Catholic San Francisco firefighters. But now, as we advance in a half crouch down the hallway, which in the past few seconds has sunk into blackness, such differences do not matter. I do not wonder, Will John back out? Will he suddenly lose his nerve and endanger those of us behind him? We do not know the things good friends know about each other—favorite colors, most embarrassing moments—but the firehouse bonds us in another way.

Lieutenant Walden is at my shoulder. He yells something at me. I push John forward—the pressure of Walden's hand increases, and he shouts to slow down, be careful, go easy. Who is this guy? I wonder. We have no time for such caution.

Just as we reach the corner of the hall, where the fire

reaches from the left, we run out of hose. We strain against it, hoping that it is momentarily caught, and then hunker down. The black settles on us like a wide hot sea, the heat on us like lazy kelp. John swings the water in a wide loop to cool us down. The water falls back searingly hot; it sneaks into my collar and down my back. When orange flashes above us, fleeting shadows of color, I pound on John's back, trying to push the words past the thick plastic of the air mask and the thicker blackness. I point upward despite the fact that I know he cannot see my hand. We can't have the fire going over us and coming down behind. It will trap us in this ugly dark corridor. We will be cremated among the maca-roni-and-cheese cartons, porn films, and old newspapers.

This is a classic fire, the crawling-down-the-hallway fire that veterans chew cigars and reminisce about. In the suffo-cating heat and claustrophobic darkness, literally at the "end of our rope"—in this case, a hose—it is easy to wonder whether something will happen to end it all. The ceiling may fall in, the heater tank nearby explode, the fire leap around and suddenly embrace us with a wide, toothy grin. I remem-ber the old Dayak chief again. "Why?" he asked. "Why do you willingly put your life in danger for something that is not yours?"

"Calculated risk" is an odd term, especially for a fire-fighter. It implies that danger can be quantified and then parceled off into neat packages to be opened at will. The idea of calculated risk is an idea I nod to, and a term I bring up with a shrug when asked, "How can you run into a fire?" Calculated risk is in some ways an apt term for firefighters who believe that they can name the odds of any game. But even as they do so they realize that there is no certainty— which is exactly why they play. Calculated risk is a fancy term for something else. It is a faith that our time has not yet come, an acceptance if it has. "I don't think I will die in this one" is what we really mean to say.

I am not the same person I was in the jungles of Borneo, though I am once again in a risky situation. Before, I thought I knew about fear. But I did not really feel it. Was it youth?

Stupidity? Too much to prove? I doubt it was courage. Now I know that bravery is to experience fear and go on anyway, with assuredness and grace. Now fear pops up like a sudden greeting. It feels interesting. It reminds me that life is fragile and precious, that there are things worth keeping, worth being a little more careful for. That life is full of small miracles easily lost. Funny, that I have just started to understand this.

If I tried to explain this to the Dayaks, however, from this hunkered-down position in a fiery hallway, they would have good reason not to believe me. But if there was time I would whisper that in the past few years I have learned that courage does not reside in physical danger. For me, courage means confronting the more emotional aspects of life. This kind of bravery means dealing with the Todd Lanes—still my nemesis years after leaving Station 4—of this world. It means confronting the contours of death, from the most banal to the most dramatic. It means interacting with all kinds of people. It means grasping the similarities and lauding the differences. I have grown up, I would say. The fire department, of all places, has given me the chance to understand that moral courage is more important than physical courage.

I swing my flashlight into the window next to me and then get up to lean through the frame to break another nearby. Lieutenant Walden grabs my coat again, yelling something through his air mask. He does not want me to lean out the window in case something falls from above. I think, in light of where we are at this moment, deep in the bowels of a burning hotel, that his concern is misplaced.

With the window open, the hallway starts to clear a little. John remains in his linebacker crouch; the fire is in no mood to back down. We and the fire are deadlocked at this corner, neither of us able to advance. It feels as if we may stay here forever, locked in a primal showdown. But we know that the fire has the advantage. It is simply gathering energy, consuming fuel, getting hotter and angrier by the second. We are simply wearing down: Soon our air packs will signal that our air is running out, or the heat will get so intense that our helmets will blister and then our ears. The crew behind us may take over or all of us may have to back out.

We hear yelling in front of us—a crew has come around the back of the hotel and taken the fire from the rear. Richard laughingly puts his arm around me when the smoke clears. "Whatsammatta, skwaaaaddddeee?" he says, elongating the words so they hang in the air as long as possible. "Had to call us to handle this one, dinnchya, huh? Huh? Dinnchya?" And his smile breaks into a gibbous moon that hangs for a long time above his mountainous shoulders.

Later we find out that this fire was arson. A prostitute, angry when the landlord told her she could not ply her trade here, returned a few hours later with a john, and together they poured gasoline in her room and dropped a match. It seems incredible that they were willing to torch the entire building and everyone in it. But fire has always been closely associated with the molten forces within us. These inner fires often consume us; they have done so through the ages. Both the God of the Old Testament and the Greek gods on Olympus used fire to wreak revenge; they knew the appropriateness of its rampant fury for their divine rage. When the Hawaiian goddess Pele is jealous, she leaks lava from her pores, and the volcano Kilauea erupts. Passion and fire are so intertwined that it is hard to see where one ends and the other begins. It is no wonder, then, that when people are enraged, they often turn to fire to express themselves. Arson is the ultimate crime of passion.

Revenge fires are actually only one kind of arson fire. Kids who play with matches are responsible for about half of the deliberately set fires in the United States. Fires set for profit are also a common type of arson fire. Unlike the other two, this type is carefully planned. These fires are usually started in the back so that they are spotted late, and near the top floor so that the roof burns through. When that happens, the building is exposed to the elements, which means a higher payment from the insurance company. Also, if the fire is near the top of the building, water from the fire hoses runs through to the floors below, causing even more damage.

Back in the 1970s and early eighties, a lot of San Francisco's real estate was torched for the insurance money. Veteran firefighters talk of whole neighborhoods on fire, night after night. "Back when the Fillmore was burning," they say, as if the fires were not just fires, but calendars by which other events were tracked: *Back when the Haight was on fire* or *while the church over on Geary was still standing . . .* And I listen, imagining whole blocks aflame.

There is speculation as to why fire calls are down these days: new building codes, fewer smokers to drop ash in their beds and on their sofas, more smoke detectors, higher property values, better fire-prevention inspections. But arson is a fire fueled by some of our most primal emotions; it will not easily disappear.

I have often seen the black smear under a window where a Molotov cocktail missed its target. Every time this happens, the procedure is the same: We pick up the pieces of glass and spray down the side of the house. I tell Alberto what a big fire it could have been, what fun we could have had, if the idiot hadn't missed. He is shocked, and tells me so. But he understands, though he pretends not to. Everyone else understands, too.

Now we climb back into the rig slowly. I am tired and my turnout coat, matted against me by water and sweat, feels punishingly heavy. "Man," John says excitedly as the rig pulls away from the curb. "Man, oh man. That was great." I laugh in agreement. The sour stench of burnt wood clings to me. "You guys wanted that nozzle, didn't you?" he continues. "You were about to slug me, I swear. And we hit the end of the hose and the corner was right there, right there, and we couldn't go any farther and it was hot! Jeez, it was hot."

I watch John. He rarely talks like this. But I understand his sudden outburst. Our everyday selves have scattered suddenly, replaced by something wilder. I watch John brim with energy. If there were more room in the rig, I am sure he would pace, back and forth, back and forth.

# UNDER THE FULL MOON

The parking lot behind Walgreen's is quiet, and I am surprised. Even though it is midnight, this is the Mission District on a Saturday night. Quiet moments are rare here. We pull into the large gray shadows, our emergency beams dropping red swatches of light like paint across the buildings. We see a few cars, an open Dumpster, a stray newspaper. Otherwise, nothing.

I look up at the sky. It's a full moon. Firefighters understand the power of a full moon—it makes people crazy. We will gaze at the sky all evening and nod: An arson fire is likely, or a few shootings. Tonight, at least, we will feel that there is some reason for the cruelty, the chaos. We can point to the large, squat moon and say, "There, that's why."

Someone steps into the headlights. It is a young man, pale and small-faced, with a faint effort of a mustache. He beckons us with the urgent flap of his hand. Now I see her, a small woman with long dark hair that hangs precisely at her belt line and seems recently brushed. The man puts his arm around her. She is pregnant. She tells us this quietly, and the man repeats it louder.

Today I am with the "B" shift, which is not my regular crew. The members of the B shift are the veterans of the Rescue Squad, a serious group left over from the days when it was known as the U-Turn Squad. Back then there were not these strange calls in the middle of the night. The few who remained after the move from Pacific Heights to the Mission District adjusted well, with the possible exception of Barney

Barret, a veteran about to retire. A sullen, craggy-faced man, he rarely talks to anyone. Though Barret does not seem to like the idea of women in the department one bit, he and I have gradually settled into a respectful working relationship based on minimum words and maximum avoidance. But Barret has been a Rescue 3 member for a long time and I am willing to risk some unsociable grunts in order to learn more about the job. His specialty is scuba diving. At first he would say nothing to me, but when he realized that I was an able swimmer and an eager, if unskilled, diver, he took to dropping small hints of advice wrapped in clipped sentences. His rare smile flakes on and off his face as if it is just another crevice of skin. Only once has he turned it to me. While cleaning up dive equipment, I remarked that I had been to one surf rescue, years ago. He straightened up and faced me fully for the first time ever. "Your wet suit was on backwards," he said. His quick smile was triumphant.

"You're pregnant?" I ask, though I heard them both clearly. I need to buy time, small seconds to repeat the steps for birthing. I see now: Her stomach is not huge, but it pushes her loose white shirt into odd creases, and the stain down her jeans indicates that her water has broken. Her labor pains are two minutes apart. The next one hits her and she sags into the man's arms. I stand and watch her, biting my lip. Okay, relax, I tell myself. You can do this, no problem. This is just a birth. It will come naturally.

"Breathe, quick breaths, like blowing out a candle," I say, and mimic the breath for her, puff, puff. She stares at me with an expression I cannot read. I remember Amy telling me about her first birth on the job. She must have seemed nervous, because the woman looked up at her mid-puff and asked, "Have you ever done this before?" Amy waved her hands as casually as possible. "No problem," she said in her most soothing Brooklynese. "My dog just had puppies, so I know how this goes."

Jamie Frank leads the woman carefully over to the bumper of the Rescue rig, and then there is a quiet shuffle as the men I work with step back. This is women's work, they are thinking. But I know less about kids than they do, and nothing about births except what the manual has taught me—a succession of questions and commands that seem far removed from the blood and pain about to happen. Jamie spreads a sheet on the concrete. We lay the woman down as another labor pain comes. She takes this like the first, with a small gasp and open eyes.

"Under a doctor's care?" I ask, kneeling on the sidewalk. Barret turns on the searchlight and the wide gray parking lot disappears, leaving only a pool of light. I notice, in that odd way that peripheral things are noticed when something essential is going on, that the cement glistens as if I kneel on new snow—little winks of silver. I can hear myself breathing in small tight breaths. Puff, puff.

*Relax,* I tell myself, this has been going on for centuries. I pick up the scissors and begin to cut her pants off.

I have been to many miscarriages, but those are different. The apartment door opens to clothes tightly wound on the floor, an effort to ward off the insistent rivulet of blood. They lead a frenzied trail to the woman, who is often still standing, one hand in her hair, walking in a dazed circle. The only baby I ever saw actually born was miscarried just before we arrived, as the woman was going to the bathroom. It dangled from her, a breech birth, the small red feet the size of my fingernails. We birthed it right there, and I stared at the tiny creature—four and a half months formed—and thought how I had never seen anything so precise. It was dark blue-red, as if still part of the woman's veins, but she stared at it with distant eyes.

I have also been to many calls for women in labor. But it has never been close enough to deliver them right then, right there. Still, a good many firefighters have attended births on the job, outside the hospital. Such births are not uncommon for women who have little or no prenatal care. And, along with the full moon, births right on the sidewalk do not seem much out of the ordinary at all.

"Oh, no, back in New York, we got a doc," the man says.

"We took the Greyhound here tonight, and we're on the way to our hotel." He says no, no drugs, no alcohol. Their doctor says it's going to be fine, just fine, a normal, full-term baby. The due date is three weeks away. I glance at the officer who is on the radio asking why the ambulance is not here yet.

Perhaps we can just coach the woman through her labor pains, and she will birth at the hospital. As much as I want to see this miracle—a birth!—I am suddenly getting cold feet at the thought of doing it myself. The pants fall away now. I peer at the woman, my body a strange, twisted genuflection, and then straighten up.

Jesus, the head is crowning.

"It's there," I say, in my calmest, most doctorlike voice. Jamie is already laying the tools out for me: gown, mask, suction bulb, umbilical-cord scissors, and ties. Barret comes over and crosses his arms as if to say *Harrumph, can't you women get it together?* but I know that he is interested. It is hard not to be; something miraculous is about to happen.

Every birth is miraculous, but to the firefighter there is something redemptive as well, as if it can wash away the stink of the day, the week, the year, all the death and injury and destruction we are called to. There are mixed feelings, because we cannot help but wonder what sort of life the infant-to-be will have, given its entrance at this absurd portico—the parking lot of Walgreen's, for God's sake.

Firefighters try to impose order, even as we know there is underlying chaos. We have seen the fire catch that errant can of paint, despite the best decisions and intentions. We know that a weak roof might fall, trapping us inside. We wear certain pants, certain socks, polish our boots, glance at the full moon, check the date of the month. We tell ourselves that we have reined in the last of the unknowns. But it is our private joke with fate, a "slamming" ritual with destiny. For all our carefully laid-out plans, our detailed decisions, we come to this job for exactly that part of life that cannot be assessed, predetermined, or calculated. We wait for whatever Chance will dish out—a fire? A stabbing? A surf rescue? When it comes, we pretend that we expected it.

"There, that's why," we say, pointing to our boots, our socks, the full moon.

Who are we, who simultaneously thrive on Chance and yet try to deny that it exists? It did not make sense to me at first, watching guys throw down Pidro cards like gauntlets, sighing when they lose, swearing that they would never do *that* again. And yet the next shift, there they are again, with another stack of cards in front of them. They like this combination of skill and luck that a game entails, just as they like fires. Fires offer similar odds.

Tonight there is the small glint of hope that this birth may prove that these forces beyond us may be benevolent after all. All that is mystery may be mystery for a good, wise reason. A birth gives hope. I snap the surgical mask to my face and glance again at the sky. To be born under a full moon is a strange and powerful omen. That, combined with the 99 CEN S FOR A SIXPA K OF COKE sign that hangs on the wall behind us.

The ambulance pulls up with a long, insistent whine. There is a shuffle and the soft exchange of words—everything is spoken in a low, almost reverent whisper tonight. The two paramedics kneel next to me. I forget that the light blue paper gown over my fire coat looks ridiculous and that I am sweating from anxiety; we are a chorus of pleased smiles.

"Yep," says the tall paramedic, his glasses glinting in the searchlight. "No time to transport. We'll just do it right here." He grunts happily, because the fire crew has handled this fine and he, too, is swept up in the excitement of a birth, even a birth on the sidewalk. His partner taps me on the shoulder. "What do you say, want to give it a go?"

"Me?" I say.

The woman's legs are bent, her feet are planted on the ground. She has perfect, solid symmetry, the geometry of birth through the ages.

"Okay, we're all ready here, and our little friend especially. At the next contraction, we want her to push."

"No puffing?"

"No, this one is for home plate. Hand on the head, gently, so nothing tears too much."

The analogy is apt. From here on in, the midwife is nothing but a catcher. It is supposed to be quick, or so the book says.

The small, tumorous appearance in front of me will soon be something recognizable! I am anxious—will I remember everything? When the head shows, okay, give a gentle downward pressure to let the shoulder pop out. Got it. Not so difficult, really, just a nudge to let nature do its thing. I nod at the paramedic. He slips a gloved hand into the woman's small palm.

"When the next pain hits, I want you to push with it," I say to the woman, who has her eyes closed now. Her small, triangular face looks translucent in the light. She bears her pain so quietly, I wonder if I will know when the labor spasm hits.

The woman gasps. "Push," I say. "Push." The paramedic leans over to watch.

He frowns. I see it, too. The head has not moved. The contraction flows through her, rippling her body enough for her to widen her eyes, but it has little effect on the baby.

"Sarah, you have to push. Push with the pain." The paramedic shifts so that he looms over her small face. The other paramedic, a gaunt man with a lower jaw that juts forward so that he reminds me of a marionette, steps forward.

"Jim, look at this," he says. He shows the underwear that I cut off to his partner.

Jim stares. He snaps his head to the woman.

"What drug are you on?" he asks. "Don't bullshit me on this one." Without waiting for an answer, he shines a light in her eyes.

"Heroin," she says, blinking.

Her underwear is stained green. I stare at it a long time.

"This baby is fucked. Load and go on this one." The paramedic spins around, waving toward the ambulance. The stretcher clatters from its bed; Barret moves fast when he has to. I get up stiffly. The sidewalk has bit into my knees and I feel it now. I know what the green stain means.

I look at the woman, whose brave calm suddenly makes sense to me. She appears even smaller on the stretcher. Her thin arms are at her sides in a stiff, straight line, and she looks at the sky. Her eyelids close slowly. When her eyes shutter back open, they appear slightly dismayed.

"You, too?" I say to the man.

"We had some this morning, yeah."

"This morning and tonight."

"Yeah."

"I asked you, and you lied," I say. I glance at Jamie Frank's face, which is pale and tight.

The green stain indicates meconium. Meconium is the baby's first stool, which, if expelled inside the mother, can indicate that the infant is in distress. Big distress.

I should have seen it, the way the woman seemed so distant, so removed. The way the contractions were dulled. The way the baby, on the very ledge of being birthed, was immobile. Maybe it held back, I want to believe, refusing to come out into this world of hard cement and glaring lights.

Meconium is a very bad sign, indeed.

The paramedics wave us off from the ambulance. They know how much this has taken out of us. We do not say anything to each other as we clean up the remnants of our hastily arranged operating room. Jamie glances at the full moon. I know what he is thinking.

*There, that's why.*

That Sunday, I find myself attending a Quaker meeting. This seems clichéd, almost satirical; people find religion in jails, in gutters next to a Jack Daniel's bottle, at the tip of a heroin needle. Am I that devastated? But I have come here less to find a God than to ensconce myself in something predictable. What could be more predictable than turning to religion for answers?

Quaker meetings are quiet affairs; people sit in silence, communing personally with their God until someone is moved to "witness" and stands to say a few words. Today no one says anything and almost the whole hour is spent in silence. There is only the soft creak of chairs and now and then a quick flutter of coughs. I stare out the window to my left, at the Golden Gate Bridge.

Miracles, I think, do not come in neat packages; they usually entail a burning bush or swarms of locusts. God could appear as a beautiful animal but decides on pestilence and the destruction of small flora instead. I should never have expected that a birth is anything other than what it has always been: a flimsy filament between life and death, a dark passageway from one world to the next, a beginning that is much like the end. I look out at the bridge, which stretches like a rain gutter across the bay and seems to grasp only tentatively the opposite shore.

# SMALL GRACES

I leave the Quaker meeting and walk slowly to my car. There have been no great epiphanies. I sit behind the wheel and stare through the windshield.

My car is a convertible; the top is down and I can feel the light brush of wind from the bay. I take a deep breath. I can still see the small round head of the infant behind my eyes, and I imagine the soft, delicate places where the skull has not yet formed. In this brief moment before I shake my head and reach for the keys to start my car, I suddenly see myself years before, in this exact position, except that the looming steel braces of the Bay Bridge whiz past me. I have nothing on my mind but getting to KPFA in time to write a newscast.

Back then I was different. I was a reporter who kept not only the news but every part of my life at arm's length. I glimpsed emotion only when I was going too fast down the luge track or cresting a large river wave. Now, after years in the fire service, it is not just fire that moves me, but the tiny fontanel of a doomed child. My growth has been opposite from that infant's. It is almost as if I were born fully armored by bone and as I grew it hardened into a barely visible but reliable shell. Only after years in the fire department did the bone begin to separate and allow the best parts of the outer world in. What moment allowed the softness to grow? Which emergency loosened the ossification? Who would I have been without the fire department? Years ago, I would never have let anything bother me enough to be a problem. I could never have come to a Quaker meeting, could never have asked for help.

I am no longer an onlooker, an observer, a reporter.

Today there is something else I have to do. I have to ask for help in a different matter. I pull into the parking lot of Station 64 and make my way to the chief's office.

Chief Kalafferty listens the way most firefighters listen; his head is cocked to one side and he nods occasionally or leans in closer. He is not the chief on my shift, but he is the chief on duty today, and the matter is urgent. There is no time to wait for Chief Masters.

"I'll need to borrow an engine. Just for an hour." I clear my throat and put my hands in the pockets of my skirt. I look off to the left, to make sure no one else hears. "The television show says that without it, they have no story. I know that's not true but . . ."

"So it's for your brother. He's in jail." There is no mockery in the chief's voice. He is a tall, handsome man whom I do not know well, and despite his thoughtful attention I am momentarily worried that I have done the wrong thing. Hat in hand, I am asking a tremendous favor. He may break out in wild laughter, for all I know, and kick me out of his office.

"He's in jail, but he is not guilty of anything," I blurt out, and then realize how ridiculous this must sound; to most people it is highly improbable that someone could be in jail and not be implicated, at least, in a crime. Even my liberal friends do not understand the grand-jury system.

My brother has now been in jail for six months. Finally, we have decided to take a different course of action to try to free him. Reluctantly, Alexandra and I concede that good old American protest procedures are not working. We have simply frozen the ends of our fingers and gone through many D cell batteries for our small, cheap megaphone. We have become recognizable figures in Spokane, as a local drunk might be. Otherwise, not much has changed. Jonathan remains in jail.

The letters that we have sent to *The New York Times*, to *60*

*Minutes,* to the ACLU, and elsewhere have focused only on the injustices of the grand jury. We have written long, passionate polemics on the sanctity of the Constitution. We have expounded on the right to free speech, waxed poetic about the proud history of political activity, and pondered sternly a country without them. In return, we receive thoughtful letters that agree, yes, the grand jury is a suspect institution that needs scrutiny. But right now, they add regretfully, there are more urgent stories to be covered. Sorry.

Finally, we realize that the Constitution and the threat of government intrusion on innocent citizens is just not hard-hitting enough. We agree that the only theme that this culture will understand centers around something more mesmerizing than even our inalienable rights. Okay. We'll give it to them. Reluctantly, we play our trump card.

*Baywatch.*

"*Baywatch* Beauty Bemoans Brother Behind Bars!" The television shows and newspapers that had ignored our earlier press releases now snap to attention. Within hours, *People* magazine and *Entertainment Tonight* have called. *The San Francisco Examiner, Hard Copy, USA Today,* and the *Sally Jessy Raphael* talk show are not far behind. Fire engines and bathing suits! they clamor. What a story! they cheer. "*Baywatch* Babe and Firegirl Team Up for Real-Life Rescue!"

"Your brother is in trouble," the chief says again. He knows nothing of the press hullabaloo that twenty-four hours from now will make me a semi-recognizable face in my own right for just about another twenty-four hours.

"Of course. Take the engine," he says. "This has to go through channels, to the chief of the department, but I'll handle it." He pats me on the shoulder. I stare after him, stunned, as he walks away. I know how much he has just done for me.

Only hours before, I had called Patricia. Until this point, none of the firefighters knew that my family had been desperately trying to get Jonathan out of jail. But now I had no one else to turn to. The television shows were asking that I drive a fire engine for their cameras. I responded with a vigorous no, anything but that. The fire department would *not understand.* Alexandra, who had just put her career on the line, looked at me with understandable disgust and an expression that said "Handle it!"

Patricia listens in silence to my fractured voice and convoluted story.

Finally she says, "It's not about being a stupid liberal, Caroline. This is about family. It is about getting your brother out of jail. Of course you have to do this. And if there is anything a firefighter understands, it's *family.* I guarantee that you will get that engine. Guarantee it."

Sure enough, as I watch the receding back of Chief Kalafferty, I think how I have once again been embraced by the fire department when I least expected it. To be able to drive a fire engine, off duty and in front of the media, is a big favor indeed. The fire department has strict guidelines about its representation in the media. The media, after all, has often portrayed the fire department as a monolithic entity. Or it does not portray it at all.

Recently, for example, the newspapers reported the heroism of a passerby who caught a baby thrown from a burning building, an event worthy of a feature story. However, not mentioned at all was the fact that four other children were also saved, pulled out of that same fire by Rescue 3. When I arrived at work the next day and heard about it, I hunted the crew down, hungry for the story. I found William first. He is square jawed and moves with the unself-conscious feline grace of a lion. He shook his head slowly.

"It was the other guys," he said. "I just followed them."

Then I found Jamie Frank, who peered at me from behind his glasses. "I just helped," he murmured. "The others are the real heroes."

"It was pretty satisfying," the officer said. "But you should get the story from the rest of the crew. I didn't do much." And so on. Since the newspaper had not bothered to cover it, I never did find out much about the rescue.

Today, however, the media is interested. From my perch on the driver's seat of the engine, I can just make out the nose of a television camera in a van next to me. The producer leans out the van's front window, which keeps pace with me, and shouts above the wind.

"Yeah, look straight ahead. You know, as if you are going on a rescue. Perfect, perfect. Okay, let's get your face a little toward me now, but keep driving. Serious, but not solemn. You know, you are speeding to rescue your brother, speeding to get him out of jail . . ."

It is hard to get just the right angle of face for the camera while driving at a decent speed and simultaneously praying that no one I know will come by.

"How about the emergency beacon?" the producer waves at me.

"The lights?" I say, yelling over the roar of the engines. *Shit.* I flip the lights on.

"Yeah, good, perfect!" shouts the producer, and we speed on down the wide, quiet street.

Within twelve hours of that absurd fire-engine drive, my brother is out of jail. The feds say that it has nothing to do with the sudden avalanche of press interest. They say that it is clear that he was not being "persuaded"—that he would never testify, and that it was time to let him go. My fellow firefighters do not ostracize me for my family's political bent. There is no shame in having a brother in jail. "How's your brother?" they ask. "That's good he didn't snitch."

*Woman hit by a train,* announces the loudspeaker. Jesus, we groan.

A woman hit by a train is not a pleasant call; there will be parts everywhere. Furthermore, the constant threat of hepatitis B and AIDS makes a call with so much blood dangerous.

The Rescue Squads are well versed in tunnels and the Bay Area Rapid Transit (BART) tunnels in particular. We have wandered the innards of this system on drills, balancing ourselves on the small space between the rail and the wall, staring at the thick ceiling, imagining what a fire down here would be like. A decade or so ago, there was a large fire and a firefighter, disoriented by the smoke, and unable to find his way to a safety door, perished. There are few pleasant ways to die on this job, but surely to do so trapped in the bowels of the city is one of the worst.

Unfortunately, I am also trained in "confined-rescue" skills, which puts me in tunnels much narrower and more uncertain than BART's. The squads are taught by earnest Midwestern firefighters, who proudly call themselves "tunnel rats." They give long, detailed lectures on tunnel rescues that they have performed, while in the back of the class San Francisco firefighters snicker. They throw in prepackaged witticisms. On helmet safety, for example, they like to say (innumerable times), "Remember, guys, don't go in a hole unprotected." Then they pause, throw an embarrassed glance at the few women in the room, and say, "Excuse the, uh, French."

We learn to use gas meters to constantly monitor dangerous gas buildup, and we learn to recognize common tunnel equipment that could alternately start a fire, slice you up, or suffocate you. The confined-rescue class does not shed an optimistic light on tunnel-rescue odds. Mostly, we pray that we will never have to use our knowledge.

Today the train is not in the tunnel, and I am relieved; it is in the station when we get there.

"She's about two cars back," a shaken conductor tells us. "Two cars back, *underneath.*"

The commuter train, he says, was pulling into the station when she jumped onto the tracks in front of it. He could not stop. I groan again. Guts, I think. It is going to be guts all over the place.

"That third rail turned off?" My probation officer, Captain Leahy, is here, too. It is good to see him again. His large, loping stature and deep voice calm the conductor, who wipes a hand along his mouth and then down the seam of his pants. The third rail carries the voltage to power the train. Turned on, it will electrocute anyone who touches it. The conductor points to it, though we all know where it is. It runs a little lower than knee-high, along the wall next to the far tracks. A thick, ominous girder of metal.

Leahy won't let anyone near the train until he is sure that the electricity is off. Even when the "all clear" is given, people are nervous. An unwitting employee at a central computer may throw the switch back on, activating the third rail while the body-recovery process is in progress.

"You ain't catching me going under that thing," someone from Engine 82 murmurs.

It does look forbidding. The snub nose of the forward car hunkers impassively in the narrow tub that holds the train flush against the platform. The cars are long. Two cars ran over her—there won't be much left. To get to the body, we must crouch and crawl under the space between the platform and the first rail. We will lug our medical equipment—oxygen, bandages, neck braces. This is being optimistic. When we get to the blood, we will confer.

Halfway down the first car, waddling and crawling single file with fellow Station 64 members, some of whom are not exactly lithe, we hear a noise.

*Oh Jesus,* I think, *she's alive.*

It is clear to the rest of my crew that only the thinnest can get under; I will crawl through to get to her. The space *is* small—so small that I have to take my turnout coat off, shedding the little protection against blood that I have, except for rubber gloves, which I snap on now. Two pair, on each hand. Butted together like cattle, it is hard to move, but James Frank manages to reach over and pat my shoulder.

When somebody loses an eyeball, a small Dixie cup will do. Tape it to the bad eye, which can then dangle protected. Then be sure to cover the good eye. If the good eye remains uncovered it will swivel, thereby causing the bad eye to swivel in unison. I think of the Dixie cup now, small and waxy with flowers around the outside—a solution so neat and practical as to be almost beautiful. But there will be more than an eyeball to worry about here.

There will be legs and arms and hands. A Dixie cup cannot help now.

I wriggle over the first rail. The ribs of the train against my back, the ribs of the rail against my stomach, I am a modern-day Jonah, trapped inside this huge, many-tonned whale, crawling toward a newly digested victim. Irrational thoughts suddenly spring up in my head: What if the train suddenly moves? What if the Big One happens right now? What if the third rail is really on?

"Get me the hell out of here," says a thin voice in front of me.

I squeeze past another network of pipes and coils.

"Are you okay?" I ask in a high, strained voice.

"Get me the motherfuck out of this place," the voice says again.

"Anything hurt?" I ask, squirming the last small distance to the second rail.

"My head hurts like a motherfucker," the voice says as I peer between a wheel and the beginnings of a thin, ragged woman lying between the second rail and the third rail on the concrete wall.

"Oh Christ," I whisper. "Oh Christ."

The woman has her hands folded across her chest. She stares straight up at the underbelly of the train and does not turn her head even as I reach out to touch her shoulder. She is thin, slightly bedraggled, in her late twenties—though it is hard to tell much in the musty gray light. She is an inch or so from the wheels of the train on the second rail. The third rail is a foot to her left and right above her.

She is completely unharmed.

I realize that my teeth have been clenched tightly only when my mouth drops open in disbelief. I had been expecting terrible carnage, severed parts, and a lot of blood. There was certain death on both sides—not including the fact that the train hit her as well. But she fell, perfectly centered, while two train cars passed over her, in the only trough that could have saved her life.

"Do you believe in God?" I whisper. "Because you will now."

"My motherfucking head hurts," she says quietly.

Extricating her is a slow process. She stares straight up almost the whole time. She is drunk, which accounts for both her stupidity and for the fact that she is alive in spite of it.

"I wanted to cross the tracks," she says as the stretcher is pushed toward me. "I just wanted to get across the goddamn tracks." I am reminded of the old joke: "Why did the chicken cross the road?"

She just wanted to cross the goddamn tracks.

Miracles come in unusual packages, like the day I saw a fire-fighter pick up his flute and play. He was a big man—a sullen man, I thought—too big for such a delicate instrument. Then he played with such softness, and he dipped and swung and sashayed to his music with such intensity, and said afterward how playing touched something in his soul, that I had to rethink my attitude. Life is too short, I now know, for small-mindedness. The fire department reminds me that generosity and an open mind are the best options, but I often forget. There are still loose ends in my life.

My mother is the loosest of the loose ends; aside from courtesy calls at holidays, we do not speak much. She has made more effort in the past years, but I am slow to respond. Second chances are not accorded often, and sometimes they are lost forever—I see that in the sudden, hapless death and destruction around me. Sometimes it just does not sink in. But today it is hard not to see the miracle in a woman run over by a speeding train and unharmed.

I pick up the phone. I clear my throat.

"I just wanted to say hello," I tell my mother.

# GRAFFITI AND TATTOOS

I check the chore board to see if I cook today—no, it is Paul's turn. The meal will be good, though in the middle of dinner Paul will frown and shake his head. "Needs more, more *something*," he will sigh. "Something. I'm not sure what." He will remain forlorn and slightly puzzled at each bite for the rest of the meal.

I hear a *click, click* behind me, and Chief Masters walks by, his bicycle shoes tap-dancing across the linoleum. He bikes twenty-five miles to work if the weather is right, and recently, on his fifty-sixth birthday, he biked those twenty-five miles home and straight to a triathlon, where he handily won in his age group and came in fourth overall. He waves a good morning to me, and the rearview mirror on his helmet bobs up and down. He has been in the department for thirty years, and has taken all the changes with good humor.

Of course, traditions die hard. I once found a hay fork in the bowels of Truck 53. The tiller operator shrugged when I held it up to him. He said it was used long ago when the horses were here (and as the last horses retired in 1921, it was a very long time ago). No one had bothered to remove it. "It's good for stuff," he said vaguely, and we put it back. Tradition is both the cornerstone and the lodestone of the San Francisco Fire Department.

But change is the law of life, and transition is difficult. Things have certainly changed since I first got in five years ago. There are eighty female firefighters now. It does not seem like a lot on the surface—still only five percent of the department—but it's a startling change from the mere fifteen or so when I began. They come from fancy colleges, too: Brown, Georgetown, Reed. I am no longer an anomaly. When once I might not have seen another female firefighter for months, now it is not uncommon for me have another woman on my shift, and today there is a female probationer from Station 72.

Cristine Prentice is a short, stocky woman with a flat top of graying hair. I do not know her well because she works on a different shift and because Truck 72, miserable at Station 64, spends as much time away as possible. We tease them often about their discomfort here. We hint that we have heard that their station will not be fully retrofitted for earthquakes until, oh, next year. Actually, they are set to leave in a few months. They have begun a gleeful countdown.

Cristine does not wear her nose ring at work, nor can you always see the tattoo on her left upper arm, but she shows it when I ask. It is a beautiful tattoo, with an intricate, artistic pattern. As I stare at it, I realize that it is made of Chinese characters.

"Mandarin," she says.

"What does it say?" I stare at the greenish-black tint.

"'It is better to die on your feet than live on your knees,'" she answers.

Despite her tattoo, and her tough, butch appearance, enhanced when she goes outside to smoke a cigarette, Cris is anything but hard-edged. I had seen her once at a fire, while she waited to be accepted into the academy, staring wistfully at the smoke and the firefighters. A part of me wanted to say "Get a life," but another part was pleased that women could be fire geeks, too.

Cris grew up with little money and describes herself as "poor white trash." Now she is an eager probationer, and walks around with the contained glee of someone whose dream has come true. It is not often, I think, that dreams come true.

"Had a fire yet?" I ask.

She shakes her head mournfully.

"It'll come."

"Not soon enough."

"Hmm."

I notice that I adopt the casual, small-sentenced attitude of one who has "seen it all," much as Tess did so many years ago.

Cris will get the quiz on fires after her first one, I decide, much like the one Patricia gave me. This "quiz" is just an informal run-through that clues the new female probationer in fire etiquette. Don't Give Up Your Equipment. The fire code behind the fire tactics. Be Aggressive. Usually, I mention these things when the woman first arrives, but Cris is not on my shift. I will wait until after her first fire, I think, and see whether she is as tough as her tattoo.

The driver from Truck 72 waves for Cris. They are going on a drill. They will be gone awhile, even though they are no longer allowed to sneak by their station to check on the work in progress. Firefighters, many of them with extensive carpentry experience, do not hold back with their opinions on the quality of the work. The contractors are tired of the squinting scrutiny. They do not like the way the men put their hands on a wall seam and run down it slowly, or harrumph through the shattered dormitory, commenting on the placement of the pole holes.

Truck 72's impatience to return to their own station is understandable. The Mission can be a depressing place. New yuppie bars have sprung up since I began working here, and eclectic cafés squeeze themselves between popular burrito places, but the sleazy, run-down hotels and housing projects remain.

There are two housing projects in what is called our "first alarm" area. Both are stiff rows of ominous, squat cement buildings. They are home to many good, decent people. Some of the grim apartments are clean and carefully decorated, but these are overwhelmed by the smell of urine in the stairwells and the wide, arrogant scrawl of graffiti in the hallways. Once only the monikers of self-aggrandizing youth, graffiti are now bizarre, belligerent headstones memorializing the death of young black men. NEVER FORGET! RIP HOMEBOY; REVENGE IS OURS; MISS YOU OUR BROTHER. They are simultaneously a war cry and a howl of grief violently splayed on the walls. Graffiti is ugly to me, and this graffiti is no different, though I have the nagging feeling that there is a story behind it that I do not understand.

There is an undeclared war between some people in the projects and anyone with a badge. Firefighters and paramedics have bottles and cans thrown at them from windows, are cursed, scorned, and ignored so that we, in turn, develop sneering or blank expressions, walk with the swagger of someone armed with an axe, or laugh or curse back. Eventually, even the decent, polite residents understand that we think the worst of them. It is a difficult situation. Perhaps it started back when the racial divide was legal, and authorities like us knew that they could do as they wanted with people they considered second-class citizens. For all the talk about "the good old days," the good old days were not good for most people. Things are beginning to change for the better now; when a firefighter walks into the projects, there is a good chance that he or she will be black, too.

But combustible human dynamics play out with the inevitability of fire when the elements—heat, fuel, oxygen, and a chain reaction—are present in the required amounts. Alter any of the factors only slightly, and a fire can be averted. If the heat source is suddenly lowered below the ignition temperature of the fuel, or eliminated completely, the day continues without mishap. Here, however, the elements are solidly balanced, a dynamic set years before. Combustion is inevitable. I am as much a part of this entrenched reaction as anyone. Before I get off the rig for even a medical call in the projects, I make sure that my helmet and jacket are securely on, as if I am preparing for battle. The tension is palpable as we walk through a crowd to the downed person. When the patient is pleasant and approachable, I am surprised, and my automatic expectation of hostility shames me.

A fire in the projects is a tricky event. Because they are

made of concrete, fire does not spread easily, but the concrete walls act as an oven would, so that the area quickly becomes unbearably hot. Backdrafts or flashovers are a concern. A flashover is when the room gets so hot that objects reach their ignition temperature and combust without direct contact with flame. A backdraft is different; here, a fire in an enclosed room will begin to produce partially combusted carbons or carbon monoxide instead of carbon dioxide. Carbon monoxide is extremely explosive at a certain range when mixed with air. This is why ventilation is imperative as early as possible. Ventilation—breaking windows, opening up the roof—will not allow carbon monoxide to build up to its explosive range. But it is also why incorrect ventilation—which will actually introduce the air required for a backdraft—is dangerous. Optimally, ventilation will be done early and above the fire so that air will not mix with carbons. But often a door must be opened to get to the fire or a window blows out from the heat and air enters below. It then rises to meet the carbon monoxide, creating an explosion. Fire has scientific properties, but firefighters do not always have the time or the group coordination to be scientific.

My few fires in the projects have been quick, hot affairs. Mostly, the garbage chute catches fire—this is especially unpleasant. Sometimes tenants ignore the garbage chute and simply throw their trash into a lightwell and it catches on fire. After one such incident, we discovered that the garbage was almost two stories high. The top layer of garbage had burned, but the rest was teeming with cockroaches. Insects do not bother me much, but it is disconcerting, to put it mildly, when the soft hill you are standing on bucks and sways with millions of small, resilient creatures. I was still a probationer at the time and cheerfully volunteered to till the charred area to make sure that nothing was still burning. The roaches ran up and down the walls around me and I had the unpleasant idea that they might find their way into my turnout boots.

We rarely expect a large fire in the projects because there is little way for it to spread easily; however, a full-box alarm there remains ominous and unpredictable. Just a few years ago, several San Francisco firefighters were burned and one firefighter died in what was initially considered a normal "room and contents" project fire. The fire was started by a five-year-old boy playing with a lighter. When the crews arrived, they lined the narrow, dark hallway outside the apartment. There was not much smoke, and little reason to worry—or so they thought. They forced open the door. Flame and superheated air catapulted down the hallway.

A fluke wind that day forced the fire abruptly out of the apartment after a back window broke from the heat. At the funeral for Lieutenant Manner, who died of his burns more than a week later, my friend Kathy still had her ears bandaged. Others had hands wrapped or could not attend because of leg burns. What had started as a routine full box ended in tragedy. We are told to expect the unexpected, but sometimes the unexpected is cloaked in mundane reality. Fire kills easily and without sentiment.

Sometimes, if the alarm comes in the dead of night, I push myself up from sleep as if fighting a gravitational pull not experienced during the day. Though my body feels leaden and unresponsive, I am able to get into my turnout pants, slide down the pole, and climb into the rig as if an unknown force guides me. If I am driving, I snap awake as I turn the key and the engine roars to life; if I am not, it sometimes takes the bright lights of an apartment or the grinning of a wide, bloody wound to shake the dullness from me. Fortunately, over the years, waking quickly and efficiently countless times in one night has become a normal part of my sleep pattern. Even at home I wake suddenly and for no apparent reason, alert and listening.

But tonight the lights in the dormitory snap on and seem to pin me to the bed. The Bee-Bop tone wraps around my head and yanks it sideways. The loudspeaker yelps an address I do not recognize at first through my haze, but I am already perched on the side of the bed as if I know that it is for me and the squad. I shake my head to clear it, and my suspenders are on my shoulders before I realize that every rig in the house is going—a full box at the nearby projects.

The flames shoot out of a fifth-floor window. I notice that they add a peculiarly beautiful edge to this otherwise grim building. But the beauty of flame is misleading. Chief Masters watches it, too, but he has other things on his mind. He coordinates the fire scene and is ultimately responsible for what happens. He is aware that Joe knows what he is doing and just nods to us as we go past.

I have rarely seen Joe run at a fire scene, but he walks fast. I have developed a walk-skip method just short of a jog to keep up with him. Behind me, Alan takes the stairs two at a time. Usually Alan is easygoing and polite; he would not ordinarily push past me on the stairs. But this is a fire, and all etiquette is out the window—both of us want to be in first. He is stronger and faster than I am—I have seen him grab a hose and climb up the scaffolding on a building to be the first to put water on a fire.

The fifth-floor hallway has the familiar gray haze that begins at the ceiling and works its way downward. After a few doors the hallway turns sharply to the right, and here the smoke thickens. A woman crouches, coughing, near an open doorway.

"Anyone in there?" Joe asks as Alan and I kneel at the threshold and pull our masks on. Joe is still moving, his air mask half on, his helmet thrown back.

"My grandson," she cries. "No, no."

Joe, who is always in calm, steady motion, stops suddenly and spins around.

"He's in there? Your grandson?"

"No! Maybe, but I don't—I don't—"

The woman, not yet in her early forties, her face grotesquely angled by too much makeup and a smear of black smoke, is clearly drunk.

"No, we got 'im," someone behind her says. "He's right here." But Alan has already plunged into the apartment. He goes to the left, so I go to the right, crawling, patting, straining wildly to see something in the thick smoke. The rasp of my air mask is loud and the air is hot. Like an oven, I think. Backdraft, flashover, what the hell. I spread my arms wide along the ground. Every few seconds I reach with my flashlight and tap the wall to make sure I keep my orientation, miss no rooms or closets, and break windows as they come up. I know that these apartments are small. I know that my crew is somewhere nearby. But in the dark the room seems fathomless; despite the hard objects I keep running into, I feel as if I'm falling. A hot fire room feels like a long molten tube into the center of the earth.

I break a window with a quick tap of my flashlight. So far, no one here. The room goes from pitch-black to cooler murky gray. Good-bye, carbons. You have not gotten us today.

I continue crawling, searching, my flashlight now casting a thin, blurred haze on the ground as the smoke escapes faster now. I am back around to the left, where Alan disappeared, and where the fire is. I hear the clamor of the engine crew advancing a line. The cool spray of water, like a sudden evening shower, trickles down my back.

Joe has been behind me the whole time, and we both lurch from the room. We both know that bodies can lie hidden under debris, and Joe wants to know once and for all where the grandson is. If he does not see him with his own eyes, he will go back in and comb the area minutely. We know too well that the human body is much the same as anything else when burned. From ashes to ashes, from dust to dust.

Alan crouches by the door. "Where's the kid?" he snaps. "I didn't find the kid." He makes a move to reenter the apartment, but Joe puts a hand on his shoulder. Alan's helmet is bent and blistered. I stare at it. Alan must have hugged the floor and tried to get through to the other side of the hallway, past the burning room. He does not notice, though it is easy to smell, the sharp tang of paint. He wants to find the kid.

"Don't worry," Joe says. "They say he's out. Can I see the kid?" he asks the grandmother, who has retreated, dull-eyed, only a few feet from the door. "I got him," says a young man behind her, and indeed, a small, scared-looking boy stands by his legs. His hands, small fists, are at his mouth, and he stares at the open doorway.

Joe walks toward the kid. I know what he is doing—he wants to know for certain that no one is dead in there, and he needs to lean in and see the kid for himself so that no mistakes are made. He needs to know why he plunged into that hot-as-hell apartment. Since that question is not easily answered, he needs to see something tangible and real—the grandson is here and all right. We all need to peer carefully and up close to the danger we face. Sometimes this comes in the persona of a kid who lit matches; we lean toward him until whatever is supposed to come into focus does, and the things that will not make sense anyway fade into the periphery. Joe leans toward the little boy. He brushes the young man's arm with his dirty turnout coat.

"Hey," the man says. "Hey, motherfucker. You got my shirt dirty."

"Sorry, buddy, I just need to talk to the kid."

"My motherfucking shirt's dirty." The man looks incredulously at his sleeve and brushes it slowly with one hand. Joe, who has just risked his life for the young man's nephew, pushes by again.

"I said get the fuck away from me, motherfucker. You're getting my shirt dirty."

Joe turns slowly toward the man. I am frozen in place, unbelieving. Alan has straightened up. He leans forward and then stands completely still, staring. There is a moment of thick, tense silence.

Joe raises one arm, his sleeve wet and dirty, and points past the man's nose. "Then get outta the fucking hallway," he says.

"It's my hallway," is the louder response.

I am astonished. Doesn't the youth realize that we have come here to save lives and property, or is everything a turf war? Part of me is uncomfortable, too, because the man is black and we are white. I feel like we are replaying an interaction that no longer makes sense, especially now, when Joe has just risked his life. I recognize the signs of a backdraft—the partially combusted carbons in the air in the form of our old prejudices, the heat generated by the small swipe of dirt on a shirt—and now we are just waiting for the slight breath of oxygen to slide out and ignite with the next exchange of words.

I pick up the six-year-old, who is crying now, and turn him away from the fight about to happen. This diverts the man, who jerks his head toward me. "Give me my nephew," he says.

"I'm going to take him to the ambulance," I say.

"Put my nephew down," the man says, stepping forward.

"Relax," I say. I imagine the sharp blow of an axe on a stubborn roof: ventilation in progress. "Let's all take care of the kid, okay?" In a fire, we know what to do and how to do it—get that roof open! Break those windows! Hot air, dangerous carbons, will rise up and out of the four-by-four hole. "Tell your son to relax." I nod to the grandmother, but even as I say this, reflexive anger rises up in me. Alan got so close to the flames that he blistered his helmet, and this guy is trying to pick a fight?

"I ain't going to beat the kid," the man says. "You think I'm going to beat him."

"I don't think that," I lie. "Let's all go down to the ambulance." I feel that just getting out of that dark cement hallway so that we can see each other in the clear night air might change perceptions, my own included. In front of the building I hand the boy to Chief Masters. He loves kids; he can handle this. I step away to stare at the thirty-year white vet and the six-year-old black boy. The boy lifts one hand. In it is a small plastic toy, shiny yellow and white. Masters reaches for it and holds it up to the streetlight.

"What's your name, little guy?" he asks as the boy stares at the toy with him. There is a quiet moment of camaraderie. And something else—hope, perhaps. Then I turn back, leaving them as silhouettes near a streetlight, to help with overhaul.

# A SEARCH

The second alarm comes in near midnight. William is driving today, and because the fire is in Hunter's Point we take the freeway. The squad shakes and groans from the strain of going so fast; the beacon casts wide swatches of red light on the overpasses. My gloves are stiff with ash from the housing-project fire, and I hold my hands in front of me to flex them. Coat, belt, helmet—they are all in place. Now all I can do is sit and wait.

The rig lunges onto the sidewalk and noses to a halt. William and I are partners tonight, which is funny because both of us have been separately reprimanded for "freelancing": when you suffer from impatience and aggressiveness and tend to leave your partner behind. In fact, the best firefighters are the ones who pause, consider the situation, make a decision, and communicate it to everyone else. Freelancing is understandably frowned upon. It is not only stupid, egotistical, and often ineffectual, it is also dangerous. Tonight, both William and I are on our best behavior.

I don't see flames, but I see that the house, a two-story family residence, is haloed in orange light. The sky is murky with smoke. We throw a quick salute to a chief who stands in the middle of the street, bent over a radio in his left hand. It is hard to hear anything above the roar of wood giving way and the shouts for more water, more ladders, more axes. Hoses lie everywhere and water sprays through leaks in couplings. Fire vehicles jam the street.

"Rescue 3 is here, Chief," William says.

"Okay, we got a report of two people still in the back room," the chief answers matter-of-factly, unfolding himself from his awkward stance. "A baby and an adult."

*Pause, look,* I say to myself as I walk quickly toward the fire. *Be as matter-of-fact as he is.* The chief is not unfeeling; he simply knows that the tone of his voice will affect the adrenaline level in his firefighters. *Pause, look,* I tell myself again, but instead, the word *baby* pounds in my head.

The garage door, at street level, is twisted and burned. Smoke cartwheels from the opening and two hose lines disappear into the darkness. "Front door," I breathe to William and bound up the steps. There is already a hose snaking its way inside: an engine company's attack.

My mask is on and I turn to make sure that William has followed me inside. I do not want to lose him or be lost by him; tonight we need to do everything perfectly. Instead, a civilian has followed me, and he is wringing his hands and pointing. There is black all over his face, and I wonder if he has been burned. He grabs my coat as if to shake me; I see that he is crying—perhaps he has grabbed me to steady himself. I cannot understand a word he says—he looks Cambodian—but I know what is going on. It is his baby inside, in the back room.

I take both his shoulders to prevent him from going farther, and he becomes frantic. He sobs and points to the far wall of the house. By this time, William is past me and on the opposite side of the room, where flashlights and dim outlines of helmets appear—the engine crew. They have not made much headway, and something has stopped them at a small hall.

I push the man back as gently—as *matter-of-factly*—as I can and join William. It is hot, very hot. "We need to get through," I say. "There are two people in the back."

"Stay back," hisses the rear firefighter, whom I do not recognize in the darkness. "We got this handled."

"There are two people in the back—" I begin again.

"Stay back!" And this time he swings his arm around to push us away.

William is trying hard to keep his voice calm. "Look, we don't want the nozzle, we're the squad and there are people trapped—"

"Don't push us forward," the large man screams, and the urgency in his voice makes me step away. The fire must be back there, and he is afraid we'll shove them into it.

I quickly check an adjacent room but there is no access to any other place. Am I missing a door in the dark? Is there a stairway I have not seen? I grab the Cambodian father.

"Is there any other way to the back?"

He points frantically again to the far wall of the room amid a hail of undistinguishable words. "Any . . . other . . . way?" I repeat in that exaggerated, idiotic way that people try to speak through language barriers. "It's your kid, I know—please, can you tell me—" And then I drop his shoulders and say, "Don't worry. We'll get them. I promise."

His eyes pin mine. I push him away from the smoke and darkness toward the outside. *I promise.*

When he has been dragged to the front door, William and I fly down the stairs. We dive into the garage. As my air hose gets caught on the bumper of a car, William melts into the dark ahead of me. *Shit,* I think. *That freelancer.* He's gone. I disentangle myself and crawl farther in. Near the front wheel, William reappears. "Can't get through! All fire!" he yells.

"The rear. Get to the rear," I answer, and we take off again, holding each other's coat sleeves, each pulling the other out of habit, out of impatience, out of urgency.

The way to the back has already been trampled by axes, chain saws, and well-aimed kicks. The neighbors say nothing as we follow the destruction through their house, out to their yard, and through a yawning hole in what was once a neat, tall fence. The smoke in the back is thick, but I can just make out a window above me. But the whole bottom of the house roils in flame. How can we get to that window?

Someone grabs my shoulder and I turn to see another chief, his white helmet gleaming against the flames, beckoning. "There's a lady here who's jumped; we need some medical help for her." Several firefighters surround a ghostly white face. Simultaneously, William reaches and jumps at a fence that lines the other side of the yard. I grab a foot and a knee and push him up. He teeters at the top and then shimmies to a small roof next to the burning building. I grab a chain saw and pass it up to him.

The chief pulls at me again. "Chief," I say, and there is apology in my voice, "we are going for someone else." I half expect him to fire me on the spot. But everyone is trained in medical work, and someone else can take care of the woman. It is our job now to get the baby; William, an astonishingly good firefighter, has managed to get into a good position to cut right into the room from the outside.

I turn my back on the chief and begin to climb the fence to follow William. The chief, yelling cautionary advice, pushes me up the last few inches. "Don't strain yourself, Chief," I manage to joke as I balance against the building. "You're not a firefighter anymore." Who knows where or why we find these vestiges of humor.

"Christ," William mutters. "This roof won't hold." He is balanced precariously on a plastic greenhouselike structure, but manages to expertly start the chain saw anyway. By now I have his belt buckle to steady him, and I crouch on the fence like a gymnast new to the balance beam. "Shit," William yells suddenly above the whine. "The damn wall is metal!" He revs the saw and tries to cut through it anyway, to no avail.

The window is a good five feet away to my left, but I think I might make it if I jump and grab enough sill. "No way," shouts William. "Then I can't back you up in there." He is right, but I know that left to his own devices, he would consider the same thing, and if anyone could do it, he could. I feel more frantic than I want to. I can still see the father's wide eyes and his stretched, grief-stricken face.

Another eight feet away, bordering the greenhouse roof, is a second-floor window into a different house. If we can make it across the flimsy plastic roof by stepping on the wooden beams . . .

William treads carefully and reaches the window. I follow him, but I am less careful. When the roof gives way, I am not thinking that I may get hurt, but that I may not be able to keep my promise. At the last second I wedge my arms out and catch myself on the beams. I hang there for a moment while William yells, "Are you okay?" I assure him I am fine, that I am going to lower myself and climb back up. Meanwhile, I think about the weight I am wearing. Air pack, turnout coat, crash axe, flashlight—fifty or so pounds extra. I hear the anguish in William's voice. "Are you okay?" he keeps saying over and over, unable to see me well in the dark and smoke. I tell him to go on ahead, that there is nothing he can do on this thin, uncertain roof, that I can handle this and meanwhile scream to myself, *You idiot!* I carefully half-slither, half-drop to the ground. There I crouch and quickly assess myself. Nothing broken, just a bruise or two and this tight chest, this pounding heart. Suddenly, my world has narrowed to the dim outline of a baby's body and a quick reassuring sentence—*Don't worry, we'll get them. I promise.* I look once at the sky, murmur something that sounds like a prayer, and force my drenched body up the fence. When I am on the roof again, this time I move gingerly, around the gaping hole I have just made, muttering advice to myself to step slowly, *here, there, now.* When I reach the window, William hauls me in.

A woman—clearly the neighbor—rushes in when she hears the sound of the chain saw. She is aghast when I unceremoniously tip her side table over to make room. William waves for her to step back, his large dark eyes wide, and swings the blade into the wall.

The hole seems to take forever to cut, but it can only be a minute, not longer. I pull at the lath and plaster with my crash axe while William pushes the blade through one house and into the next. I can only think of the small body of a baby waiting on the other side, waiting for this act of desperation to reach her. The woman has backed into a corner and then out the door as if somehow the very posture of us has told her not to try to interfere, even though we are destroying the wall of her bedroom without so much as a "Hello, I'm Caroline and this is William and we need to destroy your house as a last-ditch effort, do you mind?"

I drop my air pack. I scramble to get into the hole. Suddenly, the long beam of a flashlight hits my eyes. *"Fuck,"* I hiss, and almost collapse with exhaustion back into the room. "They're there," I manage to say, leaning against the wall. "They got the fire out and they're getting into the room." William turns away, head down. He lets the saw drop onto the queen-size bed, once neat but now covered with lath, plaster, and wood chips.

The body is found a few minutes later, but not in the room that we had labored so hard to get into. This should have been a consolation, knowing that perhaps there was never a chance, that the baby, really a four-year-old boy, had already fallen down the stairwell to the garage.

But I crawl into the closet, rake through all the furniture in that back room methodically, almost obsessively, and I do not believe that the kid is not there until William points out the small, curved body, like a cashew left in an ashtray, in the garage below us.

I lean against the wall. Could we have saved him? Did I make a wrong step, a wrong turn, a wrong decision? I want to put my head down and weep, partly from exhaustion, partly from the shock of failure. The weight of life and death is heavy, heavier than my dripping turnout coat, or my air pack, or the crash axe in my hand. I think of the father, and his frantic gestures. He had looked to me to save the most important thing in his life and I had failed.

We walk out the front door slowly. William's face, with the kind of sweet, dark good looks that your mother urges you to marry, is frozen in stunned quiet.

There is a crowd outside the front door in the same large semi-circle that must once have ringed the Coliseum as the Christians were fed to the lions, or surrounded the gallows as some hapless sinner was hanged. What is it about tragedy that rouses the blood in us? I step onto the sidewalk. Even though my head is down, I see off to the left three people huddled together. They have a blanket, probably from the Red Cross, over them. A small Cambodian woman is in the middle. Her eyes are unnaturally wide and fixed on me. I stop suddenly. To her right is a man, who has slung an arm around her and wrapped himself into her. To her left is another man whom I immediately recognize. The father. His arm grasps the other two as if they have all become a single person under the flimsy blanket. I know at that moment he recognizes me and something like hope—ridiculous, remote hope—softens his face. I want to say something, but what would it be? "Sorry"?

Sorry, but your son is dead. I hesitate, then turn away; I have said nothing, have not even let my eyes betray that I recognize him. My officer signals to us.

"Hey, the freelancers stayed together," I say to him with a small laugh. "Isn't that something?" I try to laugh again. I feel sick. I do not look back.

Some time later at the grocery store, the cashier looks at my check. "Fire department, huh?" he says. "Great work schedule. Like, you don't work that much, right? Or you watch TV or something. Very cool."

I stare at my groceries and bag them carefully. "Gosh, I'd like to have it that easy," he continues, not maliciously.

I reach for the receipt. For a moment, I think I will say something back to him, something that will explain it all, to him and to me. I see the wide, plaintive eyes of that father, the empty, broken face of the mother.

"Yeah, well, have a good day," I say quietly.

# THE FINAL ALARM

The phone wakes me at eight A.M. I sit up quickly, look around. I am at home, a cat sprawled on my legs. Jesus, I have slept late. I did not sleep well, waking several times for no reason. I get up to answer the phone.

"Caroline. It's Karen." I am surprised to hear from her. A police officer on the night shift, she should be sleeping now. Karen often swings her police car through my neighborhood and quietly checks on my house. Like many police officers, she is certain that the world is a grim and terrible place, and that her friends need to be constantly protected. And like many police officers, she divides people strictly into two categories: the good guys and the bad guys. I, too, used to believe in this simple paradigm, but no longer. The firefighter's world is full of gray areas. Things do not happen according to a moral guidebook but from a combination of luck, choice, and an ineffable element some might call destiny, others God. Whenever I run into Karen, I am secretly and sheepishly glad for the change of perspective, to a world that seems controllable, if only by a gun and a badge.

"Are you okay?" she asks.

"I just woke up," I say, thinking that perhaps my voice sounds slow and flu-like.

"No. I mean, you're okay, right?" There is something odd in her voice.

"Yes, sure." Karen is always protective, but this sounds different. "What do you mean?" The cat I have disturbed winds around my legs. I lean down and run my hand over her fur absently.

"Caroline, there was a big fire last night." Karen pauses, but already, instinctively, I know what she is going to say. I lean against the door. "Some firefighters were killed. One of them was a woman. I thought it might be you. Thank God it isn't."

It had been a stormy night. In fact, it had been the brutal kind of storm that reminds us city dwellers that San Francisco is still a port town, subject to the furies of the ocean. The rain fell hard and copiously. The wind howled at up to sixty miles an hour. Trees shed branches and leaves under the onslaught, and visibility was terrible.

Probationer Cristine Prentice was sent to Station 50. She was teased about the detail; Station 50 is a sleepy station. It sits high on a hill with a beautiful view of downtown and the Bay Bridge. It also overlooks Noe Valley and Station 64's own Mission District. The common joke is that Station 50 will see every fire in the city, even if they never go to any of them. Probationers shouldn't go to Station 50, people laugh, because they might get comfortable and lazy and stay there forever.

A call of an activated residential smoke alarm came in at one o'clock in the morning. The alarm-monitoring company that called the Fire Department Communications Center reported an activated smoke alarm but did not indicate that this was a confirmed fire. As a result, the Communications Center dispatched it as a "2-1 box," which means that a full box or a full first-alarm contingent are judged unnecessary. Engine 50, with probationer Cristine Prentice, rookie Gavin Wong, and Lieutenant Thomas Shore, a veteran of twenty-six years, arrived alone.

The house was set into the hill to maximize the views. The garage was flush with the sidewalk; the rest of the house extended down behind the hill. This is a common design for Bay Area homes, and there seemed nothing unusual, not even smoke, when they pulled up. The owner was backing his Jaguar out of the garage. He said the fire, which had started at an outdoor electrical outlet, had been blown inside by the wind. Attempts to extinguish it had failed, so the family had dialed 911 soon after their alarm company had called. A full-box contingent was on the way. Shore radioed in a "working fire."

Conditions changed dramatically as the crew walked into the house. What was at first a small fire quickly became a large one because the shape of the house acted like a chimney for the high winds that night. As conditions worsened, Shore sent Wong back outside to help pump operator Dan Beckwith. Wong followed the hose through the now-thick smoke, crawling through the blackness, and suddenly hit a solid wall. The hose was still in his hands; what could be the problem? Just moments before, the hose had led outside and to the engine. Now the unthinkable had happened.

The garage door had closed.

Meanwhile, Truck 72 was at a call for a wire down just a few blocks away. The storm was playing havoc with the streets, but Truck 72 could find no problem wire. Just then, the call for a full box went over the radio. Because Truck 72 had been dispatched on this "wire down" call, they were not called to the fire, though they would have been otherwise. Nick was the temporary lieutenant today, and he grabbed the radio phone. Like all firefighters, Truck 72 wanted to go to a fire, and besides, they were only a few blocks away. However, to prevent rogue crews from arriving at fires, the dispatch center does not take kindly to requests to change initial dispatches. This is understandable; crews might leave medical or other scenes early in order to get to a fire. Truck 72 was curtly told that they were not dispatched to the fire. Nick and his crew drove to the fire anyway.

There was no truck when they arrived. They noticed nothing wrong with Engine 50. Pump operator Beckwith was at the pump control panel, which was faced away from the garage. Beckwith could not see the disaster that had just happened.

From here on the stories that fly around the firehouse vary. John Benoit, who prophesies doom, heard what he thought were cries for help and later he said, with his head in his hand, that he knows that it was Cristine's voice. Someone else said that Gavin Wong's hand was sticking out of a grate he had kicked out. Everybody said that the smoke was so heavy around the garage that you could not see the door.

Someone began yelling that there was a crew inside. People rushed at the door with axes. The smoke was so thick they could only take a few swings before retreating for air. Then they would lunge back in. From the roof, Nick saw Benoit start a large circular saw and walk straight into the smoke. This was a forbidden, dangerous move, and Nick was stunned. Only then did he realize that Engine 50 was down, inside.

They got the door open. Two turnout coats were barely visible on the right side, another one on the left. There is nothing so terrible, Nick later told me, than seeing a firefighter down. "Those black and yellow coats, man, motionless. Just motionless," he said. In heavy smoke and fire, the crews dragged out Shore, Wong, and Cristine.

Here was Nick's personal nightmare—*burns, man*—right in front of him. Shore, his face badly burnt, was still. He did not respond at all. John Fisher, who was working that night, initiated CPR and stayed with it all the way to the hospital, even though he knew that Shore had died in the garage. You just don't give up if it is a firefighter. You hold on, ridiculously, to hope. You keep doing CPR until they pull you off.

Cristine and Gavin were both responsive. Gavin walked around in a small circle, dazed. Cristine, initially unconscious, waved off help. "Take care of the others," she said. "I'm fine." But Nick, a paramedic, saw immediately that she was badly burned and in imminent respiratory danger. She had inhaled superheated gases and seared her lungs.

"She is *not* fine," Nick yelled. "Get her to the hospital *NOW*."

On a video that a civilian filmed I see Nick pulling the gurney with Cristine on it. He has a determined expression on his face; his large eyes look enormous. His helmet is off and his hair is plastered to his forehead. The rain is torrential. The wind is so high that people lean far forward as they run, straining against an invisible force. The trees whip around frantically; embers are flying everywhere. I imagine Benoit staring up at the sky and wondering how he could have miscalculated. It was not September 9, but surely this was Armaggedon. Later, someone who had been in Vietnam said that the fire was the worst thing he had ever seen. Worse than a strafing, he said.

Sharks and burns. Firefighters down. A nightmare come true.

I call Station 64 immediately. They tell me the news: Cristine is in critical condition and she is not expected to live. Lieutenant Thomas Shore is dead. Gavin Wong, though burned on his hands and neck, will survive.

There is no one else in my house except the cats, who watch me warily as I begin to cry. I cry at first as if trying to expel the tightness in my belly, and then with a flood of grief that makes me wonder who I am really crying for—them or myself.

I wonder if Cristine regretted it, being a firefighter. Maybe a little, just at the moment when the heat overtook them. I wonder how I would feel, if I would regret it.

Cristine is not only another woman, she is a probationer at my station. Though I did not know her well, the fire department has taught me about inherent loyalties. A few years ago, I would have kept my grief to myself. But I have learned much since then. Still, I do not know what to do. Firefighters are being told not to go to the hospital. Otherwise, it would be packed. For all I know, Cristine has already died. I take a few deep breaths and pick up the phone. There is one person to call, one person who will know what to do.

Patricia answers cheerily. I am determined not to cry on the phone—Patricia is the last person I want to cry in front of—but I can only get out a "Hello, Patricia?" before I have to stop. She clearly has not heard about the fire yet.

"Go to the hospital," she says. She, too, is in shock. She did not know Wong or Cristine, but she knows Lieutenant Shore. "A real gentleman," she murmurs. "Go to the hospital," she says again. "Who the fuck cares that they said not to? This is about another firefighter."

Patricia is right, once again.

A small waiting room has been set up. The food spread out by the Local is untouched, but coffee flows freely. Everyone looks terrible. People hug or touch elbows. Through the grief and the shock, I realize that something feels different inside me. I have felt that I am part of the Rescue Squad and part of Station 64. But today I feel, for perhaps the first time, unequivocally a part of the San Francisco Fire Department.

Joe McGinnis, of the union, walks up to me. He is a handsome man with exuberant gestures. Even now his energy is uncontainable, though his eyes are red and swollen. He shakes my hand in wide, earnest arcs.

"We need to contact Cristine's friends, her family. We know she has a sister in Connecticut and there is a brother on the way." He lowers his voice. "But does she have a, you know, girlfriend we should call?" He stares at me earnestly. "This whole thing is unbelievable, with Tommie and . . ." His voice trails off. He blinks.

Jonathan Hunt is here, and he makes his way quickly to me.

"How's Cristine?" I ask.

"It doesn't look good. Second-degree burns and some third-degree over fifty percent of her body. The second-degree can still revert to third—it is all still burning in there. The lungs are the big problem. They took X-rays. Good lungs are black and bad lungs come up gray. About twenty percent of her lungs are white."

Stories are whirling around now, competing versions of the same incident. They weren't wearing air packs. They were, but they didn't use them. Wong lived because he turned his air pack down to save air (this last statement is obviously incorrect; the new air packs do not have a regulatory valve, though the old ones did). Cristine Prentice pulled her mask off in a panic before her air was out. The owner in the Jaguar closed the garage door by accident. The fire shorted the wires out, and the garage door closed. The firefighters leaned on the inside button as they entered the house; they closed the door unwittingly and sealed their fate.

There is no way to know the true story yet. Gavin and Cristine are unconscious. Thomas Shore is dead. A full investigation will happen later. Still, there is something comforting in trying to make sense of it all. There, we could say. That's why.

The intensive-care staff is patient with the growing crowd in the halls. Firefighters keep showing up. The long vigil begins.

At Station 50, there is already a black wreath on the door. The flag is at half-mast. A television crew pulls up as I get out of my car. The camera operator aims his camera at the station. He zooms in on the wreath. Another man primps in the side mirror of the television van, ready to translate this tragedy into catchy sound bites.

The communications room mills with firefighters, both on- and off-duty. The phone rings incessantly. One firefighter blinks hard as he greets me, but the captain of the station lets tears stream down his face unchecked. He hugs me and asks about Cristine, wiping his face with one hand.

"It looks bad," I say. "She's been given last rites." This is true; the department chaplain, fearing her imminent death, has administered them by the hospital bed. Unfortunately, Cristine is decidedly not Catholic. Perhaps, from her distant place in a coma, this last-minute conversion strikes her as funny, or at least ironic. Perhaps, on the other hand, she is angry that she is being given up on so easily.

I came here for Cristine's belongings, so I walk reluctantly into the dorm. Her gear bag is in the corner, as if she will come back any minute and pack it up. Her sleeping bag is pushed aside, and I imagine that she was quick to get out of her bunk and into her turnout gear. She was an eager, earnest probationer. This was her dream job.

I gather her stuff. As I pass through the apparatus floor, I catch sight of three sets of dirty, wet turnout gear strewn on the floor. Air packs are nearby. I turn my head away. I have caught a glimpse of ghosts, and I do not want to see any more. As I leave, more television vans pull up.

Cristine does not die the first day. On the second day the intensive-care staff allows firefighters to enter two at a time and stand at the glass windows of each of the rooms. I decline. Only by mid-afternoon, when about twelve female firefighters have gathered, do I decide to go in. We ask for a few minutes with Cristine. The head nurse nods. "Only a few minutes, though," she adds. She is large and imposing, and she crosses her arms across her bosom as she speaks.

We stand at the glass. Nothing could prepare us for this sight. Cristine is heavily bandaged. Her face is grotesquely swollen and bright-red and shiny, as if just polished. She is hooked up to an immense number of tubes and machines. They blink and squirm monotonously. I try to interpret the meaning of the numbers they show, though I know that my rudimentary medical skills are not up to it. Tears run down our faces, but nothing is said. Even Amy, never at a loss for words, is silent. Behind us is Gavin's intensive-care room, but curtains are drawn over the glass. As we turn to leave, each one of us stops in front of his glass for a moment. We stare at the curtains. I want to scream something to a power I doubt can even exist. *Fuck you* is one option. *Why?* is another. Either would shatter the stillness of this place.

Captain Trent Lee is out in the hall. I am relieved. He inspires confidence, and his low, calm manner, laced with his signature sarcasm, makes him a soothing presence. He quickly begins to make sure that Cristine's family is taken care of.

Cristine's mother is almost seventy. She has flown in

from Hawaii and has the exhausted, drawn expression any parent would have at this moment. She is accompanied by Cristine's best friend, who has extremely short dyed hair and a ring through her lower lip. More of Cristine's friends arrive. Their hair, too, is dyed in various colors and they wear rings through their noses or lips. It is a strange scene: uniformed personnel dispersed among orange-haired, multi-tattooed, pierced women and men. Two subcultures, vastly different, meeting and mingling. *Only in the fire department,* I think as I watch Trent nod and extend a hand to a petite woman with a mermaid tattooed on her forearm.

I tell my family. My father inhales sharply, and I know he has gone pale on the other end of the phone line. He is silent, just as he was when I first told him about the fire department. This time, he does not think about "phases." He thinks about losing his daughter, but he does not say this. He says "Be careful" before we hang up, but he does not mention today, as he usually does, that I give him all the gray hairs that he has. Today it would not be funny. It would be too close to the truth.

Cris has made it through the first thirty-six hours. This is a miracle, though the head doctor pulls me aside and shakes his head. "We are not telling the family this," he says. "But it won't be long now."

At this moment someone else from Truck 72 pushes out of the intensive-care doors. He wipes his eyes. "I just stood there and stood there," he murmurs, shaking his head. "Tears falling like crazy."

The funeral for Thomas Shore is held in a large white church, with a marble patio half a city block long. Here most of the off-duty department gathers, boots finely polished and dress jackets pressed. It is raining hard, so people mill around the sprawling staircase, or snap umbrellas shut and walk into the church. When the wind picks up, I am reminded of the storm that started all this. I am an usher today; Amy and I will seat Shore family friends. White gloves are passed around, and emergency workers begin to walk into the rain to line up in long, dark rows. There are thousands, many from other fire departments around the state. Police officers have come, because Lieutenant Shore's son is a police officer, but there are also highway patrol personnel, sheriffs, paramedics, and retired city workers. The expanse in front of the church is now almost full, the dark rows of personnel striping the marble like a flag.

I smile and nod to the people I know—almost everyone from the San Francisco Fire Department. *Six years,* I think. Even those I only recognize murmur greetings. There is an unspoken, collective understanding of what each of us might face at any time.

*Coulda been me,* our minds whisper. A different shift, a different station, a different detail. Each of us calculates the distance between ourselves and that fateful day. For some, the distance is small. For me, it was a shift away. In fact, next shift I am up for the detail, though I do not know it yet, and I will be sent to Station 50. *Oooh,* fellow firefighters will tease, *the bad-luck detail from Station 64,* and I will wave nonchalantly and laugh, too. For others, especially the two firefighters at 50 who were replaced by Gavin and Cris, that fateful day was very close indeed.

"Hey," someone says. It is Ritch, from my academy class, his long hand lightly on my elbow, nodding slowly. His cap is slightly off kilter. It makes him look young. "Good to see you," he says.

His narrow blue eyes are expressionless. He pauses and I know what we are both thinking. *Glad you didn't eat it, kick the can, bite the big one, blow the pop top, crash and burn, terminate, deactivate . . .*

"How's Rescue 3?" he asks.

*. . . amp out, lose the lolly, bite it, catch the crispy . . .*

"Good, good. It's home now." I smile slowly.

*. . . DOA, rigor out, decease, pass on . . .*

"We're getting on, that's for sure."

*. . . pass away . . .*

"Yup. Shoot. It's been six years."

*. . . die.*

I watch him walk away. He had promised once that it would be simple. "Little fire, little hose. Big fire, big hose"; it has never been that easy.

I watch Thomas, who has always looked out for me, shake rain from his sleeve. Then there is Chief Kalafferty, who without hesitation bent every department rule on the strength of my word. Across a pew, Chief Masters waves. He looks tired. He goes to the hospital every shift to bring food to the Prentice family and friends. Other firefighters, too, arrive with food, their crisp, straight creases and belted pants incongruous against the loose leather jackets and baggy jeans of Cristine's friends.

As the casket is lifted from the back of Engine 50, a bell, signaling the final alarm of Lieutenant Thomas Shore, is tolled. The resonance of each ring rolls over us for a long time, while we hold a salute. The rain continues.

With each toll, I imagine Thomas Shore's soul rising upward a little higher. On the final toll, I strain to hear the last wisp of sound as the casket, with his helmet placed on it, comes slowly up the marble aisle. The firefighters who carry it are tight faced and pale. Some cry openly.

The service is short and somber. The church, the largest I have ever seen, is overflowing with mourners.

At this moment, Engine 50's pump operator is on the other side of the city. He is found stumbling around in the rain, crying, at the scene of the fire. The house is now silent, girded with yellow police tape. Flowers lie at the garage door.

At the end of the service, the firefighters and police officers file out. Amy and I follow, taking our places once more in the long, straight rows. The color guard calls out a command, and a salute thousands of hands long snaps to attention. The coffin makes its slow way back to Engine 50 as taps is played.

Now the long, thin cry of the siren begins. It is the sound we hear every day, as familiar to us as a telephone ring to a business executive. It never fails to raise the hair at the back of my neck, to race my heart. Today I get the chill again, but there is a mixture of melancholy and apprehension. I close my eyes. Do we take the job precisely because we might die? Or in spite of the possibility? Perhaps it is a perfect balance of both.

People ask me if I still want to do this work. I think that it is an odd question. We go into this career knowing that death and injury are inherent possibilities. Today is not a surprise. My feelings about fire will not change, nor will I be more fearful of it. I have always known its potential to ravage and destroy. However, the constant possibility of serious injury or death has changed me. I am no longer as reckless as I once was. I understand more about life—its transient, wispy quality, the way it can so easily fade. In this job I have seen that the insight I sought so fervently in my twenties is close at hand and comes with compassion more than adrenaline, with open-mindedness more than adventure. People like Kalafferty, Masters, Jackie, and Trent Lee have shown me this.

An old-timer said to me once, years ago, it seems, "You gotta be scared of fire. Anyone tells you they ain't scared of fire, they're either lying or they've never really been in a good one. Gotta be scared by it, because then you'll respect it. Then you'll live to fu— excuse me, sleep with your wife, play with the kids—smell the flowers, as they say." This is fire's most important lesson.

The casket is lifted and laid in the hose bed. The siren continues. Even when we drop our salute—two thousand swishes of wool sleeves slapped against thighs—no one moves.

The procession is hundreds of rigs long. It travels slowly—this is the way grief moves. People stop on the sidewalk, pushing their umbrellas back to look. Homeless people stop their swaddled shopping carts. If they are military vets, they snap to a perfect salute and stand that way until the whole procession passes. Mothers lean to their children, whispering. The children stare, chewing on their hands, wide-eyed.

"A firefighter died," they will say. "In a big, bad fire. See, sweetheart, all the lights? A firefighter died and this is a very sad day."

Police and parking-control officers stop traffic and then swivel around to pay their respects. People twist in their cars to see. The procession is silent, a long line of flashing lights, but I imagine I hear the slow, insistent wail of Engine 50. As they make their way to the burial ground, fire engines wait at each overpass. The casket passes underneath, and each new engine crew responds overhead with a long, silent salute. The emergency beacons glint like halos, with the slow, solemn pulse of a last alarm.

# FULL CIRCLE

It had been a bad day, and then the building collapsed.

I feel better after watching it fall. It falls with a kind of outraged dignity—first the inside in bits and pieces, jerkily and unwilling, and then the outside with a huge crash. My crew was first in on the west side, and I was on the nozzle—you can't beat that. It was a bad morning, but now I feel better.

I have the kind of cold that makes my nose sag and my throat heavy. Right at the shift change this morning the Bee-Bop sounded; it was for a person with AIDS over on Mariposa Street. Later, when I left the Mariposa Street apartment, I was worried about my stuffed-up nose and the man inside was still curled over in agony. All we could do was put an oxygen mask onto his face. It started to rain.

"That's the sort of place you gotta breathe shallow in, ya know?" someone once said, back when AIDS was still a fairly new phenomenon. He said this without missing a beat, his right hand bending down to his shoe and applying a thick layer of polish. He had washed his hands as soon as he got back to the station, changed his shirt and shaken out his turnout coat. "They say you can't get it by being close," he had added. "But they all lie. All of them. You just can't be too careful."

Things have changed now. There is less fear, and more awareness. There is also more protection for the fire-fighter—gloves, masks, and adequate information. AIDS has hit San Francisco hard, but it is not just the gay population that gets it. This disease is open to everyone, straights and non-drug-users, too. I have seen a sixty-year-old grandmother with AIDS; all we could do was put an oxygen mask on her as well.

Now I want to wash this morning's image out of my mind, the image of that drawn, wasted body, with the skin that looks like crackly paper. The mother, gray-haired and bulbous, had put her hand lightly on my arm. She picked up my helmet for me as we turned to leave, and cried into my shoulder.

I think of Mrs. Prentice, standing vigil over her daughter. Cris is still in the hospital. She survived the critical first forty-eight-hour window. Since then, she has also survived pneumonia, pancreatitis, lung collapse, and burn infection. Before work this morning, I stop by the emergency room to check on Cris's mother and her friends, who keep a twenty-four-hour-a-day vigil. They talk, sing, and laugh to her. They rub her feet and hands. They play her favorite music, from Al Green to Johnny Cash. The intensive-care staff encourages this—all part of the healing process, they say. If you watch through the glass, you can see Mrs. Prentice nodding to Cash's "A Boy Named Sue." When I walk into the small room that the hospital has given the family to sleep in, I startle Cris's mother. She thinks I am a nurse arriving with bad news. She sits up from the sofa, disheveled from the night before. She greets me with a smile, then puts her head in her hands and weeps in convulsing movements. No mother should endure this, I think. Day in and day out—a month now—she watches her daughter, mutilated and unconscious, unreachable.

I arrive back at the station. I check the pockets of my turnout coat. It's all there—the hose spanner, the carabiners, the extra rubber gloves, the small paper medical mask, and the work gloves. There is also a prusic loop, ready to loop around a rope, and a piece of webbing pre-tied to become a quick seat in case we have to pick someone off of a ledge or a cliff. There are batteries, size D, perfect for throwing at windows for ventilation. And—a new addition—a portable air-filter mask, good in case my air pack fails. I will have to remind myself to sling it around my neck before every full box. On my belt are medical scissors. Next to them is a knife that Alberto gave me. It is more than a knife—it is a good-luck charm. I am ready, packed like the tool chest of a slightly deranged carpenter.

I head for the coffeepot with a nod at Alan. Paul pats the sofa beside him and I sit down, holding the coffee I will hardly touch. Today I will drive, because Miller is not here. I remember that it is Joe's day off as well. I wonder who our officer will be. I sit down at a table and glance at the Rescue officer's desk. I almost choke on my small sip of coffee.

Todd Lane stands there. I have only seen him three times since I left Station 4, and that was at fires where I could duck my chin into my collar and slide behind a rig. If I could not avoid him, I turned my head away, without a word. But I would recognize him anywhere. He is stamped indelibly on my mind.

"Who's the squad boss today?" I ask Paul. Paul is on the engine, so he is not likely to know. I want to ask Alan, but I do not want him to see that I am bothered. He knows about the trouble with Todd Lane; he was there that day. As a pro-bationer, all he could do was watch in silence, but later he quietly shook his head.

"Lane, I think," Paul says.

"Uh-huh," I say, as casually as possible.

Lane looks up from the desk. He walks toward the kitchen, frowning. He holds the list of today's squad mem-bers in his hand. I know that he is trying to figure out who his driver and his emergency medical technician for the day will be. I should be driving, but this would mean that I would spend the whole day in the cab, with him sitting next to me. This seems unthinkable, to have only a gear shift between me and the person who has, for all these years, symbolized to me the narrow-mindedness and fear of this institution. On the other hand, why should I let Todd Lane run my life? I want to drive. If I do not drive because he is there, then he wins.

Forget it. I'm not going to drive. I want to be as far away from him as possible. My stomach feels tight and my throat is dry, even after all these years. Alan can drive and I will be in the back as the EMT, a thick wall of steel and noise between us. Todd Lane is a loutish, malicious person.

Lane stops at the head of the table, interrupting my thoughts. He looks the same, heavy-jowled and angrily mustached.

"Who's on the squad?" he asks. Alan waves in response.

"I am, too," I say. Lane looks back with a slight quizzical air. He hesitates and then says, "And you are . . . ?"

He does not know my name. Momentarily, this astounds me. I have affixed his every mean feature in my head, would recognize his every arrogant gesture from one hundred yards away. There is only one incident between us, and I cannot even repeat it to people without a profound physiological change coming over me. I feel myself become pale, and the prickly beginnings of sweat start at my collar. My voice becomes tight and my eyes go flat. The incident is vivid in my mind, and the emotions associated with it remain etched in my psyche. He has affected the way I interact with the department. But he does not even remember who I am.

"I'm the driver today," I say.

Today's rain falls in a small, grim spray that makes the hot May day seem heavier and hotter. Soon it stops. The sky breaks blue. I wrestle with whether to talk to Lane at all; maybe I will just maintain a stony silence. Let him be uncomfortable for a while. I practice various versions of *Okay, asshole, why were you so hateful four years ago?*

I have been taught that politeness is next to godliness, and I decide that I would suffer more than he from a stony silence. I settle for a tone that is businesslike and sentences that are short and to the point. But I will not succumb to the almost irresistible urge to be "nice," the need to be liked. Todd Lane will not play on my insecurities a second time.

"We need batteries for a flashlight, and we can go without gas for the rig today," is all I tell him.

The morning is quiet, and we head into the afternoon with no calls at all. This is highly unusual for Rescue 3, especially on a hot day. Fate, God, and Lady Luck all seem to agree: No sense in my having to be in the cab with him.

At the kitchen table a listless game of Pidro is played. I enjoy watching the men play cards, but I am not at all interested in the game; instead, I like to watch their hands. They hold their cards softly and jealously, as they might the fingers of a lover. I like these hands, especially the stubby fingers. They look like the heads of hammered copper rivets nailed onto big rough palms. I admire the ableness of those hands and the wear of the fingers through the years. They tell an important story to the younger generation of this tribe that I am now a part of. I wonder how the wear of fire fighting will tell on my fingers. Many people wonder how women's bodies in general will stand up to the physical demands of the job. In this culture, men become ornery, gray, and wiry. Women just become fragile. Supposedly.

The glide of the cards continues. I am intrigued by the intensity around the table, though the game is slow and methodical. There is talk of the latest diet bet going on. Who can lose twenty pounds in a month? In the final week, participants start to panic. They cut out liquor. They jog in layers of heavy clothing around the station house. The ones who were smart enough to weigh in with five large eight-ounce glasses of water in them and a full bladder try to think up new tricks. If someone on your shift is in the diet bet, you cook his favorite meal that night and snicker while he watches everyone eat it from behind his glass of SlimFast.

Finally, at five-thirty in the afternoon, a call comes in. It is a shooting at the housing projects. Luckily, there is no time to talk as we dodge and duck in and out of afternoon traffic, sirens and airhorn blaring. When the patient has been "packaged," extra hands are needed in the ambulance to help the paramedics on the way to the hospital. Lane and I will follow in the rig.

"That is where my old high school was," Lane says, pointing. I nod and let out a sound in my throat that I want to be acknowledgment but not interest. "Sure seems like a long time ago," he adds. He seems to be trying to be pleasant, but then again, I will not be a fool this time. Luckily, there is little more to say, because we are at the hospital. Alan and Riley hop on and we head back to Station 64, which is only five minutes or so away.

A full box comes in within half an hour. *Many phone calls,* the dispatcher adds, and we know that it will be good—*big.* And we are right; we see the smoke from the bottom of the hill, still ten blocks away. We already know what the first engine to arrive radios in: "Working fire and give us a second alarm!"

The building—a paint factory—is "fully involved" when we pull up; large billows of smoke belch from the roof, and flames have already broken through. Lane is not used to the gear of a *skwwwaaaadee,* and I notice with satisfaction that he has entangled himself in the officer's belt and not yet thrown on his air pack. I will not wait for him; I enter the warehouse next to the paint factory. Its wide, roll-up doors have been flung open, and it is crowded with cardboard boxes. With an axe in one hand and a nozzle in the other, I clamber up the stacks of boxes and toward the lath and plaster wall. If we get through the wall, we can get water on the fire and, we hope, advance to its seat.

I begin to chop at the lath and plaster, cradling the nozzle between my knees. It is awkward, but it works. The wall shears off easily, revealing metal corrugation underneath. I swing at the metal, but someone yells my name. Todd Lane stands there with a chain saw.

He is known for his work with a chain saw as someone else might be known for facility with a gun. Sure enough, he is confident and precise, and the corrugation sags with each quick cut. I stand to one side, ready with the nozzle in case of fire right behind the wall. It is not lost on me, this sudden camaraderie. Lane may not think a woman can do this job, but he knows that if there is fire behind the wall, I am the one he must rely on.

When the flames leap through, and they do, with vehemence, we see that the paint factory is completely enveloped. There will be no entrance here.

A third alarm is pulled and the roof begins to collapse. The loud sounds of exploding paint rat-tat the air. By now, we have moved deeper into the warehouse, chopping holes in the corrugation and sending streams of water in. Todd Lane is nearby, but I doubt he even notices me. We know the paint factory is lost. Our goal is to contain the fire now and to save the warehouse and the residences on the south side.

More paint explodes nearby. Everyone ducks. Thick black smoke shrouds the nearby freeway. Traffic comes to a standstill. Long white rivers of paint stream down the streets. A fourth alarm is pulled.

The warehouse we are in is a large, open space with only skeletal partitions. An open staircase leads to a platform with rudimentary railings. Next to this is an open attic space that provides perfect access to the paint factory, now burning virulently. With a slightly higher angle on the fire, perhaps the hose can beat back the flames. But this, we realize, is wishful thinking. Aiming a small line on this paint-fueled fire is clearly inadequate.

A further inconvenience is that the floor is not a floor, but ribs of wood surrounded by fiberglass insulation. This means that we must swing our axes while balancing on the stripes of two-by-fours.

The rest of the fire goes like this: chop holes, find a hose line, aim it into the paint factory, which vents easily now. Most visibility problems come from the steam of the master streams that rain down from the aerial ladders. The flames persist. As firefighters say to describe a good greater alarm, "There is enough fire for everyone."

I squat by a hole I have made with the large, powerful circular saw. There is not much to see because of the steam, but I can hear. Fire like this sounds like an oncoming train. The building creaks and groans and cracks. Every so often more paint explodes, sending what looks like fireworks into the air. Timbers give way with muffled thumps, and the metal corrugation whines as it bends. Every so often, too, the air will clear slightly and I will make out the gangly remains of the structure. It is defeated now, splayed out and tired.

I have left my air pack far behind, but I remember the respirator in my pocket. It helps some, and when the roof is mostly collapsed, it allows me to crawl into the factory with a hose. Even with the respirator, however, I can feel that toxic edge to the fumes. Tomorrow, health officials will assure the public that there was nothing dangerous in the air, no need to worry about airborne contaminants. I know differently: My throat stings in a special way and my eyes feel swollen and sore. Every so often I cannot breathe at all.

The paint keeps exploding, but now with less vigor. I stay perched in my peculiar doorway, which is badly cut because I do not have the tool skills that Lane has. I watch the remains of the building heave and sigh. And there is something else, too, a hard space inside me, heavy and sealed like the paint cans, that splits and begins to leak away. A crew from Station 27 wanders by. They pick up hose and kick through the ankle-deep water to check for sunken equipment—axes, ceiling hooks, air packs. Patricia is their pump operator today—she is four blocks away at a hydrant. I laugh. From her vantage point, all she will see is the smoke rise and change color according to whether her colleagues are winning or losing the battle. She will be fretful that she can only watch.

"Tell her she missed a good one," I tell her crew, knowing that my remark will further infuriate her. The thought makes me smile. I look back at the stricken warehouse. There is something about a fire that saps anger. It is replaced with something closer to a state of grace.

It had been a bad day, until the building collapsed. I feel better now, watching it fall.

There is nothing more to do except make my way to the front and reconnect with my crew. Lane is already there, making one last hole in a wall. It seems that he is soldered to this saw. I steady the metal for him while he cuts. Paint streams from the factory, thick and white. This fire will smolder for a long time, and crews will be posted on "fire watch" all night and into the next day. For now the squad's job is over. Lane and I straighten up and stare at the factory, now only a vast space full of debris. Darkened, splintered posts hint of the structure it was. The building beside it is intact except for the many holes gnawed out of one side. Behind, the two-story houses that abutted the factory have long black streaks of fire damage down their sides. But they remain standing.

"Good job," says Lane, nodding my way.

Perhaps it is the adrenaline still kinked inside the interstitial places. Perhaps fire simply wipes away small cautions. Or is it the sheer joy of watching something so huge and powerful coil and bellow and leap so close to you, like a beautiful animal in the wild? Whatever the reason, I turn to him and look him straight in the eye.

"You're joking, right?" I say. I shake and laugh, almost delighted. "After all, you hate me. You once told everyone you wanted to make my life miserable, and in your small way, you did."

He looks shocked. There is a pause, and then his face changes as recognition hits. Before he can respond, Masters walks up. "Squad, go home," he says, nodding at the both of us. "And great job."

In the cab of the rig, Lane clears his throat.

"You know," he says. He looks at the dashboard. He speaks slowly. "I'm not excusing what I may have done, but, women coming in, it was hard."

I stare straight ahead.

"This might sound odd," he continues, "but the fire department was the best men's club in the world. And then women came in and it all changed. It was not easy. Change is not easy." He pauses. "But I'm different now. I've changed. You've got to change—more women are in and they're going to keep coming in. I see men who refuse to change, who hang on and they are bitter and it's killing them, eating them up. I'm different now."

I nod. I am suspicious. Why should I listen to him? He sounds sincere, but he may go back to Station 4 and laugh.

Remember that girl, he will say, that girl—what's her name? And he will tell the whole story as if I am an idiot.

"I think I get along pretty well with some of the women." He sounds slightly confused. "Maybe some of the old-time women, the women who first got in, they hate me, but what can you do? I have a son now; he's two years old. And women come up to me and say, 'Hey, Todd, how's your son?' "

I flick the emergency lights on and veer left across the street to back into the station. They throw a blink of color across the firehouse. We back in and I cut the engine. He stares at me and for the first time, I realize that he is a handsome man.

"I'm not like I was. I'm not proud of everything I've done."

"Okay," I answer slowly. "I believe you. I appreciate your telling me."

Without another word, we exit the cab. I begin to take off the dirty tools and switch the tanks on the air packs.

Alan walks up. You cannot get much by him. "Everything okay?" he asks, turning on a hose to help me clean the equipment, which smells sour with paint and ash. "I know you two don't get along too well," he adds quietly.

"You won't believe what happened," I say. And I tell him.

Alan shakes his head. "And you believe him? People don't just change like that," he says.

"You know, I am the last person to trust Todd Lane. Or to like him. But yes, I believe him. I can't say why, exactly, but I do."

Alan frowns and shrugs. We go back to wiping off tools and air packs, and hosing our boots down.

An hour and a half later, the other crews start drifting back. There is much milling around, tellings and retellings of the fire. Everyone's skin is streaked with black and white, and everyone's hair is awry. Suddenly, from the Rescue desk, Todd Lane beckons me over.

He hitches his pants and clears his throat. "Listen," he

says, his voice low. "Is it too late, four years too late, to say I'm sorry?"

Funny, when you wait for a moment for years, and then there it is and you can't think of anything to say and, worse, you can't even summon up the kind of satisfaction you thought you would feel. Instead, there is only relief, and something else, an inner quietness perhaps. "No," I say. "It's never too late." I watch as Lane walks away, wiping paint and ash off his hair.

# EPILOGUE

I feel my skin burn, but I do not move. It will not be a bad one, and besides, I am up front with the nozzle. Someone is yelling to back out, but I feel fine; I already know how I will bail out if more hell breaks loose. The stairwell banister is to my right and it will not be so bad a fall. The air is hot and I guess that just a few feet above me it has reached about one thousand degrees, so I lie down completely flat, which is when I feel the burn on both shins. Embers, perhaps. Or steam from the heated water.

I don't know who is behind me. It does not matter. They are doing a good job relieving the weight of the hose. In front of me, it sounds as if a giant rock slide is beginning, and the entire room reaches that viscous orange texture familiar to anyone who has stared closely and deeply at a campfire. The space around me dances and screams. The water falls back in rumbles and roars. The heat is suffocating.

I start to smile.

I took the line out of the firefighter's hands as he crouched on the sidewalk, too far from the building, really, for an aggressive attack. He did not have gloves on. I pointed this out to him and then reached for the nozzle, as if doing him a favor.

"Put on your gloves," I hissed. I acted astonished at this breach of safety, and then snatched the nozzle and dragged the hose toward the stairwell. Right inside the doorway it became dark almost immediately, except for the streams of flame that fell with the wood from the walls above. I had time to think how beautiful it was before some of the roof fell in, too, and knocked me and my newly gloved partner back momentarily. But we moved quickly up the stairs after this, spraying into the eerie, luminescent darkness unique to a good, hot fire. Which is how I find myself here, with the fire in front of me, roaring. Here, amidst the incredible heat, the angry, twisting beauty, and the sharp feeling below my knees.

Later I will find out that the fire got around us, and behind. It does not matter now, and it is perhaps better that I do not know. Someone from Station 64 falls through the roof. He hangs there while truckies scramble to grab him. I do not see any of this, and later, when he tells the story, he acts as if it is nothing. He laughs that his large belly stopped his fall. "Food saved my life," he says. We laugh, too, but we know that he is lucky. We are all lucky.

Cris is out of her coma. Despite terrible odds, she is alive. But she is blind.

She shouldn't even have lived, the doctors say. It is a miracle. The burns up her legs are bad, though in time they will heal. Her eyes will not. She goes from the darkness of the garage to the darkness of a coma and now to a new darkness. Crazily enough, all she wants is to be a firefighter again. This seems impossible, but who knows? She's tough. She has beaten all the odds before.

She hangs out with two retired firefighters. They got into the San Francisco Fire Department just after the Second World War, almost fifty years ago, back when it was unthinkable that a woman could do the job. Cris's friends have drifted away, as friends do when the drama of tragedy is over and the monotony of tragedy begins, but these retired firefighters are different. They call her every few days. "Hey, Cris, hiya," they say. "Let's have dinner tomorrow." Other times, they take her for walks. They go slowly, because her legs are still wrapped in bandages, and I have seen them put their arms out protectively when they think that she might fall. It does not matter to them that Cris is a woman. She is a firefighter. To them, she is a member of their own big-armed, chain-smoking, hard-drinking crew.

The firefighters at Lieutenant Shore's station finished work on a house for his wife. It was a house in the country that Lieutenant Shore had started to build and had planned to retire to.

Station 4 raised one thousand dollars for Cris.

Life goes on here at Station 64. The largest station in San Francisco, it is a good mix of men, women, blacks, whites, Asians, Hispanics, and "other." September 9 came and went; the world remained intact, despite the predictions of John Benoit. The endless cycle of birth, life, and death continues in the Mission District, and everywhere else.

The fire triangle has finally been changed to the fire tetrahedron, or so I saw in a recent fire magazine.

The San Francisco Fire Department has its first black chief, appointed by the city's first black mayor.

San Francisco's Department of Public Health will soon merge into the fire department. This means that ambulances will be stationed in firehouses and that paramedic work will become part of the fire department. A lot of firefighters are unhappy about this, including me. What about fires? we moan. What about the good old days?

Change is hard, after all.

There is talk of closing down some firehouses altogether. Money, as usual. I hope that San Franciscans won't allow it. It's like canceling the insurance policy. Everyone says, "It won't happen to me." And then it does, and each minute counts.

Alexandra will soon leave *Baywatch*. She likes her work there, but her agents tell her it is time to move on. The producers want to marry her character off, but she insists on death during a rescue and poignant last words. Jonathan moves on, too, to Oregon. He is deep in the backcountry, living near both Earth First! environmentalists and radical white separatists. He is happy, powering his life with solar panels and hydropower from a nearby creek. He organizes anti-logging demonstrations.

My mother and I talk every couple of weeks or so. I like it when she visits. We are making up for lost time. My father calls every other day. He tells me again that I gave him all his gray hairs. I tell him that Alexandra and Jonathan deserve equal credit.

The burn on my legs is not so bad, just blisters that rise and then wither in a few weeks. There are worse burns. I stare at the dark patches and know that in some perverse way I am glad for the way the moment has marked me. It is a moment when in the dark and heat, life is finally precious. Finally, for me, it is truly and deeply felt.

As for this book, it began as a story of an institution and the people who changed it. But really, it is about the way the institution and its struggles changed me. But that is the way it is with a Fire Story. Everyone has one, and you never really know how it ends until you get there.

# DAVID POYER

## AUTHOR OF *THE GULF* AND *THE MED*

"There can be no better writer of modern sea adventure around today."

—Clive Cussler

The tight-lipped residents of Hatteras Island aren't talking about the bodies of the three U-boat crewmen that have mysteriously surfaced after more than forty years. But their reappearance has unleashed a tide of powerful forces—Nazis with a ruthless plan to corner the South American drug market, and a shadowy figure with his own dangerous agenda.

Whatever's out there, someone besides salvage diver Tiller Galloway is interested. Someone prepared to bomb his boat and kill any witnesses. And when Tiller finally meets face-to-face with his pursuers, it's in a violent, gut-wrenching firefight that climaxes hundreds of feet below the surface.

"I couldn't turn the pages fast enough!"

—Greg Dinallo, author of *Purpose of Evasion*

# HATTERAS BLUE

HATTERAS BLUE
David Poyer
_____ 92749-5 $5.99 U.S./$7.99 Can.

In all of New York's Chinatown, there is no one like P.I. Lydia Chin, who has a nose for trouble, a disapproving Chinese mother, and a partner named Bill Smith who's been living above a bar for sixteen years.

Hired to find some precious stolen porcelain, Lydia follows a trail of clues from highbrow art dealers into a world of Chinese gangs. Suddenly, this case has become as complex as her community itself—and as deadly as a killer on the loose...

# China Trade

## S. J. Rozan